Praise for *The Girl Who 1*

'The opening descriptions of Bonnie's misadventures in the Great Australian Bight had me hooked. And her retelling made me understand the enormity of the adventure – crocodiles, sharks and even sea snakes included. I loved hearing about the fantastic characters who became part of the adventures along the way.

'Hearing about Bonnie's experience growing up made me realise how important it is to be all-consumed and committed to sport and goals through those tricky teenage years.

'Bonnie's ability to endure extreme physical pain paddling for such a long time is a testament to what humans are made of – or can be if inclined to such craziness! Her passion for endurance is impressive and motivating. Thank you, Bonnie, for the motivation' **Jessica Watson**, author, adventurer and sailor

'Bonnie is bravery and determination personified. Her strength is brought to life with an incredible story, and if you want to feel like everything is possible, this is the story for you. Bonnie will show you that when life offers a challenge, she will return serve and do it in style' **Leisel Jones**, Olympian

'As you read this book, prepare to be both moved and inspired. Through engaging anecdotes, heartfelt moments and vivid descriptions, you will intimately experience the joys, triumphs, and hurdles Bonnie encounters along her courageous journey' **Gus Worland**, Gotcha4Life

'I'm in awe of Bonnie's almighty leap of faith to set out on this expedition into the complete unknown. A challenge that would test every part of her being, forcing Bonnie and her amazing team to dig deeper than they ever thought possible.

'It's not only the unbelievable physical bravery and athleticism that's on display, but the courage to face the relentless knock at the door by her inner fears. Showing up to answer those knocks every single day both in and out of the ski is part of Bonnie's journey that I admire most.

'Every time I paddle out into the surf after reading about Bonnie's epic adventure, I stare out to the horizon, imagining her paddling into the abyss and think how proud I am that a friend accomplished one of the craziest world-record attempts' **Sally Fitzgibbons**, surfing champion

A professional ironwoman by age 17, Bonnie Hancock has competed in seven Nutri-Grain IronWoman series and represented Australia in surf lifesaving. In 2022 she completed a gruelling 12,700-kilometre journey around Australia solo in an ocean ski, becoming the fastest-ever paddler to circumnavigate the continent, the first Australian woman to circumnavigate the continent by paddle, and the youngest person to do so. She also achieved a new world record for the longest 24-hour paddle, covering a distance of 235 kilometres. Bonnie is currently an ambassador for Gotcha4Life and a speaker on leadership and mental health. She is an accredited practising dietitian with a passion for working alongside clients to look at holistic factors to achieve their best physical and mental health.

THE GIRL
WHO
TOUCHED
THE STARS

BONNIE HANCOCK

ABC
BOOKS

The ABC 'Wave' device is a trademark of the
Australian Broadcasting Corporation and is used
under licence by HarperCollins*Publishers* Australia.

HarperCollins*Publishers*
Australia • Brazil • Canada • France • Germany • Holland • India
Italy • Japan • Mexico • New Zealand • Poland • Spain • Sweden
Switzerland • United Kingdom • United States of America

HarperCollins acknowledges the Traditional Custodians
of the lands upon which we live and work, and pays respect
to Elders past and present.

First published on Gadigal Country in Australia in 2024
by HarperCollins*Publishers* Australia Pty Limited
ABN 36 009 913 517
harpercollins.com.au

A catalogue record for this book is available from the National Library of Australia

ISBN 978 0 7333 4335 3 (paperback)
ISBN 978 1 4607 1714 1 (ebook)

Cover design by Louisa Maggio, HarperCollins Design Studio
Cover images by Ben Lavery (front) and Karlee Nurthen (back)
Author photo by Blake Bradford
Typeset in Adobe Garamond Pro by Kirby Jones
Printed and bound in Australia by McPherson's Printing Group

For Matt.

When I told you about my crazy idea, you had a choice.

Thank you for opting to go all in.

And for every person who's never had that one big win,
this one's for you.

CONTENTS

FOREWORD

It is with great delight and warmth in my heart that I share with you this captivating book, which tells the extraordinary story of a remarkable friend who embodies bravery and passion like no other. Within these pages, you will embark on a journey that will ignite your spirit and remind you of the incredible power that lies within the bounds of mental fitness.

In a world where bravery can often be overshadowed by fear, this book serves as a beacon of hope and inspiration. Through the lens of Bonnie's epic journey, you will witness the unwavering courage that propels her forward as she embraces the challenge head-on and fearlessly pursues her goals. Her story reminds us that bravery is not the absence of fear but rather the strength to face it with an indomitable spirit.

The passion that emanates from Bonnie is truly contagious. Her enthusiasm and dedication to her pursuits are awe-inspiring, igniting a fire within those fortunate enough to witness it. Her unwavering commitment to what she believes in serves as a testament to the incredible heights that can be reached when we follow our hearts and pursue our passions with fervour.

As you read this book, prepare to be both moved and inspired. Through engaging anecdotes, heartfelt moments and vivid descriptions, you will intimately experience the joys, triumphs and hurdles Bonnie encountered during her courageous journey. Her story will remind you that bravery and passion go hand in hand, fuelling each other and shaping our lives in profound ways.

It is my sincere hope that as you turn the pages of this book, you will not only come to know and love Bonnie as I do but also reflect upon the power of your own bravery and passion. May her story serve as a gentle reminder that within each of us lies the potential for greatness, and that friendship has the remarkable ability to ignite our souls and bring out the best in us.

So fasten your seatbelt, for you are about to embark on an unforgettable adventure filled with bravery, passion and the unbreakable bonds of friendship. Prepare to be inspired, motivated and uplifted as you witness this remarkable journey.

Gus Worland, founder of Gotcha4Life

PROLOGUE

I COULD HEAR THE CREW SHOUTING AT ME. THEIR CALLS came ringing through the night air.

'Bonnie, say something! Do you need us to jump in?'

My lips formed the words that would rescue me but only a whisper came out.

'Help!' I murmured hoarsely. 'I can't get back in the ski.'

Just a week ago, it had all seemed like such an exciting adventure. And now here I was – cold, scared and floating in the dark waters of the Great Australian Bight.

The 1200-kilometre stretch of water that runs along Australia's base is notorious, with sailors considering it testing at best. And at worst, the Bight is treacherous, unpredictable and even fatal.

The difference between my crossing and that of well-equipped sailors is that instead of a multi-tonne boat beneath me, I was making the crossing with just nine kilograms of floating carbon fibre between me and the precarious ocean.

If successful, I would be the first person in history to cross the Great Australian Bight by paddle. This was just one part of an even bigger goal – to be the fifth person in history, as well as the youngest and the fastest, to circumnavigate mainland Australia by paddle. This challenge was expected to take me at least eight months.

But all of that faded into insignificance, as I floated in the freezing waters, barely able to call for help. I just wanted to be home.

As I desperately tried to climb back into the ski, I could see my support crew working overtime to turn the boat back around, the wind and swell pushing the vessel further away, at first 20 metres, then 50 metres and now 200 metres. The ten-tonne catamaran was built to ride the swells, and the strength of Mother Nature was on full display as she continued to extend the distance between me and my sole source of safety. I had no GPS beacon on me. Without my support boat, I would perish.

In the bitingly cold nine-degree water, my body was rapidly losing energy and I didn't have the strength to perform the chin-up style movement required to safely remount my ski.

As I tried yet again to haul myself up, a huge gust of wind ripped across the water and flipped the ski, driving the hard edge into the top of my head. I heard the sickening thud as it landed, and my body reeled in pain after the initial shock wore off.

Every day for three months I'd put myself into life-threatening situations – encountering sharks, swells as high as buildings, sharp rocks and cliff faces, near run-ins with my support boat, and seasickness so severe it had left me doubled over for most of the day, unable to stop the vomiting.

Was this it?

A strange sense of calm overtook me.

Realising the helplessness of the situation, the panic I'd felt was replaced by a sense of acceptance.

Lying back in the water, I caught sight of the most beautiful night sky I'd ever seen.

There was not a hint of light pollution, just the full moon providing an illuminating glow. The stars appeared like handfuls of glitter thrown at a black silk sheet. Overwhelmed with awe, I considered the power of nature and how small we really are in the grand scheme of creation.

My focus shifted to what was beneath the surface of the water, where I observed a blue light radiating from my feet. Other than the burning balls of glittering stars above, the only light source should have been the tiny LED light on the back of my ski, but I accepted this new discovery without question.

A feeling of warmth had started to overtake my body. Beginning in my chest and spreading to my extremities, the feeling wasn't unpleasant. In fact, it was almost soothing. No longer able to hold onto the ski and slowly growing weaker, I looked back up to the Southern Cross constellation shining brightly above me.

Suddenly, a second gust of wind lifted the ski high out of the water and drove it back down into my cheekbone, this time creating a significant cracking sound.

Lifting a hand to check for blood, I prayed the impact hadn't broken my skin. Sharks are attracted to blood, and out here in the middle of the ocean at night, I was a sitting duck.

There was no blood but an immediate lump had formed at the spot I'd been hit.

The sensation of warmth continued to increase, as did the pins and needles in my toes and fingers, and I looked again at the beautiful night sky.

A searing pain shot up my cheek as the shock from the impact wore off, and I snapped back to reality. *What was I doing, floating on my back in the middle of Australia's most dangerous stretch of ocean?*

Lying there, 500 kilometres out to sea, letting my body temperature drop, was the worst thing I could do. Remaining stationary was the enemy. I needed to keep moving.

With no strength left to pull myself to my ski, I knew I needed to resort to the final option.

Swim.

My legs were barely able to muster the strength to generate a kick, so I desperately started to doggy paddle in the direction of the boat. The crew had managed to turn around and I could see the support vessel was now less than 100 metres away.

The safety line between me and my ski was still clipped to my waist and the ski dragged behind me, creating significant resistance as I pulled it along. I struggled to keep my head above the dark water.

Eventually I was close enough to hear the calls from the crew once again. As the boat manoeuvred backwards to pick me up, I could hear shouts of encouragement over the sounds of the motor. They were willing me to keep going. Just a few more strokes.

Edging painfully closer, I clawed my way towards the red port-side light of the boat, which cast an eerie glow over the water's surface.

Finally close enough, I summoned one last surge of effort to lunge at the boat.

The first figure I made out was Blake. Backlit by the deck lights, he appeared to me like a guardian angel. As he reached down, unclipped my safety line and hauled me up onto the back step to safety, my limp body acted as a dead weight, my muscles unable to offer any assistance.

Shaking uncontrollably, I managed to crawl up the back steps, still unable to speak.

My hands were purple and my teeth chattering as the first bucket of hot water was poured over my head. By now my body was so numb that I didn't yet register the water's warmth.

The second bucket offered the first bit of relief and with it hope that maybe I was going to be okay. The space blanket from the previously untouched first-aid cupboard was draped around me and felt like a cocoon, shielding me from the relentless elements.

I became aware of a hairdryer starting and felt its warm blast streaming over my chest. As it warmed me, I was overwhelmed by gratitude for my crew. In this moment, they were my life savers. Without them, I was done. I didn't have the strength to provide my body with the first aid that would restore my temperature to a safe level.

No one spoke. No one was willing to voice what we all were thinking. We were 500 kilometres out to sea, a few days away from help at a full motor. A long way out of helicopter range.

We found out later that it takes 12 minutes of submersion in the Great Australian Bight to become hypothermic.

I'd been in the water for ten.

I also learnt that a feeling of warmth and tingling in the extremities is one of the first stages of hypothermia. As for the blue light? I was most likely concussed.

It was day eight of our perilous 15-day Bight crossing. We were only just past half of the way across, with 450 kilometres still to paddle. I know what you're thinking – how did I get myself into such a dangerous situation? What possesses someone to paddle 500 kilometres out to sea, in the dark, on a tiny ocean ski?

This book is my chance to tell you.

CHAPTER 1

WHY NOT?

WORD OF THE GLOBAL COVID-19 PANDEMIC FIRST SPREAD ON the Gold Coast as some sort of joke. We thought of Covid as a bizarre happening on the other side of the world and considered ourselves safe within our bubble of golden beaches, busy cafes and Friday night pizza shop lines.

But in March 2020, that all changed. A visitor to the Queensland Surf Life Saving Titles tested positive, and all athletes, officials and attendees were advised to get tested immediately. The surf-lifesaving community was abuzz with talk that the highlight of the competition calendar, the Australian Surf Life Saving Titles, or 'Aussies', as the event was affectionately called, would be cancelled. I had participated in these titles since the age of 14. The pinnacle of the surf-lifesaving season, the Aussies provides competitors with the opportunity to race against the best in the world and a shot at winning a coveted Australian gold medal. Having won 12 Australian gold medals over 16 years as a surf lifesaver, I had trained hard over the past six months to give myself every chance of winning another. Unfortunately, though, I would have to wait because the rumours were true; not only were the Aussies cancelled, but soon the government enforced strict lockdowns that required us to stay home unless we needed to go out for work in an essential industry, for medical purposes, to exercise or to shop for food.

As I negotiated this new world where toilet paper became a prized commodity, supermarkets were staffed by security guards to ensure people didn't buy more than one packet of pasta, and businesses such as cafes and restaurants were closing their doors, I found myself turning to the local library.

In primary school, I had openly stated my desire to be a librarian, my love for books only overtaken by sport. By my late twenties, I had gravitated to autobiographies as my genre of choice and took pride in my ability to learn about politics, horse racing, pop culture and sport from the pages I enthusiastically turned.

In April 2020, amid the Covid pandemic, I swiped three books through the check-out of Broadbeach Library. Shane Warne's autobiography was first, and the second was a read on the equine industry. The third was a black-covered biography titled *Fearless*, written by Joe Glickman. Its cover featured a woman holding two paddles, crossed in front of her like swords. The woman was Freya Hoffmeister, a German sea kayaker, who, in 2009, had successfully circumnavigated Australia by paddle, becoming the fastest ever recorded to do so.

From the first mention of crocodiles stalking Freya for 100 kilometres and sharks continuously bumping her ski, I was hooked. I couldn't believe I had never heard her story. Freya was the fourth person to achieve the feat, the first being Paul Caffyn in 1989.

Finishing the final page of Glickman's eloquently written book, I immediately had a thought: *I wonder if I could do that?* Rather than feeling terror, the thought of the expedition excited me; I couldn't think of a greater challenge than taking on every metre of coastline our beautiful country has to offer. In my time competing as a professional ironwoman in the Nutri-Grain Ironwoman Series, I had seen much of New South Wales and Queensland, as the races were predominantly held at beaches in these states. However, my geographical knowledge of Western Australia, the Northern Territory and South Australia was poor. Much of the coastline in these states is remote, almost uninhabitable due to harsh conditions, crocodiles and lack of access. Paddling along these areas seemed impossible, yet apparently it wasn't.

A week after finishing the book, I told my husband, Matt, of Freya's story. Like me, he was intrigued but could never have predicted the next words I spoke.

'I think I could do it,' I said slowly, not quite believing what I was saying.

'What's that?' he answered warily, unsure of where the conversation was headed.

'Paddle around Australia. I think I could do it.'

My words were met with a silence that hung in the air, and I realised that Matt simply didn't know what to say.

I could hardly blame him. Half of the world was still stuck in strict lockdowns, and closer to home, residents in Australia's southern state of Victoria were advised by their premier that they couldn't venture beyond a five-kilometre radius from their own home. Yet here I was, eager to plan a circumnavigation of the entire coastline of Australia.

It wasn't the first time Matt had listened to one of my crazy ideas. We began dating in 2014 when he moved from Mackay to the Gold Coast to pursue a career as a high-performance coach in the Australian Football League. Matt had then followed me all over the globe as I chased podiums in some of the toughest ironwoman and ski paddling races in the world, many of which took place in the middle of the ocean.

My need for adventure and craving for a race win would often result in Matt hanging on for dear life to the rails of a support boat driven by a crazy skipper, watching me launch into the next runner on my ocean ski. Just 45 centimetres wide and nine kilograms in weight, the carbon fibre craft requires a significant amount of skill to control, particularly in rough seas, and many times I have found myself lying flat against the back of my ski to keep its nose from burying into the deep blue sea.

But this idea was different. To paddle around Australia wasn't crazy. It was ludicrous. Big seas were just the start. One third of the Australian coastline is inhabited by fearsome saltwater crocodiles, and the cold waters of South Australia are home to the infamous great white shark.

To his credit, never once did Matt tell me the idea was crazy or that I should forget it – though perhaps he hoped I would come to the realisation on my own.

'Why don't you do a bit of research on it?' His answer, which came several minutes after the idea was proposed, was typical of who he is. Thorough. Matt is a planner, whereas my nature is to jump first and think later.

To humour Matt, I began diving into the online information on nautical expeditions. Visiting Freya's website, I studied the photos and blog entries she had posted throughout the journey and viewed articles on Paul Caffyn, Stuart Truman and Jason Beachcroft, who had completed the big loop before Freya. Obsessively studying the Australian coastline through the maps application on my phone, I learnt which stretches of coast were remote and which sections would require me to paddle a long way offshore if I wanted to beat Freya's record.

In two particular sections of coastline, I would be faced with the tough decision of whether to play it safe, hugging the coastline but adding extra distance in doing so, or take a big gamble in taking the direct line across, which would see me paddle hundreds of kilometres offshore. Freya had completed 14,000 kilometres of paddling in 10 months and 22 days, but though she'd saved distance by cutting straight across the Gulf of Carpentaria, she had hugged the coastline of the Great Australian Bight. I had a thought – if I cut straight across the Bight, I would save 1000 kilometres of paddling and create an instant buffer on the record. I didn't once stop to think how incredibly dangerous it would be to paddle an ocean ski that far out in open ocean, in an area known for huge sharks and wild seas.

My plan was to complete the circumnavigation faster than had been done before and become the new Guinness World Record holder. It would be great if I could also raise money for a charity. I had been alarmed by the threat to mental health that Covid seemed to be causing.

There were a few ways to achieve a new record; firstly, I would need to cover a greater number of kilometres a day than Freya, so I set my target at 80–100 kilometres a day on average, accounting for the occasional rest day due to poor weather. The second factor that influenced the time taken is the total number of kilometres covered throughout the circumnavigation. Four people had paddled around Australia previously, and the total kilometres completed throughout the expeditions ranged from 22,000 kilometres down to 14,000 kilometres (Freya). The variation in distance came down to whether the paddler stayed close to shore, hugging the coastline, or dared to venture further out to sea, paddling in a straight line between headlands. While the latter option was appealing, as it resulted in less distance covered, it required a paddler to head out as far as 500 kilometres to sea in certain sections, as Australia's coast is definitely not a perfect circle.

There was no way I was going to paddle in the middle of the ocean on my own without a support boat. My background is in elite ironwoman racing rather than navigating, therefore a solo trip would almost certainly lead to disaster. Having a support boat to navigate for me and provide me with nutrition meant I could focus on pushing my body beyond the realms of what was previously considered possible. But though it sounds nice to paddle next to a support boat, I knew that while on my ski, it would not be wise to get within 50–100 metres of the boat. A collision with a boat on my ski could be fatal and conversations with my crew on a windy day would be limited to physical signals or a few words shouted over the breeze.

But before worrying about communication breakdown with my crew, I had to find one. With the enormous cost of hiring a boat, skipper, fuel, food and safety equipment, we simply couldn't afford to pay a crew, so we would be relying on enthusiastic individuals who were not only willing to volunteer their time, but were competent across areas of videography, cooking and managing elite athletes. Theoretically, half of the crew would be on the support boat and the other half would tow a jet ski on land. The jet ski would be a back-up option in case the support boat required servicing or encountered problems.

Overwhelmed by the enormous logistical challenges and expense involved, I eventually closed my notebook of planning with a sense of disappointment, writing the circumnavigation off as another one of my silly ideas and deciding to forget about it.

In an attempt to quell the feeling of disappointment that came with abandoning the venture, I conceived an alternate plan which was less risky: what if I just paddled from the Gold Coast to Sydney? The 1000-odd kilometres was more than decent, and surely challenging enough to raise funds for mental fitness. But after settling on the idea, I suddenly realised I'd be selling myself short. If I was going to plan an expedition, why not find out where my true limits were? I knew they weren't going to be found in the well-travelled waters of the east coast of Australia, so I decided to back myself in paddling the whole way around.

For six months I went back and forth on the idea of the circumnavigation, trying my best to get on with life as normal. That meant training with my local surf club at Mermaid Beach for fitness and tending to the dietitian business I had spent the better part of a decade building up. But as I sat in traffic on the way to work or ambled up the supermarket aisle searching for toilet paper, something was different. A fire had been lit within. It was as though the idea of the circumnavigation was calling to me, the urge slowly building until I could no longer ignore it.

And then I had a premonition: I envisioned myself as an 80-year-old woman sitting in her rocking chair, bitterly wondering if she could have done it. She'd never know because she never gave it a shot. The thought was terrifying. *Stuff that*, I thought, realising I would rather try and fail than regret not trying at all.

After I first conceived this plan to paddle around Australia, I'd asked myself, *Why?* Why would I want to take this on? Were my reasons valid enough to face the risks associated with such a mission? But now I decided to ask myself a different question. *Why not?* What did I have to lose? As a 30-year-old woman without children, there would never be a better time to take on such a challenge. The vision of an older me full of regret provided extra motivation. From that moment, I was going to go all in. After all, hadn't I been preparing for this my whole life?

*

I had grown up with the beach as my backyard. My parents, Richard and Julie, had decided the idyllic coastal town of Sawtell, New South Wales, would be the perfect place to raise my three sisters – Georgia, Courtney and India – and me. This meant that when we were growing up, the beach was just a 200-metre walk from home.

When not at school, my sisters and I had spent much of our time at Sawtell Surf Club, where we were nippers from the age of five, developing into junior and later senior surf lifesavers. With Georgia and Courtney a few years my senior, I was forced to sit on the beach and watch them train with head coach Mr De Carle until I was old enough. I'd watch the training squad crash through the surf with their fibreglass boards and imitate the action with my boogie board.

When I turned seven, I was given one of Georgia's old nipper boards made from foam. A foamie board is used as the learner board for children just starting their surf-lifesaving journey, before they move on to a board made of fibreglass the following year. It was finally my time. I'll never forget the feeling of paddling into the Sawtell shore dump with my very own board. The once shiny stickers had almost entirely peeled off and dints were scattered over the nose, but to me it felt like the most valuable board in the world. Grasping the front handle, I tore into the water after my sisters to take on the three-foot walls of white water, never once looking back towards shore.

My obsession with the surf would continue, and after winning consecutive board titles at the New South Wales State Championships, my mind was set on becoming a professional ironwoman, an idea cemented through watching my idol, Karla Gilbert.

After training, Courtney and I would race home to watch the Meadow Lea Ironwomen and Uncle Toby's Ironmen on the television. For over a decade, Karla was the queen of ironwoman racing, and both Courtney and I worshipped her. A dedicated athlete known for stepping up and delivering her best performances under pressure, Karla epitomised everything a champion was. She raced under the yellow star of Surfers Paradise and as she ran up the beach, leading her fellow competitors around the course, I imagined myself one day doing the same.

I loved discipline and from the age of 11 often trained twice daily. On the Coffs Coast in the 90s and 2000s, good coaches were hard to come by, so my dad took on most of that responsibility himself. With his wiry build, Dad was a natural runner and, in his late twenties, had taken up long-distance running, completing multiple marathons. He would join my sisters and me as we'd head to the pool or hit the streets of Sawtell for a run. In single-digit temperatures, we'd lace up our shoes, zip up our tracksuits and get going.

Dad's favourite routes included those around the Sawtell water towers and local caravan park. The 'Water Tower Run' consisted of timed loops starting from the northern end of Sawtell Beach, up the stairs and along a path that looked over a pristine right-handed surf break off Boambee Beach. We would then take a sharp left turn and face a 300-metre near-vertical climb to the water towers at the top before proceeding back down to the sand.

That was one loop.

We would do a minimum of five.

As I chased my older sisters up to the top of the water-tower hill, I pictured it as the chute to the finish of a professional ironwoman race, an audience either side clapping as we came through as winners. Until the day I left Sawtell as a late teen, I continued to do this loop, and both Courtney and I credit it as contributing to our success as athletes. There was nowhere to hide on that loop, and our shared mindset of taking no shortcuts in training was forged somewhere between the bottom and top of that hill.

But my sense of resilience was ingrained at a far younger age. Starting school at the age of four meant I was a year younger than most of my peers. While mentally capable, I physically struggled with many of the tasks we had to tackle in those first few years. Red-faced and head down, I would reluctantly ask my fellow classmates if they could tie my laces for me. I was the last to get my pen licence, as my fine motor skills had yet to catch up to those of my older peers, and I scrubbed out my pencilled mistakes with an eraser while my classmates finished sentences with a flourish in biro.

Struggling with physical tasks, I was left feeling frustrated and humiliated, but I learnt a valuable lesson in patience. My teacher's insistence on my completing each task instead of giving me an easy way out meant my coordination improved and I caught up with the other kids. I might have had to work longer and harder at each task but after many failed attempts, I got there.

Perhaps the early feeling of being behind the mark, of being the underdog, was where my competitiveness was born. Significantly smaller in stature than my three sisters, including the youngest, India, I felt a need to prove myself. I carried this need into adulthood where I would retain an urge to strive for perfection in training and study. A blessing and a curse, this need to achieve would drive me to reach great heights from a young age, but it also meant that no prize ever seemed to be enough. A win or placing, while quieting the beast within temporarily, would soon give way to a gaping emptiness, and the high of success was too often followed by a crippling low.

Racing nearly every weekend of my teenage years meant my life was a rollercoaster of achievement and disappointment – but sacrifice was a constant. For instance, I had to make a tough decision in Year 10. My end-of-year school graduation ceremony was on the same day as a surf-lifesaving competition in Sydney that served as selection for the New South Wales State Representative Team. Though graduation was a fun chance to wear heels and makeup, I never once regretted my choice as I pulled on my goggles and put my foot on the line to race that weekend. By that stage, sacrifices were second nature to me, and I saw them as a necessity if I was going to follow in Karla Gilbert's footsteps as a professional ironwoman.

But I wasn't the only one who made sacrifices to achieve my lofty goals. Every other weekend, my sisters and I would pile into the car with Mum and Dad and head south on the M1 to take on the best young surf lifesavers in the state. My parents did this without complaint. I don't think you ever fully appreciate the extent of the sacrifices your parents make for you until many years later.

While growing up in Sawtell was a blessing and the local beaches my training grounds, if I wanted to make it as a professional athlete, I needed to make a move. After finishing high school, Courtney had taken the trip north to the hub of surf lifesaving that is the Gold Coast. So after my Year 12 graduation, I packed up my belongings and followed her. Courtney had already shown enormous improvement under the punishing regime of Pat O'Keefe at Northcliffe Surf Club, and I was excited to follow in her footsteps.

Pat's name was synonymous with surf lifesaving. Coaching a young Karla Gilbert to superstardom had brought Pat legendary status, and in 2003, he was appointed head coach at Northcliffe Surf Club, transforming a little-known club into a stable of champions.

On my first day there, Pat handed me a training program that detailed the sessions for the week. At first, I thought I'd read the timetable incorrectly. In addition to swimming six kilometres in the pool of a morning and a ten-kilometre board or ski session in the ocean of an afternoon, there was a third session of running or boxing at 10am. That couldn't be right. Three sessions a day?

I quickly learnt there was no mistake. In Pat's squad, three sessions a day was the norm, and if you didn't make the mid-morning workout, you'd receive a call from Pat immediately after the missed session.

As well as ensuring we were physically primed, Pat's regime provided us with a mental edge. One memorable afternoon, Pat drove the squad to the famous point break of Snapper Rocks on the Gold Coast, located 20 kilometres south of Northcliffe. Once we arrived, he helped us unload the trailer he'd towed, which was packed with our surf skis, and then instructed us to paddle back to Northcliffe Surf Club and promptly drove off. We had no other option; there was no one coming to get us so the only way back was to paddle. Looking back to the Gold Coast hinterland, I saw the sun beginning to dip below the mountains and realised we weren't going to get to the club before dark. There are few things scarier than paddling in the dark along an unfamiliar section of coastline, but as night fell when we were only halfway back to the club, we had no choice but to keep going, using the glow of the full moon as a guide.

If Pat was still alive, I would thank him for experiences like that one. I had no way of knowing at the time that 15 years later I'd be paddling thousands of kilometres in isolated areas at night during my circumnavigation of Australia.

While I was training with Pat, I was also studying nutrition and dietetics at Griffith University in Brisbane, driving my beaten-up Nissan TRX back and forth along the Gold Coast Highway, while juggling the enormous load of study and training and the extra responsibilities of cooking and cleaning now that I lived out of home. Revelling in my newfound independence, I slowly progressed from cooking mince and pasta every evening to preparing more complex meals.

Though my fellow athletes gave me insight into the best cafes on the coast, money was incredibly tight, and the most I could afford was a small hot chocolate. With just $250 a week in assistance from government benefits, this was my budget for food, fuel and everything in between. Though Pat arranged financial help for Courtney and me in terms of rent, I was soon living below the poverty line like so many aspiring athletes in Australia. But as everyone around me lived a similar low-budget lifestyle, it felt normal to forgo any luxuries.

Under Pat, I reached a state of physical fitness and mental fortitude I never considered possible, and three months after leaving the sheltered shores of Sawtell, I qualified for my first professional Ironwoman Series.

The trial for the series consisted of eight brutal races in the dead flat waters of Brisbane's Redcliffe Beach. By the end of the weekend, my legs ached, and my arms felt as though they'd drop off, but as I scanned the leader board to see my name in the top ten, confirming my position in the professional series, the feeling of pride was overwhelming. Courtney had secured her placing as well, meaning there were two Hancocks who had achieved their lifelong goal of following in the footsteps of Karla Gilbert, as we'd planned all those years ago.

Though I showed lots of promise as a rookie, what followed was three years of near misses. I finished just off the podium in professional races time after time. Finishing second or third at a less prestigious carnival, I would face the same field the next week in the professional series only to be relegated to sixth.

There were so many races when I'd lead for the first half but then fall short, which was endlessly frustrating. After so many disappointments I had to ask myself whether the issue was more mental than physical. Those around me tried to empower me, reassuring me I had so much potential. Potential. A word I came to resent. Maybe I simply wasn't good enough. Yet the desire to reach the podium in a professional race grew; I felt I needed that to have my potential fulfilled, my internal critic silenced. Convinced that once the first win came, the floodgates would open, I continued to compete, but as the years went by, that win never came.

When I turned 23, I became so frustrated at having never won a major title that I began skipping meals to reduce my body fat and sneaking in extra sessions on my own; any chance to gain an edge over my competitors. Underfuelling my body and overtraining caught up with me, however, and after a few months my immune system wasn't coping. I was constantly sick, and my results began to decline. The glands in my neck felt like they were on fire and blood tests confirmed I had contracted glandular fever. What eventuated was two years spent out of the sport I loved, away from the network I'd built, seeing my name replaced by a new competitor. It was a time of bitter disappointment. It took me a couple of months to see a silver lining in that it gave me the chance to fully apply myself to my university studies, after which I proudly graduated as an accredited practising dietitian. Following graduation, I found work as a private dietitian in general practice clinics, and I fulfilled my passion for helping people manage diabetes, heart disease and other health conditions that can be greatly improved through changes to diet.

Studying nutrition allowed me to better improve my own health. After two years, my immune system grew strong enough to allow me to exercise again, and I began to consider the idea of returning to competitive racing. Eventually I entered several ironwoman events, to varying degrees of success: on the podium one weekend, I'd finish at the back of the field the next. My passion for training wasn't what it used to be, hence the inconsistency in results, but I did notice that my ski paddling had greatly improved since returning.

Sitting on the floor of the shower after a tough ironwoman session, I had a thought. Maybe balancing the ski, board, swim and run was too much. *Why don't I give specialist ski paddling a try?*

Differing vastly from the 15-minute ironwoman event, the three-minute surf ski race is about speed and power. Surf-ski paddlers possessed a strength I had always admired, and

I suddenly craved to be on the line against these powerhouse women, battling my way through the surf on the trickiest craft in surf lifesaving.

So began my quest to become a specialist ski paddler.

Once I switched into the sprint event, it was a relief not to have to juggle the three other disciplines of the ironwoman event and in only needing to train one to two times a day as opposed to three, I had more balance in my life.

In my first year as a specialist ski paddler, I achieved the consistency I'd never had as an ironwoman. My speed off the start became my greatest asset as I found a strength in my upper body that came with age and specificity of training.

Loving my pivot into ski paddling, I soon stumbled across a social-media post which sparked my interest in long-distance ocean ski paddling. The 52-kilometre Molokai race is held annually in Hawaii and sees competitors race each other in huge swells in the middle of the ocean. *That looks like my type of fun!* I thought.

I only gave myself two months to train for the event, but managed to cross the line in fifth place. Though I hadn't finished on the podium, my fellow competitors were full of encouragement and the experience lit a fire within me. I made plans to travel around the world, racing on my ski in the middle of the ocean. Such plans were soon interrupted, however, as the Covid pandemic spread across the globe in 2020. Any idea of travelling had to be abandoned, but I still paddled most days and the training broke up the monotony of lockdown.

And so it was mid-Covid when I picked up that book about Freya Hoffmeister and experienced the strong gut feeling that told me I needed to face this new challenge. I realised that if I was to make it happen, I'd need to go all in and use every resource I had and every connection I'd ever made to pull off this enormous expedition.

Once I decided to go for it, Matt and I looked at each other and agreed there could be no shortcuts in planning. It was May 2021, and I had my mind set on starting the expedition at the end of the year, which meant one thing: we needed to hustle.

CHAPTER 2

THE HUSTLE

We split the tasks. Matt's job would be to find the crew, jet ski and car. Though he had initially been hesitant when I'd floated the idea of the expedition with him, once he saw my passion for the project and agreed to help with planning, he entered into a zone of tunnel-vision focus. In his role as High Performance Director at the Southport Sharks VFL club, Matt was heavily involved in organising logistics for the team when they travelled, and, fortunately for me, coordinating various moving parts of a project is among his greatest strengths.

Freya's world record for the circumnavigation stood at 10 months and 22 days, and my aim was to significantly better the mark. Initially, six months was the lofty goal I had in mind, but when we factored in days off due to bad weather, we came to realise that a timeframe of eight months was more realistic. To achieve the record, we required a competent crew, a jet ski and a car to tow the jet ski. With no sponsors, minimal savings in the bank after the purchase of our home, and no evidence that I would be successful in the record attempt, we needed to somehow find the $200,000 required to fund the project. To kickstart our fundraising pool, Matt selflessly suggested we sell our cars. In handing over both sets of keys to the respective buyers, we raised a combined total of $45,000, which helped but wouldn't get me around Australia. So Matt put on his athlete manager's hat and began planning a sponsorship pitch to entice prospective companies.

Meanwhile, I faced the intimidating task of finding a support boat and skipper. As a young woman with no background in sailing, I knew it wouldn't be an easy task, but I started small by visiting local marinas and chatting to boating contacts. Initially I failed to find anyone willing to take a chance on me and join what I was pitching as 'the adventure of a lifetime'. But in speaking to contacts within the marine community, I did learn valuable information about weather patterns, currents and climate that would impact my decision regarding when to start the paddle and the direction in which I would complete the circumnavigation.

After hearing first-hand from sailors about the freezing waters of the Bass Strait (between the Australian mainland and Tasmania) in winter, I knew that to give myself every chance of avoiding hypothermia, I needed to time my run to attack the southern stretch of coastline in the warmer months of January, February and March. Next, I had to make a choice between paddling around the country clockwise or anti-clockwise. Though the four paddlers who had previously completed the journey had all circumnavigated in an anti-clockwise direction, I eventually made the decision to go clockwise thanks to a current made famous by a well-known children's movie.

Known as a 'superhighway' in the 2003 film *Finding Nemo*, the East Australian Current (EAC) flows down the east coast of Australia, carrying warm, low-nutrient water from the Great Barrier Reef to the cold southern waters of Tasmania. In the movie, the EAC allows Nemo to catch a ride with his newfound turtle friends towards Sydney. The EAC has been flowing more strongly in recent years, a factor which has been attributed to climate change and warmer water temperatures. The EAC was mentioned to me by top meteorologist Sir Roger 'Clouds' Badham OAM as an advantage I could use to gain a buffer on the previous world record. Clouds believed the EAC would make paddling both easier and faster, allowing me to gain an extra two to three kilometres an hour in speed. However, he pointed out, the most challenging part of completing the trip in a clockwise direction would be the southeasterly tradewinds I would face on my way back down the Queensland coast north of the Great Barrier Reef at the end of the paddle.

Figuring my body would be conditioned to handle it after six to seven months of paddling, I made the decision to paddle around Australia clockwise. Not only would I receive assistance from the EAC, but it would allow me to start at the end of the year and take on the colder states in the summer. After talking through the options with Matt, I decided on 19 December as our start date.

If considered too carefully, the prospect of nearly 13,000 kilometres of paddling is potentially overwhelming. Once the date for the paddle was set, I pulled up the map of Australia on my phone in satellite mode and began scrutinising the coastline in detail. As it turned out, there were far more sections of uninhabited coastline than I had anticipated; I knew that much of the northern part of Western Australia was sparsely populated, but so, I could see, was a lot of the Northern Territory and Far North Queensland. Along certain sections of coast, you could travel for hundreds of kilometres without bumping into a single soul; running out of food, fuel or water in these areas could prove fatal. My stomach dropped as I envisioned being deserted on a beach in the middle of nowhere, with no reception or supplies.

Fortunately, our plan to start on the east coast and head south meant I'd be paddling the most populated section of coast first. The stretch of water from the Gold Coast to Sydney would be a warm-up of sorts, a chance for the crew and me to test our protocols and get to know each other before we took on the freezing, isolated waters of the southern states. But once we crossed the border into Victoria, we'd be in a different league altogether.

With the commencement date set but no skipper or boat locked in, I decided to harness social media, figuring it was the most effective way to reach a large population of people in a short space of time, ideally allowing us to find financial assistance as well as a skipper and crew. In June 2021, I released an Instagram video that detailed my intentions to paddle around Australia and break the current record, urging businesses to come forward if they could help. Across Instagram and Facebook, the video received thousands of views and likes, along with hundreds of comments about the expedition.

The reactions were overwhelmingly positive, but the video didn't manage to attract any sponsors. With the social-media campaign not yielding the results hoped for, our approach would need to be more targeted.

Shaw and Partners Financial Services are a very successful investment firm based in Australia and internationally, and the co-CEOs, Earl Evans and Allan Zion, are huge supporters of both surf lifesaving and ocean ski paddling. Champions of female athletes, Earl and Allan are responsible for increasing the women's prize money to be equal with that of the male athletes. From its inception in the early 1990s, ocean ski racing had awarded women significantly less prize money than their male counterparts. The female winner of a major event would complete the same distance as the male winner but would open her prize envelope to find a cheque worth half the amount her male counterpart had been awarded. Sure, there were greater numbers of competitors in the men's races, but was it fair to have this affect the opportunity for the top women to earn decent money?

Top female ocean ski paddler Hayley Nixon described the situation at the time as a self-fulfilling prophecy: if you didn't provide adequate prize money for the top women, the numbers in the women's field would continue to be below that of the men's. Professional female athletes were usually left out of pocket once they factored in travel and accommodation costs and time off work. Increase the prize money, Hayley explained, and the numbers in the women's field would grow, and the standard continue to rise.

After years of female athletes and their supporters calling for pay parity, the change finally came when Earl and Allan, as major sponsors for the big ocean-racing events, pledged to match the prize money for both genders. Effective immediately, the women who fought their way into the top placings would receive the same prize money as the men. The cheers of women could be heard across the globe; for so long accepted as the norm, unequal pay between genders was now no longer acceptable in this sport.

I was fortunate to enter the sport of ocean ski paddling at a time when these changes were being made, and I benefited greatly. In the past, finishing fifth would have meant being out of pocket, but I was able to take home decent money while striving to finish at the top of the podium.

Now, as I was facing the enormous task of funding my expedition, it hit me. Earl. I needed to contact him. Perhaps he could be my saviour.

I mulled over how to make the approach without sounding desperate. How do you casually tell someone of your plans to paddle around Australia and say, 'By the way, could you please help me fund the damn thing?'

To Earl's credit, the reply to my carefully worded email was prompt. The next professional ocean ski race was coming up in

Forster, New South Wales, and he suggested we meet there to discuss my proposal.

And so, on a sunny Saturday at the Forster Surf Club cafe – my knees shaking under the table and my hands tightly gripping my glass of water – I told Earl of my plans to paddle around Australia. Deciding transparency was best, I explained that I had no way to fund the paddle and needed his help. I told him that I admired the way that he had helped both the sport of ocean ski paddling and female athletes, and I believed my journey would align with the values that Shaw and Partners staff work hard to embody. Taking his time to digest the information I'd presented him, Earl showed interest in the project and arranged a Zoom call the following week to discuss the specifics in terms of our estimated budget.

The call was the final stage of securing sponsorship. I'd never had to do a pitch before, let alone for a project I was incredibly passionate about. Connecting to Zoom, I saw Shaw and Partners' general manager Britt on screen, who informed me that Earl was in a meeting and running slightly late. It was apparent that my time to pitch had just been reduced. My nerves increased; I was going to have one shot at this. When Earl arrived, he apologised for being late and confirmed that we had just five minutes. 'Tell me more about the project.' Earl didn't muck around with small talk. 'What can Shaw and Partners do for you?'

Here we go, I thought, clearing my throat to speak.

Five minutes later, Earl spoke. 'I'm keen,' he said, 'but I need to see what Allan thinks.'

I waited anxiously while he signed off to make the call to Allan. Within two minutes, Earl called back and spoke the three words that enabled the entire project to go ahead: 'We are in.'

I'm not sure exactly what it was that convinced Earl and Allan to take a chance on me. Perhaps they valued my attitude and willingness to put myself outside my comfort zone, to take a risk and back myself, as they were required to do on a daily basis in their field. Whatever it was, I am eternally grateful they said yes, because if their answer had been different, I may never have got to the start line.

Feeling elated as I ended the call, I jumped up to hug Matt who had patiently waited in the other room. We shared a look. Things had just got real. Instead of an incredibly bold idea that would never come to fruition, we now knew that on 19 December 2021, I would set out from the shores of the Gold Coast to do what many considered impossible: paddle a piece of floating carbon fibre around the entire continent of Australia. We might not have had all the money we needed, but we figured that as the paddle gained media attention, we'd have leverage to push for further sponsorship.

In planning the expedition, there were many unknowns, but three things I knew for certain. Firstly, I wanted to break a world record. Secondly, I wanted to share the journey. With many people still in lockdown, I had a desire to take people on the paddle with me by capturing footage of the amazing parts of the country I visited, and so therefore I needed to find a videographer (more on that later). And thirdly, I wanted to do some good and raise funds and awareness for a cause I thought was worthwhile – and as fate would have it, the Shaw and Partners deal would lead me to a cause I grew to be incredibly passionate about.

Throughout the pandemic, mental-health statistics were climbing. People were more anxious and depressed, and the rates of suicide had increased. Shaw and Partners had always had an affiliation with Gotcha4Life, a charity that had a clear mission to reduce the suicide rate to zero. With nine people lost to suicide every day, enough was enough, said Gotcha4Life founder Gus Worland. He had started the foundation to provide mental fitness workshops in schools, businesses and sporting communities after losing his friend and mentor to suicide. I loved that the charity used terms like 'mental fitness' and 'emotional muscle', and once I learnt that they tailored workshops for school-aged children, I was in. Little did I know at the time of pledging to raise $100,000 for Gotcha4Life that I would gain a community of people who followed my journey, people who'd been affected by the loss of someone close to them to suicide or who struggled with their own mental fitness. Now an ambassador for the charity and delivering the workshops myself, I consider it fate that I pursued Shaw and Partners as a sponsor, as their passion for Gotcha4Life would soon feed my own.

The Shaw and Partners deal ensured I was able to start the paddle, but there were still crucial pieces of the puzzle to put into place, such as organising a crew, boat and car. And with plans set to start paddling in just a few months, the pressure was on.

Thankfully, I wasn't facing the daunting task on my own. Matt looks at the world differently to most people, and while I consider myself an extraverted introvert who prefers quality one-on-one conversations, Matt is a true people person. His ability to easily relate to people of different backgrounds, genders and ages allows him to make connections and see opportunities I am completely ignorant to. Matt was therefore able to link me in with people who could help me with one of the missing pieces of the expedition: the car.

Dave Gardner, the owner of Gardner Cars on the Gold Coast, lived in our building and, after a few conversations, Matt had arranged with Dave for the use of a Ford Ranger for the journey. It was not just any old Ranger; it was an almost new vehicle, complete with a suspension lift to handle the rough terrain; extra-large durable wheels to withstand the unsealed roads, sand and mud; and a wrap featuring the major sponsors of the expedition. Australia is renowned for its sections of remote coastline and the car would need to carry two of our crew and tow a jet ski over rough terrain. We would be asking it to take on everything from the soft sand of Western Australia to the red dirt of the Northern Territory. We needed a beast, and Dave delivered in spades.

Now it was time to find perhaps the most important component of the whole project: the ski I would spend the next eight months in.

I'd first met Mick Herden in 2019, when the desire to begin ocean ski paddling had led me to his paddling shop. Walking into the shop, I had no idea where to start but Mick provided me with a crash course in ocean skis and the equipment required, and I'd walked out with everything I needed to get started.

Mick was to help me again in 2021, when he arranged three brand-new ocean skis for the circumnavigation. Those who had completed the expedition prior had done so on craft that were much heavier than the nine-kilogram Nordic Nitro Mick recommended for me. The Nordic Nitro is the lightest ski on the market, a rocket through the water but with an emphasis on comfort. While I had struggled to sit in other skis for longer than a few hours at a time without my backside feeling numb, this ski was comfortable for sitting in all day. It has a wider seat compared to other brands of ski, a feature I would be grateful for on every day of my paddle.

Mick also recommended that I take an intermediate ski and a 30-kilogram plastic ski as back-ups. I wondered aloud about the purpose of carting a plastic ski around Australia. It was slow and a nuisance to transport; surely it wasn't necessary? Mick then reminded me that one third of Australia's coastline is populated with the fearsome saltwater crocodile, and the much heavier plastic ski would be more stable if it was bumped than the nine-kilogram lightweight carbon fibre ski.

I had picked up the three skis and was just walking out the door when Mick asked me one final question.

'Bonnie,' he said slowly, 'you get scared paddling five kilometres offshore here on the Gold Coast. How will you go in the middle of the ocean?'

It was a fair point. On multiple occasions, I'd paddled with Mick and his squad at Currumbin, and as we'd head out to sea, beyond the protection of the bay, I'd freak out. Moving in close to the person next to me, I'd rationalise that sharks wouldn't attack a group of paddlers because we looked too big bunched together. But when I took off on the circumnavigation of Australia, there would be no paddlers to move in close to. Other than my support boat, I would be alone in the water. Up to 500 kilometres out to sea. And as I would come to learn, both sharks and crocodiles are very interested in a paddler on her own.

'I'm really not sure how I'll go with it,' I eventually replied, a mix of nervousness and excitement swirling in my stomach. 'But I guess I'll find out.'

As I drove away from the warehouse, I pondered Mick's question. There were so many unknown quantities about this paddle, but instead of deterring me, the challenges excited me. Maybe it was the experience of Covid lockdowns, the feeling of Groundhog Day where one week blended into the next, that caused me to revel in the prospect of the unknown. I started to get the sense that while the world record was the initial reason for planning the journey, the self-growth I would undoubtedly experience would prove far more significant than any title.

*

Though I was having difficulty securing a boat and crew, Matt had not only found a car but had used his network to lock in a support crew to accompany me for the journey. If I was to break the world record, the crew would be absolutely crucial in assisting me not only physically but mentally. I just hoped Matt had made the right choices.

The first thing I noticed about Blake Bradford was his confidence. With a penchant for loud shirts, Blake is no shrinking violet; you could take him anywhere and he'd walk away with a list of contacts to add to his ever-growing network. Quick to joke and slow to anger, you'd be forgiven for thinking that he hadn't experienced hardship in his life. I would come to learn that quite the contrary is true. I would also come to rely on him to help me through some of the toughest stretches of water in the world. He would save my life on multiple occasions over the eight months.

Matt knew Blake through mutual friends in Mackay. They had been in contact on and off over the years, and at a recent charity swim I had completed, Matt had engaged Blake as the videographer for the occasion, and we asked him to come on for the paddle not long after. For 23 kilometres, I had ploughed my way up and down the pool as friends and family watched from the sideline. It took half the day to complete the swim and not only did Blake capture the swim in a way that was raw and moving, at every stop he was full of encouragement and optimism.

From the outset, Matt told me he was looking for crew members who were a 'hybrid' of skill and the right personality. Blake had overhauled his life just 12 months prior when he left his job of seven years as an auto-electrician in the mines to live in a van. He had spent a large part of the year between the Gold Coast and the south coast of New South Wales and had developed a keen interest in photography and content creation for social media. In terms of finding a hybrid, Blake was our man. We had our first crew member locked in. Now to find the next.

Growing up in Sawtell, I was used to the laid-back nature of people who hail from rural areas, and Ben Lavery embodied the easy-going personality I so admire. He is the quintessential country kid. Standing at 6 foot 2, the talented basketballer and runner moved from the tiny New South Wales town of Nymboida to the bright lights of the Gold Coast a week after his eighteenth birthday. Ben was midway through completing a master's degree in Environmental and Protected Area Management when Matt asked him to come on the adventure of a lifetime. Often lacking a filter, Ben's direct nature and problem-solving ability were traits we greatly valued. Throughout the paddle, his dry wit proved an asset in moments when I experienced despair and doubt.

Like Blake, I'd met Ben only once before he was engaged on the project. As the owner of a van and with a love of travel, Ben jumped at the chance to join the crew, with the intention of continuing to study online as we made our way around the country. He was also keen to get his jet-ski licence, an asset that would prove highly valuable in the remote parts of the Western Australian coast, when we were in between support boats.

So, we had our jet-ski and support-vehicle driver in Ben, our videographer in Blake and logistics manager in Matt.

When Blake committed to the paddle, he was to be the sole videographer for the trip. Trying to hold a camera steady on a catamaran in the middle of the ocean for eight months straight while helping with support and sailing the boat? It became clear he would need some help. By fate or chance, Blake's friend Jaime Sallows had finished a stint working in the snow fields the week Blake extended an invitation, and so Jaime jumped at the opportunity to join us for the duration of the trip. The timing was impeccable.

Jaime was born and raised on the southern end of the Gold Coast. A lifelong surfer, Jaime was the crew member who had the most prior knowledge of the ocean and the influence of wind and current, and throughout the expedition, he and I would share moments of excitement as we witnessed perfect barrels peeling off islands and broken swells that carried for 200 metres in the middle of the ocean. Jaime had a background in filmography (with a skill set so valued he lent his hand to the production of Baz Luhrmann's *Elvis*), and he and Blake had immediately hit it off during a chance encounter at a cafe.

Some people are born generous, and Jaime Sallows is one of them. I met Jaime the week before I was to spend eight months with him in some of the most testing conditions imaginable, and within the first five minutes, he had given me a gift. After approaching a local jeweller to sponsor the paddle, Jaime arrived at our house on the week of the paddle with a handmade ring and necklace for each of the crew. His selflessness and generosity would remain a constant through the journey.

Two weeks out from the start of the paddle, we'd finalised our crew, and though I didn't appreciate it then, we'd struck gold with these young men. The project would ask more of them than was demanded of most people in their lifetime and they would stand up to any challenge thrown at them. Though we couldn't pay them, I promised one hell of an adventure and can confidently say I made good on my word.

With the crew locked in, Matt's assigned tasks were completed. Fortunately, I'd finally managed to have success with my delegated assignments and had lined up a 38-foot catamaran, skipper and crew. The boat was anchored at a Brisbane marina, and I'd spent a trial day paddling 23 kilometres alongside it. After several meetings with the skipper, we officially had a support boat. Blake had also had success in sourcing a jet ski, which was donated through the company his sister worked at. With a jet ski to provide back-up support if the catamaran had mechanical issues, I now felt confident that we had all our bases covered. We had one month until the start date and we were nearly ready.

One of the final steps in preparation for the journey was speaking to our respective work colleagues. Over the previous ten years I had established three nutrition clinics on the Gold Coast, so I had to break the news of the paddle to the clinic managers. The idea was that I would return to the clinics after completing my circumnavigation, but as I walked out of the doors for the final time, I wondered again if I was making the right decision.

By far the hardest part of the preparation for the expedition was realising that for Matt to accompany me for the duration of the expedition, he would need to give up the job he adored as the High Performance Director for the Southport Sharks. I have never seen anyone lit up in the way Matt would be when he walked in the door after a Tuesday or Thursday night spent at the footy club coaching players. Throughout the season, Matt would work with the players, both individually and as a group, to help them achieve their goals. He loved that job.

Matt had already made sacrifices for my athletic career, beginning seven years prior when he'd supported me in the tail end of my ironwoman career. He'd been an ear and trusted confidant on hard training days and throughout the ups and downs of racing, listening as I sat in the shower after a race an emotional mess, devastated after just losing a major title. He would bring a juice and muffin down to the beach after training and gently guide me on which sponsorship avenues to pursue. Once, when struggling for money, we'd flown to Sydney for a competition using the last of the money in our bank account. Although we had only $30 to both of our names, Matt made sure that I didn't miss the opportunity to put my hard training into practice. He was my rock.

Now as we discussed whether he would accompany me on this latest venture, I wanted it to be his decision.

'You don't have to come,' I assured him, promising it would be okay if he stayed at home. The silence that followed was telling.

I'd be starting the challenge without enough money in the bank to finish, and while I was paddling hundreds of kilometres out at sea, there would be no way for me to contact sponsors let alone raise the extra $100,000 that we had calculated was required to get to the finish line. I would also be pushing myself harder than I'd ever done before, against elements not limited to big surf, crocodiles and sharks. We both knew the truth. If I was going to make it around, Matt needed to come.

'I would never stay home while you are risking your life every day. I couldn't do it.' Matt's words were soft but genuine.

And so, in the latest of many decisions that proved Matt's love and loyalty to me, he left the job he loved to support me on an expedition I wasn't guaranteed to complete.

Just two months before we set off, I watched Matt adjust his tie and put on his best boots for the Southport Sharks presentation dinner, feeling a pang of guilt I'd be happy never to experience again. Here he was, so proud of the role he'd worked incredibly hard to achieve, now saying farewell to the community in which he felt most at home. Checking the Southport Sharks' social-media accounts throughout the night, I saw a post put up around 8pm.

'Thank you, Matt,' the caption read, beneath a photo of Matt receiving an envelope and a bottle of wine to mark the club's gratitude for his service. Matt had given up his time and money and put his career on hold for his wife. The irony of the situation wasn't lost on me as I was acutely aware that it is so often the other way around, with women sacrificing their own ambitions for the sake of their male partner.

I had a car, jet ski, boat and crew. And a husband who was willing to go above and beyond to make this project successful, and I would come to rely on him in more ways than I could have ever imagined.

In our first year of dating, Matt's father, Dave, had passed away, and it brought us extremely close in a short amount of time. But the paddle would test us beyond anything we could have expected. Not only would I be risking my life in the middle of the ocean, but also my marriage, which would bend so close to breaking that I would many times question whether pursuing this lofty goal was worth it.

CHAPTER 3

GAME DAY

RAISING MONEY REMAINED A CONSTANT OBJECTIVE, AND A month out from the start of the paddle, I organised two sportswomen's breakfasts in the cause. My vision was to have a panel of some of the best female athletes and a mix of both genders in the crowd. Leaning heavily on my contacts, I managed to secure top-class athletes for both events.

With no experience in event management, Matt and I worked as a team to create mornings that we were proud of. As the women on the panel spoke passionately about their experiences, I watched the crowd listening intently and felt I had earned a reward greater than the $5000 we made from the event. We finished the second breakfast feeling like we'd done everything we could to raise as much as possible, and in the process had played a small part in helping to elevate female athletes.

One of my wishes for future generations of girls and young women is that they never know the feeling of racing for half the prize money as the men or having to sell their car to fund a sporting project. I will continue to do everything in my power to help make equality real.

As well as preparing financially and logistically for the paddle, I was readying myself physically, though not in the way most people would assume. My research had taught me that my estimated caloric expenditure would be around 10,000 calories a day. An active woman needs approximately 1500 to 1800 calories in an ordinary day, meaning I'd need to consume more than five times what I was currently eating, much of which would have to be eaten while balancing in an ocean ski. The maths didn't add up. So, getting on the front foot, for the six months leading into the paddle, I began to purposefully gain weight. Logic told me the extra body fat would come off once I started the paddle, and even if I didn't lose it all, the extra weight would assist me in the near freezing conditions of the Victorian and South Australian coastlines at the bottom of the country.

The first thing I did to gain weight was stop running. As a dietitian and athlete, I'm aware of the high energy expenditure associated with running, so I stopped the activity altogether. I increased the calories I was consuming by doubling the portion sizes of my meals, and I also increased my dietary fat intake. At nine calories a gram, fats have more than double the energy of protein and carbohydrate, which have four calories a gram. After finishing my usual lunch of a chicken salad roll or scrambled eggs on toast, I would follow up with a Nutella croissant and a smoothie. The change in diet soon began to show in my physique. Over the course of six months, I put on 12 kilograms to weigh 77 kilograms. It was the heaviest I'd ever been and I didn't fit into most of my clothing. Once a size 8, I was forced to purchase a new wardrobe of clothing in size 12. I knew clothes would be falling off me as I shed weight on the journey, but I resolved to purchase new items as I went because there was minimal storage space on the catamaran, and starting off with clothing in multiple sizes was simply not realistic.

The weight gain was a social experiment of sorts. I felt insecure about my changing physique; as an athlete I had always striven for muscular tone and a low body-fat percentage. This was the first test for me and the people around me. In what is perhaps the biggest testament to the quality of my family, not one of them commented negatively on the weight gain, and Matt was more than supportive. For my own part, I figured if feeling uncomfortable and heavy for a temporary amount of time was required to set a record, so be it.

As well as gaining weight in the name of the project, I would also need to sacrifice my inherent need for privacy. It was not always going to be practical to climb aboard the catamaran to use the toilet. I would need to either dive off my ski and do my business in the water or risk soiling myself in the craft. The prospect of the latter terrified me, but I needed to trust that my crew would have no judgement and be there to support me no matter how ugly things got.

As we counted down the days, I was in a state of conflicting emotions. I was excited and daunted but also feeling heavy and uncomfortable from keeping my calories up and my training sessions regular but not excessive. I didn't want to arrive at day one with niggles such as tennis or golf elbow – common ailments of motivated paddlers who attack pre-season with a little too much vigour – so I limited the distance paddled in training sessions to ten kilometres. I knew if I could stay injury free, my body would condition to the huge load as time went on, just as it had done under Pat's regime at Northcliffe all those years before.

One week prior to the start, our little Mermaid Beach unit looked like a warehouse as we packed our clothes and personal items away into cardboard boxes. The catamaran was to be our home for the next eight months and at 38 feet in length, it was the size of a large living room. We would have no choice but to be minimalists, as space would be tight. Trying to think practically, I packed my paddling gear and accessories into one large bag and my clothes into the other. That was it. My entire wardrobe for eight months in two bags. Vanity would have to wait.

*

The morning of 19 December finally arrived. Game day. Changing into my swimwear, paddling tights and rash shirt, I took a long look in the mirror and walked out the door, knowing that the woman who returned wouldn't be the same.

The sun was high in the sky and the temperature was already nearing 30 degrees as I attended media commitments with Seven Sunrise and Triple M radio, which had been scheduled with assistance from a PR agent in Sydney. My background as a professional athlete allowed me to stay calm under the pressure of live television and radio. With a healthy crowd beginning to build on the beach to witness the start of my paddle, I told the interviewers how I had recently discovered a sense of clear purpose, as though my whole life had been leading to the expedition. All of the mistakes I'd made, both as an athlete and in my personal life, had brought me to an emotional maturity that had been absent in my twenties. I was ready. Though I didn't know what was around the corner, I was prepared to work harder than ever before. And indeed, the work ethic that had been nurtured in me as a child, rounded as a young athlete and polished in the years since was an attribute that would be tested every day for the next eight months.

At 8am, it was finally time. After a hug and kiss for Matt, I made my way around to each of my immediate family members. Barely managing to contain my emotions, I cuddled my little nephews who were only one, three and ten years old, trying not to think of how much bigger they would be by the time I returned and the milestones I would miss. Their first step, first word, first swimming lesson. Not yet with children of my own, I took great pleasure in spending time with Georgia's three children and the thought of being away from them for nearly a year was heartbreaking.

Propping my ski up onto my hip, I grasped my paddle tightly and set off towards the ocean. Jaime followed with camera in hand, recording the occasion. Blake was already aboard the support catamaran, which was to meet me out the back of the break, and Ben was waiting on the jet ski; he would accompany me for the first few days as extra support. So Matt and Jaime were the ones beside me at the start. But it wasn't just the three of us present that day; forming a guard of honour was a crowd of over a hundred people, made up of my friends, family and members from my surf lifesaving and ocean swimming group.

Making my way towards the ocean, I was buoyed by the loud cheers of the crowd. I enjoyed the warmth of the white sand between my toes, and the prospect of surfing runners later in the afternoon excited me. By 2pm, I could look forward to 25-knot tailwinds, which would guarantee fun. As paddlers, we want the wind at our backs or 'tail' to push us along. A strong tailwind made the paddling highly enjoyable and far easier, often whipping up little waves, making it possible to 'surf' runners for hundreds of metres at a time. A headwind, on the other hand, feels like a giant fan blasting a paddler in the face, creating resistance and causing a paddler to grip the shaft of their paddle tighter, losing form with technique and expending twice the energy to keep the ski moving forward.

Sitting down into my ski and propping my feet on the pedals, I took the first strokes in my circumnavigation around Australia. The ocean was a pleasant 23 degrees and I enjoyed the warmth of the sun on my back. Our target was Byron Bay, roughly 70 kilometres away and further than I'd ever paddled in a single day. I tried not to let the small voice of self-doubt in.

A group of my local ocean-swimming friends joined me for the first 200 metres, then turned and headed back to shore.

A small group of paddlers remained, Mick Herden included. Leaning forward to reach for the tube of my water bladder, I was shocked to find it wasn't in my ski as intended. How careless I had been! When I was growing up, my coaches had always emphasised that as athletes we check our gear – and on the biggest day of my athletic career so far, I'd forgotten this golden rule.

Kicking myself for the mistake, I knew it simply wasn't realistic or smart to paddle all day without water, so I needed to acquire some from my crew. But a lack of water wasn't my only problem. Placing my legs into my ski, I immediately felt that my pedals were too far away, requiring me to stretch out with pointed toes to reach them. *Damn it.* The ski had been shipped brand new from Europe and had just arrived the week prior, and I hadn't had the chance to try it yet. It was still set up to fit an average man; and the leg length setting was far too long for me. It was a simple procedure to slide the pedals back towards me, but that was on land, something else I'd forgotten to do in the excitement of launch day.

With no water bladder in my ski, my feet barely able to touch the pedals, and facing 70 kilometres of paddling ahead, I looked around for help. Ben was shadowing me on the jet ski, and I called out to him, remembering that in the frenzy of the pre-paddle festivities, I'd also forgotten sunscreen and food. Ben rode the jet ski towards me like a knight in shining armour, equipped with water bottle, sunscreen and a small bag of bananas and lollies. Leaning against the jet ski for balance, I managed to fiddle around with the clip and adjust the footplate to fit my leg length. Crisis averted.

Throughout the morning, the accompanying paddlers dropped off until it was just Mick and me paddling towards the border of Queensland and New South Wales, lone silhouettes against the backdrop of Gold Coast high rises. The view of the coast was spectacular, but the sightseeing was soon interrupted when a fishing boat sped past us, cutting close and chopping up the water around us. Suddenly, I felt a wet slap across my face. Confused, I looked down to see something wriggling on my lap. On closer inspection, I saw it was a fish, flailing away, desperate to be returned to the ocean. The boaties had thrown the fish at me, and it had connected perhaps better than intended. Their shrieks of laughter were lost in the whirr of the boat's engine as they tore away, leaving Mick and me to comprehend what had happened. We eventually decided to laugh about it. If I was ever at risk of thinking I was special with the media attention I had recently received, my ego received a check when that cold, wet fish connected with my cheek.

The New South Wales border was Mick's final destination, and after a fist bump and a word of good luck, it was time for us to part ways. Turning back, I watched him fade into the distance, the outline of his ski growing smaller and eventually disappearing completely. The catamaran was several hundred metres further out to sea and Ben was trailing 100 metres behind me to give me space to enjoy the occasion.

Taking a sip of water, I allowed the moment to sink in. This was it. My paddle around Australia had begun. Then the roar of the jet ski interrupted my thoughts as Matt and Ben came zooming up behind me.

The plan was for me to follow the line of the catamaran, which set a course for the most direct path around Australia. The more we hugged the coast, the more kilometres we added to the trip, and so it was time to head out to sea. Though paddling 100 kilometres offshore was something I'd never imagined myself capable of, it was a necessity if I was going to better the previous times. It would take a few weeks to get used to the dark blue water of the deep sea, and the lack of sound that came with being so far removed from civilisation. In the beginning, I would jump at the shadow of a cloud passing overhead and squeal at every splash. Looking towards my crew on the boat, I would try to draw strength from their presence, reminding myself that putting myself outside of my comfort zone would be necessary to break the world record. But even then, I would whimper as I felt a bump against my ski, unsure if I'd run over a jellyfish or something far more sinister.

Peering into the distance towards Byron Bay, I felt the breeze pick up and the tail of my ski lift with each swell. A lifetime spent in the ocean allowed me to estimate, from the ease of my paddling and the size of the ocean chop, how strong the wind was. Sensing the gusts to be around 20 knots, I reached forward to secure my leg leash around my ankle. One of the key safety elements in ocean ski paddling is the leash that attaches a paddler to their ski and prevents the ski being carried away with the wind if the paddler falls off.

As a rookie ocean ski paddler, I'd once taken safety measures too lightly and paid for it. In 2019, I made the mistake of paddling in rough conditions without a leg leash and lifejacket. After a 50-kilometre paddle in 5–6-metre swells, I'd been hit from the side by a rogue wave and thrown out to float alone in the Gold Coast Seaway, a spot renowned for its aggressive bull sharks. Fortunately, a group of tourists on the rock wall spotted me and called for help, and within 15 minutes the volunteer marine rescue crew had managed to haul both me and my ski into their boat. I'd been lucky, they told me. Others in a similar situation hadn't lived to tell the tale. I was adamant I wouldn't make the same mistake again.

Two years later, with the leg leash tightly fastened around my ankle and a lifejacket secured around my core, I began to lift my stroke rate to surf the increasingly larger swells. The wind, as predicted, was up to 25 knots, and the conditions had become borderline dangerous. At 60 kilometres into the paddle, my arms were full of lactic acid, a result of asking more of my body than I ever had before. But I wanted to keep going. I knew people were tracking the distance I paddled on the first day through Strava (an app which allows people to record and publicly share times and distances achieved in a workout), and my ego overshadowed the care I owed myself and my crew.

In the months leading up to the circumnavigation, dozens of people had questioned my ability to finish. Social media had transformed from a platform I used to communicate with my friends to a vessel for opinions on the paddle, both positive and negative. From the day I announced my ambition, I'd received hundreds of messages from people sharing their thoughts, many of them questioning my ability. Too far, too dangerous, too crocodile infested; I'd heard it all.

To finish the day at Ballina instead of Byron Bay would extend the paddle by 15 kilometres but would result in 88 kilometres total, a distance members of the surf ski community would find impressive. My obsession with what others thought was a problem I took into the journey and would take a while to shake, and on the first day I had a point to prove.

From the jet ski, Matt relayed options from the skipper via the two-way radio strapped to his chest. Though he suggested I call it quits at Byron Bay, which lay five kilometres further ahead, I ignored the advice and continued to paddle without replying. Matt's voice grew sterner, as he asserted that it was unsafe for the jet ski and the boat to continue.

I snapped. 'I want to go to Ballina,' I shouted above the breeze.

I noticed Ben's shocked reaction at my tone.

But Matt held his ground. Staring each other down in the middle of the ocean, I eventually realised I wasn't going to win the battle. Seething, I reluctantly agreed to head to shore at Byron Bay.

Paddling into the popular Wategos Beach of Byron Bay, 73 kilometres from where we'd started at Mermaid Beach that morning, we noticed odd looks from the professional lifeguards as well as members of the public. At first, I thought the sight of a young woman paddling in huge winds with two men following on a jet ski was causing the confusion, but we soon learnt that there is no jet-ski access allowed on Wategos because of the rocky bottom of the beach and its steep shore dump, which made it too dangerous for motor craft to enter or exit. Fortunately, we were able to avoid a reprimand from the friendly lifeguard, who suggested we drive the jet ski around to the back beach. Having just gained his jet-ski licence the week before, Ben was pushed beyond his comfort zone as he revved the craft into the side chop, but without hesitation he stepped up, as he would continue to do for the next eight months.

Far from the flashes of cameras and applause earlier in the day, I struggled up the beach with my ski and paddle. I shivered as my wet rash shirt clung to my body and tried to ignore the cries of pain from my overused muscles.

Matt and I barely spoke as we waited for Ben to return with Jaime, who'd driven our Ranger south down the highway to pick us up. We had rarely fought before the paddle, but the pressure was getting to us. Adding more tension was the fact that I was starving hungry because I hadn't eaten enough during the day, my lips were cracked thanks to windburn, and I was resentful at having to wait under a tree after paddling further than I ever had in my life. By the time the boys arrived, my lips were purple, but I had to wait still longer until we arrived at the marina for a hot shower.

When I finally got under the marina shower I let the water run over my aching body and my core temperature slowly returned to normal. Logistics were one part of the challenge, but keeping my body together would be a key element of the project. I unfastened the velcro of the back brace I was wearing and let it fall to the floor, wincing as I did so. The brace had held my muscles together and supported my back throughout the paddle. I'd laughed when Matt brought the accessory home from the chemist, but now I was thankful to have a husband who knew the benefits it offered for posture and injury prevention.

Walking back to the catamaran from the bathroom, I saw the boat crew cooking dinner while Matt, Ben, Blake and Jaime sat on the trampoline at the front of the boat and debriefed. The tone of the conversation was serious. Prior to the paddle, we'd held an orientation day on the boat but I'd had limited time to practise paddling beside it, meaning we would need to refine our protocols as we went. Leaving the boys to their discussion, I sat alone on the back deck. I opened my phone to find dozens of messages of support, several missed calls and my social media going off.

Starting from the most recent, I began replying to those who sent their well wishes, a habit I would continue for the duration of the expedition. Engaging with the paddling and wider community was something I'd come to embrace, and it never felt a chore to write back to someone who had taken the time to send well wishes. As comes with the territory of social media, however, the messages weren't always positive, and one particularly persistent follower would regularly make contact to let me know how crazy I was and how I was never going to make it.

Following a quintessential Australian dinner of steak and veggies, we crowded around the table for a meeting to unpack the day's events. Now that I was over my dummy spit, I was keen to start planning for the next day, but I was soon given reason to retreat back into my dark mood. Taking turns to provide input, we each stated what we believed could have been done better. When it was Blake's turn, he noted that I'd appeared 'distressed' towards the end of the paddle. Having just met Blake, I immediately felt annoyed. Frustrated at having to finish earlier than expected, yes, but 'distressed' I was not. Not wanting to start a debate, and with little rapport with anyone else but Matt, I didn't reject the idea. Not yet confident to lead, I let others run the meeting, and it was only after several weeks of withholding my opinion that I started to speak up.

We were eager to start day two with a bang. The Guinness World Record guidelines for circumnavigation attempts state that the participant must start and finish in the exact same spot each time. This data would be recorded in the boat's navigation system and through the watch I wore, which had GPS data. So I needed to paddle out from the rocky shores of Wategos Beach where we'd landed the previous day.

Ben was to escort me with the jet ski for the day. It isn't often mentioned, likely due to the prevalence of tourism in the northern New South Wales area, but the stretch of coast we were to cover had seen several great white shark attacks in the previous few years. And yet here I was, floating on my tiny ocean ski on top of the dark grey water, and this time my shivering was not due to the cold.

The hum of the jet ski helped to soothe me as I took my first few strokes. Unsure whether it was thanks to his experience of being an older sibling or the fact that he was physically a lot taller than most, I felt safe when Ben was beside me.

His protective instincts were about to be tested. Making our way towards Ballina, I forced my arms to move quickly, propelling my ski forward through the choppy water. Though my arms were aching from the enormous distance I'd paddled the day before, I did everything I could to keep my speed up so I wouldn't be seen as an easy target from below. I was idly making conversation to distract myself from the eeriness of the situation when a splash in front of me suddenly alerted my senses.

'Did you see that?' I asked Ben.

'Bait ball,' came his swift reply.

Soon after, the singular splash turned into an enormous ripple that carried across the water for 50 metres. A frenzy of movement confirmed that I had indeed paddled straight into a bait ball, a mass of tiny fish that move together. A common rule among surfers and paddlers alike is to avoid bait balls at all costs. These tiny fish attract bigger fish and, in turn, sharks. One of the more terrifying sights for ocean-goers is a bait ball parting up the middle, the result of something very large making its way through.

An ocean ski is steered through a rudder system, which is controlled by the pedals at the front of the ski, so I slammed my foot down hard on the left pedal, forcing my ski to turn sharply back out to sea to steer clear of the bait ball. Simultaneously, I heard Ben whip into action revving the jet ski hard, hoping the excessive noise would ward off any unwelcome visitors lurking below. He then proceeded to drive 'doughnuts', or large circles, around me with the jet ski, churning up the water as he did so. Sharks are extremely sensitive to noise and in that moment I felt indebted to Ben, knowing that without the jet ski I would have been in an extremely precarious position. Paddling hard, I was grateful to reach the other side of the huge ball of fish.

Another enormous bait ball awaited us just one kilometre further down the coast, and we employed the same tactics. Ben made as much noise as possible as I paddled around the masses of fish, and we passed by unharmed. We reached the end of the isolated stretch of coast to meet the catamaran just outside the Yamba marina, signalling a total of 95 kilometres for the day. While safe, I was slightly rattled by the experience. Standing under the hot shower at the marina I was relieved both to be over the day's paddling and onto the next leg towards my hometown of Coffs Harbour. That stretch of coastline was far less isolated than the one we had just navigated.

The next day, as I made my way south from Yamba, the catamaran and crew coasted alongside me in the 25-knot tailwind. The extra support of the jet ski had been helpful for the first two days as I grew used to paddling the huge stints, but with the cost of fuel at an all-time high, it wasn't economical to have the jet ski with me each day, so it was now on the highway, being towed by Jaime and Ben, as Matt and Blake accompanied the skipper and his three crew on the boat.

Positioning myself 50–100 metres beside the catamaran, I ensured the skipper and I had a clear view of each other. With the catamaran weighing ten tonnes, a collision with my nine-kilogram carbon fibre boat could be potentially fatal. The side-by-side dynamic was highly enjoyable, and I could hear shouts of encouragement from Matt and Blake over the wind, lifting me to keep up the hot pace of 13–14 kilometres an hour.

Navigating the break wall at the Coffs Harbour jetty cemented my first time completing more than 100 kilometres in a single day. I'd managed 108 kilometres in total, and throughout the final 20 kilometres of the day I'd been joined by a pod of dolphins who playfully coasted either side of me. The feeling of having a dozen dolphins – among them a mix of adults and babies – surfing the swells alongside you is indescribable. The pain in my back that had been plaguing me all day subsided and I felt a child-like delight. The dolphins were welcoming me home.

Since childhood, I'd been a workhorse. Balancing a schedule of academia and training had set me up for a successful transition into university and a professional athletic career. Refusing to be outworked built me up for an exciting life in the fast lane but, in the process, my unrelenting pursuit of success had killed my sense of curiosity. They say you don't know what you've got until it's gone, but maybe I didn't know what I was missing until I found it.

That pod of dolphins, gliding effortlessly down the swells, reminded me that there's more to life than work. Though I had lost my sense of spirituality over the years, there I was at 31, in the middle of the ocean with not a place to be other than right there, sharing the water with what I'd come to call my kindred spirits.

As my crewmates hauled me onto the back of the catamaran at the end of the day, my back muscles were on fire, but I was grinning from ear to ear. This was never about a world record. There was a greater purpose to this project, and I was going to find it.

CHAPTER 4

JUST ONE MORE MONTH

IN INTERVIEWS WITH ULTRA-ENDURANCE ATHLETES — THOSE people who have pushed themselves beyond what was previously considered the realms of possibility — one question is almost guaranteed to pop up.

Did you ever want to quit?

Since the paddle, I've been asked the question over a hundred times. In schools by students and teachers, in the boardrooms of multi-billion-dollar companies, by coaches, fellow athletes, parents of surf lifesavers, friends, family and those who crewed the trip. And each time I answer without hesitation.

Yes.

I wanted to quit when the top layer of flesh from my lips peeled off from sunburn and the salt water bit into the raw new skin, preventing my lips from healing. I contemplated throwing in the towel when my finger joints seized up from gripping my paddle all day and refused to straighten, rendering me useless when it came to everyday tasks like opening bottles and writing with a pen. I longed to call it a day when all that was left to throw up was stomach acid, the full contents of my gut long ago emptied over the side of my ski, the seasickness relentless.

And long before any of that happened, I also wanted to quit. The first time being a few days past Coffs Harbour, near the tiny coastal town of South West Rocks.

One week into the paddle, Covid-19 was still running rampant throughout the country and the world. Every time humankind tried to get back on its feet, the virus would bring us to our knees once more. We had planned to run workshops as we made our way along the coast, the aim being to highlight the importance of mental fitness and raise funds for Gotcha4Life. Our first workshop was to be held at the Coffs Harbour Surf Club, and the hard work of my uncle Pete and friend Megan had ensured a full house for the event. Raffle and auction items were ready. I was excited to sit down for dinner with people I hadn't seen for years, many of whom had played an important part in shaping my future as an athlete.

But one day out from the event, a surf-club employee contracted Covid and the whole surf club had to shut down. The event was off. And so were we, the very next day. With no chance to postpone, we were forced to cancel. The unfortunate timing of the incident was a stark reminder that the virus was still dictating our lives more than we liked to admit.

Covid threatened to end the paddle at any given moment; if one of our crew contracted the virus, as close contacts we'd all need to isolate for two weeks and the world-record attempt would be over. As per the Guinness World Record rules, I wouldn't be able to remain stationary for longer than two weeks at a time throughout the attempt.

The threat of state border closures also loomed, particularly in Western Australia where the border had been closed by the premier, Mark McGowan. During the pandemic, McGowan had declared that no one was to enter or leave Western Australia, meaning many residents hadn't seen friends and family for over two years. The border was due to open on 5 February, but, of course, there was every chance that this could change, meaning there was every possibility I would paddle over 3000 kilometres to reach Western Australia and get turned back around if the state decided to close its borders again.

Sharks, bad weather and financial challenges were all hurdles I could accept, as scary as they were to face, but being forced to retire due to border closures would be hard to handle. All I could do was trust in Matt, who was constantly monitoring the situation and had taken on the responsibility of applying for an exemption for us to enter the state if the borders closed before we got there.

And so, a few days past Coffs Harbour, having been denied the opportunity to see lifelong friends at the workshop, and with the threat of border closures lingering, I experienced the first urge to quit. Twenty kilometres offshore, I could feel the assistance I was getting from the EAC. The current is known to work as close as five to six kilometres off the coast of Byron Bay, but in staying further offshore, we were in the strongest part. Though the skipper gave me regular updates as to its strength, I knew that when the paddling felt easy, the current was at its strongest. Spending many hours in the ski each day, I began to feel like part of the ocean and developed the ability to predict the wind strength to within a knot and the water temperature to within a degree or two.

But even with the assistance of the EAC, my body was in agony. My back was incredibly inflamed and I could barely stand a gentle prod let alone massage to relieve my knotted muscles. Not yet used to paddling so far out to sea, I was scared to get in the water each day. Loneliness also became an issue, as I was unable to communicate with my crew beyond a few words at a time, as my skills didn't yet allow me to paddle close enough to the catamaran to hold a conversation.

Just one week in, the novelty of the experience was wearing off, and I was missing my comfortable life on the Gold Coast. The familiar sinking feeling in the pit of my stomach told me I was out of my depth. Matt and I had given up everything we'd worked for to make the expedition happen and perhaps it was all a waste. Maybe capabilities and ambitions can get so mixed up, and the thing you'd been so sure you were destined for just wasn't in reach after all.

As these thoughts crossed my mind, I heard an internal voice fighting against the negative thoughts. At first faint and then louder.

Just one more month.

It was no more than a few words, but the message was clear, urging me to hang in there for 30 more days. To not back down. Yet.

Just one more month.

The angel on my shoulder worked hard to quiet the devil that would persist with its negative message until the day I paddled back into the Gold Coast or called it quits before I got there. Which one would win out?

Okay, I rationalised, *I'll give it a month.*

In one month, I'd be near the border of Victoria, an isolated stretch of coastline and a less embarrassing place to pull out. Others would see that at least I had made it that far.

My measure of successful feedback was still primarily external. What would others think? How would I be perceived? The people pleaser within me that had been present since childhood was still dictating my decisions. Thankfully, the paddle gave me the opportunity to change this. In the isolated waters of the Northern Territory, when I was without phone reception for three weeks, where I witnessed a giant shark leap out of the water in front of me and where huge sea snakes were coiled up ready to strike as I passed, it was no longer about who was watching. An environment that harsh strips back all layers, forcing you to look at the true reasons you are putting your body through hell. The approval of others by then was simply not enough to keep going.

But for now, my key motivator to continue was to avoid the shame of pulling out; I couldn't be seen as a loser. And so, somewhere off South West Rocks, atop the EAC, the quiet inner urging became a pact I made with myself. *Just one more month.*

Struggling through each painful kilometre, I downplayed my physical and mental suffering to the crew. I didn't want to burden the people who would be giving eight months of their life to help me. My hands were blistered from gripping my paddle for 12–14 hours each day. We had discovered early into the expedition that the thin paddling gloves I'd packed were not durable enough to handle the huge load. Jaime had suggested I use his spearing gloves instead. Designed to protect spearfishermen when handling fish, the gloves were far thicker than the paddling gloves and had, to my relief, solved the problem of the blisters. I did, however, still experience aching in the joints of my fingers due to the pressure placed upon them as I gripped my paddle, and the dull pain became more pronounced as each day passed.

Along with the pain and self-doubt, I was also dealing with a loneliness I hadn't experienced before. In the water on my own, I'd often look up and see the crew sharing jokes and conversations and feel a longing to join them. While I'd put my hand up to do the paddle and the physical pain was mine to carry, I still desired human connection. I wanted to show that my value as a person went far beyond my ability to paddle 12 hours a day, and I wanted to share stories of childhood and life back home, instead of paddling and logistics.

As I grew more stable in the ski over the passing weeks, I developed the ability to surf in a zig-zag pattern, paddling in towards the boat, which allowed me to hold a brief conversation with a crew member on the side then paddle away from the boat to safety if I got too close and risked a collision. The only problem was that every word could be heard by the whole crew, meaning a private interaction was impossible. Privacy is important to me and to have it stripped away left me feeling vulnerable. Even if I felt the need to share my struggles with Matt or Blake, I wasn't yet ready for the whole boat to hear about it, and so I mostly kept my problems to myself or waited until the end of the day when I could share them privately.

Fortunately, in the early days when I was craving a personal chat and missing my friends, assistance was to arrive in the shape of an ironwoman.

One of the youngest ever to qualify for the professional Nutri-Grain IronWoman series, Lizzie Welborn is a certified champion. A passionate surf lifesaver, Lizzie cares deeply about our waterways and the environment, and you'd be hard-pushed to find an athlete who is more giving of their time in promoting a cause to benefit others.

Lizzie was holidaying with her family at Seal Rocks, north of Newcastle, when she heard I was paddling past the area. It was Christmas Day, and following breakfast with her family, Lizzie paddled out to accompany me. Seeing Lizzie in her Santa hat, I instantly felt lighter. For six kilometres, we chatted non-stop and the dark feeling that had been building over the past week all but dissipated.

The universe has a strange way of rewarding those who persist, and I believe Lizzie was meant to come into my orbit that day.

The encounter helped me through Christmas Day and also the following week. Lizzie's positivity reenergised me.

Eighty kilometres later, I finished the paddling day at Port Stephens near Newcastle. Enjoying a seafood lunch and opening presents there, I felt life wasn't too bad. With a few scheduled days off due to some bad weather rolling in, the crew was in great spirits as we explored the stunning coastal town, gathering ourselves mentally and physically before the push towards Victoria.

A few days later, I made my way through the heads of Sydney Harbour on New Year's Eve. In planning the expedition, I hadn't anticipated spending the last day of 2021 watching fireworks light up the sky in the most iconic location in Australia, but the timing was perfect. Sunbaking on the front deck of the catamaran, watching local revellers anchor up around us in preparation for the evening, vibes were high.

Early in the day, I paddled with a crewmate up to the iconic Sydney Harbour Bridge and underneath it. Opened in 1932, the bridge spans 500 metres and stands an impressive 134 metres above the waters of Sydney Harbour. Casting a huge shadow over the water below, the bridge is a masterpiece and from our skis we were able to view it from an angle few would ever experience. The significance of the occasion wasn't lost on me, and goosebumps lined my arms as I made my way to the sunny waters on the other side of the bridge, taking in the sights of Luna Park on my right.

As we welcomed in the new year, I appreciated how far I had come physically and mentally. I had weathered the low spirits following the disappointment at Coffs Harbour; I'd battled a few days of nasty headwinds off Port Macquarie; I'd worked through some of my loneliness; my crew had spotted several hammerhead sharks tailing me; but I was nowhere near my limit yet. Not even close.

Once we crossed into Victorian waters, the games would truly begin. Past the border of New South Wales and Victoria, the water changes from cool to near freezing, and the risk of great white shark attacks doubles, and then triples once you get to the waters of South Australia.

As we headed south, I'd paddle approximately 100 kilometres offshore in taking the shortest route, and while crossing the Great Australian Bight, I'd be 500 kilometres out to sea, with the depth of the ocean reaching three kilometres in some sections. The water is different that far out. The sea is darker in colour. You can sense the depth and huge volume of water underneath, yet on a cloudy day you can't even see below the surface. It's enough to make you start seeing things. *Was that shadow a piece of seaweed or something more deadly? Was that bump on my rudder caused by a tuna or killer whale? What lies beneath?* It's easy to lose your mind if you let your imagination get carried away.

But on New Year's Eve, I enjoyed spectacular fireworks with my crew on one of the most populated bodies of water. Looking back now, I can see that the young woman who listened to the sounds of Indigenous music echoing around the Opera House that evening was incredibly naive. She who admired the work of the pyrotechnics as the sky lit up and laughed as the crowd grew rowdier with intoxication was someone not yet exposed to the cruelty of Mother Nature. I was an athlete who had pushed beyond myself physically but hadn't yet found my limits and then been forced to go beyond them. I had no idea what was to come.

But the naivety was also protective; it allowed me to plan with enthusiasm and optimism. Ignorance allowed me to pretend, even just for a day, that I was a regular person. On that day, I was just a girl on a boat watching the pretty lights sparkle in the sky.

The next day we were back to work. The glassy conditions were gone but the tailwinds were back, and we knew we had to make the most of the good paddling conditions. Pushing hard, I was sore at the end of the day but less sore than the week prior; my muscles were slowly becoming accustomed to the hell I was inflicting on them.

Luxuries on the high seas are rare, but a highlight remained the 'bucket bath' I would receive when I came onto the catamaran after a day of paddling. On a boat, saving water is essential. Fresh water is made through desalination or sourced from tanks, which are filled up at the marina. The bucket bath was exactly what it sounds like: a bucket filled with warm water, tipped over my head to wash off the salt. If I was lucky, a second bucket of water was tipped over my head, but I learnt to cherish that first bucket and its power to wash away not just the salt but the mental load of the day.

I was the only one allowed to use a hairdryer on the boat due to the large amount of power the accessory uses, and the engines would be revved as I dried my hair to ensure I didn't drain all the power from the boat. My hairdryer, at first brought onboard for vanity, would prove one of the most valuable items I had with me. The blast of warmth heated me to my core and when used in conjunction with a space blanket would save me from hypothermia on more than one occasion. By the end of the first week, the routine was set: bucket bath, change into dry clothes, hairdryer and dinner.

In the first few weeks, I would look forward to the dinner served by the crew member rostered on for that evening. But as conditions grew rougher and seasickness set in, the meal often ended in a sprint to the back deck to empty the contents of my stomach. There's something cruel about watching the person next to you holding down a wholesome meal while your nutrient-starved body rejects it. Theodore Roosevelt once said, 'Comparison is the thief of joy,' and I tried hard to abide by the warning in this statement. While paddling 100 kilometres, I tried not to feel like I was missing out on conversations on the boat. Running to the back step to vomit, I tried not to envy my crewmates who held down their food. I tried to stay in my lane and not compare, but my lane was often a lonely place to be.

Making our way down the south coast of New South Wales, the water temperature and coastline began to change and in a single day of paddling, I would notice the temperature of the ocean drop. Early in the paddle, the skipper informed us that after passing Sydney, the distance between anchorages would grow longer, with fewer headlands and safe places to stop. Sighting boats became a rarity and scenic bays gave way to long deserted stretches of beach. As the coastline became more remote, we started to catch our first views of the wind turbines that occupy large stretches of headlands on the south coast.

The wind increased to 25 knots on some days, and as the ambient and water temperature plunged, I went from wearing swimmers and paddling shorts to a wetsuit with a jacket over the top. Australian brand Vaikobi supplied me with as much gear as needed. With a background in elite sailing and a lifetime spent on the water, owner Pat Langley was well versed in the durability of garments, but even he admitted he wasn't sure how the gear would stand up to the elements over such a long period of time and under the enormous paddling load. Fortunately, the gear not only stood up to the test, it exceeded my expectations in every way. My Vaikobi paddling steamer wetsuit was made of three- to four-inch thick neoprene material and allowed me to paddle in ten-degree water all day without getting hypothermic until I was able to change back to lighter paddling gear in the heat of Western Australia.

Approaching Jervis Bay on the far south coast of New South Wales, I began to fall out of my ski quite frequently. The mix of ground swells, wind chop and currents meant the ocean's surface was no longer pleasant, and several times a day, a stray swell would throw me off my ski into the icy water. Wearing several layers of clothing, as well as carrying a radio, it was incredibly taxing to heave myself back up and into my ski.

At the beginning of the day, the fall-outs were comical and led to open laughter from myself and the crew, who were watching closely from the boat, as a lapse of concentration or mistimed lunge to grab a food bag tipped me off. Towards the end of a day, however, with the ocean growing rougher and the sky darker, the response was different. No longer a joke, my priority was getting back into the ski as quickly as possible, before my body temperature plummeted or a shark became interested in the splashing. The key was not to rush; it was better to take my time and nail the remount first go, instead of failing and plunging back into the icy water. As my upper body grew stronger, remounting my ski became easier but in the early days the process was quite an ordeal.

One place that is less than ideal to fall out is next to the cliff faces off Jervis Bay, south of Wollongong in New South Wales. Looming high above the ocean, the huge rock walls created a backwash that could be felt for kilometres out to sea, making it incredibly difficult to balance along the rare stretches of coastline where I was just a few kilometres offshore. The backwash and ocean turbulence caused by the cliffs affected my stomach, and multiple times in the day, the expensive electrolyte drinks I'd consumed went to waste in the frothy ocean as I vomited over the side of the ski.

As the Jervis Bay cliff faces loomed larger, the skipper informed me that the boat had to keep a certain distance away, so as not to enter shallow water. Curious to get a closer look at these natural beauties, I left my usual position 50 metres off to the starboard side of the catamaran and paddled towards the cliffs. Matt's shouts to be careful were just audible above the wind. Soon I was several hundred metres from the boat, and just 100 metres from some caves I could see beneath the cliffs, with thousands of litres of water swirling beneath me. I edged closer until I could see the moss on the cliff edges and hear the rumbling as the water angrily crashed into the caves below.

Suddenly, a large black fin surfaced 50 metres ahead. At first glimpse, it's impossible to tell whether a fin belongs to a dolphin or a shark, but on a second sighting, it's usually clear. The fin failed to reappear, which I knew wasn't a good sign, as dolphins surface frequently. Gut instinct told me to get out of the area immediately, so quickly slamming my left pedal down, I angled back out to the boat, where the crew was waiting anxiously.

'I'm going to stay close,' I called. My arms were beginning to drop with fatigue from the huge paddling load, and the sun was starting to set over the headland we were aiming for.

Looking across to see Matt's gaze fixed on me intently, it was as though he was seeing into my soul. Seven years together meant he knew me better than anyone, and though it wasn't obvious to the rest of the crew, he could see I was struggling. My lip visibly quivering in the cold may have been the giveaway, or perhaps it was my knuckles, which had turned white from gripping the paddle in fear. Matt knew I was spent. Scared, cold and fatigued, I looked at him in despair.

With half of his life spent around elite footballers, Matt always seemed to know what to say when the chips were down.

'Never go silent on your athletes' was a mantra he lived by, and he was quick with a word of encouragement when it was needed. Considering the situation carefully, he kept his words brief but effective.

'The anchorage is just up here. A few kilometres. Hang in there.' His voice was carried from boat to ski by the northeasterly wind that continued to increase.

Even though I wanted nothing more than to quit, Matt's words inspired me to hang tough. Just a few more kilometres and I'd be sitting on the back deck as the warm water of the bucket bath trickled over my head. Numb from over 13 hours of immersion in the cold water, I glanced down at my watch to see I'd racked up 122 kilometres for the daily total.

As I continued to grind out kilometre after painful kilometre, the sky and water growing increasingly dark, I entered a zone of laser focus, channelling my energy into each stroke.

Three kilometres later, the skipper called it: 'Time for that bucket bath.'

These were the words I'd paddled 125 kilometres to hear.

Several minutes later, slouched on the back deck, my crewmate brushing the knots from my matted hair and the sweet fragrance of conditioner lingering in the air as the sky darkened, I pondered the fact that I'd achieved 125 kilometres of paddling in a single day. That was further than I'd ever paddled before in a single stint and added another layer to the shield of resilience I'd been welding since day one of the paddle. The achievement overshadowed any sense of doubt I'd felt; the 125-kilometre effort proved I was capable. Maybe I was in with a fighting chance of pulling the whole thing off after all.

At South West Rocks, when I had wanted to quit more than anything, I'd made a pact to complete one month. Just one week later, not yet a month into the paddle, I realised I was growing stronger every day. With the border of Victoria soon approaching, I would have a choice to make. Pull out or push on?

There's a saying I love: *Diamonds are forged under pressure.* When I was training with the world's best ironwomen, our coach Pat would send us to the local gym to lift weights and run on the treadmill. That quote was printed on the wall behind the treadmill and during every session, as I pushed my legs to run faster, I studied the words.

Diamonds are forged under pressure.

Ten years on, I thought of those words once more. Maybe, if I could find a way to withstand the pressure of the wind, swells, shark encounters, hypothermia, aching muscles, fear and doubt, I would be forged into a diamond.

CHAPTER 5

STATUES OF THE SEA

EDEN IS A COASTAL SETTLEMENT ON THE FAR SOUTH COAST of New South Wales. With a population just shy of 3000, the town sits between rugged cliffs to the south and a surf beach to the north. As the most southern town in New South Wales, it was the last point of land contact before we crossed into Victorian waters.

Arriving in Eden on 5 January, I'd enjoyed a 73-kilometre paddle soaking up the gorgeous coastline of neighbouring Tathra and Merimbula. The tailwinds were still following me, and I'd essentially been blown down the east coast, facing just a few days of headwinds since beginning the expedition. Blessed with 15–20-knot northerly winds for the majority of the past three weeks, the favourable conditions not only increased my speed but took a great deal of strain off my body, giving me a chance to condition to the huge paddling load without the injury risk that would accompany 10–12 hours of pushing into headwinds.

But I knew my luck wouldn't last. Eventually the wind would turn, and instead of 100-kilometre days, I'd be looking at achieving 60–70 kilometres in the same timeframe. It was therefore crucial that when the wind was behind us I put my head down and paddled. When the tailwinds were pumping, any thought of a day off was forgotten and aching muscles were ignored; instead, I needed to paddle harder than I had in my life. The tailwinds provided a chance to put a buffer on the previous world record, but also gave us time up our sleeve should any obstacles arise: be they Covid outbreaks, bad weather or injury. The plan was to put days, weeks and eventually months between myself and the previous mark; I already knew I'd never repeat the expedition, so this was my one and only chance.

Dinner in Eden was delivered by a friend of Blake's who lived in the area. Mid-paddle that day, Blake had asked whether I preferred chicken or tofu in the poke bowls being prepared and, choosing the latter, I was excited by the prospect of one of my favourite meals. Blake met his friend onshore to receive the meals, then handed individual poke bowls to each crew member. The food looked delicious and was packed with valuable nutrients: vegetables, quality protein and slow-release carbohydrate in the brown-rice base. The dietitian within me approved. Grabbing a fork, I began scooping up the first chunks of tofu and avocado, savouring the fresh ingredients as they hit my tastebuds. My joy lasted only two minutes. At first my salivary glands began to work overtime, followed by nausea. I knew what was coming. Quickly putting down the bowl, I sprinted to the back deck, making it only just in time to empty the entire contents of my stomach over the side.

Returning to the group, I was reluctant to share what had happened considering Blake had put so much effort into organising dinner. However, the crew was full of sympathy and encouraged me to try something that might be better received by my gastrointestinal system.

Deciding to trial a Jatz, I figured I could use the high amount of salt in the biscuits. Carefully placing the first cracker into my mouth, I waited to see what happened. Not sensing an immediate rejection, I slowly swallowed the masticated salty, buttery goodness. I consumed a second biscuit and then several handfuls more, and quite soon I'd devoured nearly the whole box. I scanned the nutrition information and calculated the calories in a box as opposed to a serve and was shocked to find I'd consumed over 1000 calories: more than half of an average woman's daily intake. And I was still hungry.

Deciding to prioritise calories over nutritional value, I returned to the snack cupboard to see what other treats lay within. That's when I spotted the jar of Nutella. A delicious blend of hazelnuts, cocoa, sugar and oil, Nutella has been spread on toast, sandwiches and eaten by the spoonful by Australians for decades. It also happens to be one of the highest calorie foods per gram you can find at the supermarket. Grabbing the jar and a spoon, I returned to the bench at the back of the boat; if I was going to be introducing new foods to my unsettled stomach, I wanted to do so just one lunge away from the water.

Though my stomach seemingly rejected anything nutritious, the Nutella went down like a charm. Savouring the smooth, chocolatey treat, I finally started to feel full. Following the Nutella with half a packet of Tim Tams, which stayed down without a drama, I decided to push things a little further and attempted a punnet of blueberries. This had me hanging over the railing once more. That evening began my expedition-long obsession with Jatz biscuits and Nutella; the foods became a regular treat but also supplemented my diet with vital calories when I was in a significant calorie deficit.

The next morning, the sky turned a menacing grey. As rain started to fall in the protected waters of the harbour, we checked the forecast: further out to sea, things were getting ugly. The wind had picked up to 30 knots and marine-safety authorities had put out a warning to the boating community to be careful in the rough conditions.

As Matt and I sat at the semi-circular shaped table that served as a meeting place, games area and dinner space, he studied me closely.

'The skipper has said he will support either decision,' he assured me. 'There's no pressure either way.'

Perhaps Matt already knew my answer before it was given, and perhaps he prayed it would be different. But those who know me as well as he does also know a challenge like this is not something I would pass up.

'Let's do it,' I replied.

There was a massive 226 kilometres from our haven at Eden

to Lakes Entrance, our first stop in Victoria. This was a huge distance to cover to reach the next marina. But though it would be risky, I was confident we could handle it. The tailwind was pumping and the thought of leaning back and surfing huge swells towards Victoria excited me.

Retreating down to the cabin to change into my thermals, I wanted to be as comfortable and warm as possible in the conditions, as there would be no chance of stopping to climb aboard the catamaran once I had started. My ski would be flying with the huge wind gusts, and boarding the catamaran would be far too dangerous.

Setting off mid-morning, we called marine safety to inform them of our plan. With limited safe anchorages en route to Lakes Entrance, we'd need to anchor behind a headland or cliff that evening. Assessing the chart, the skipper chose Point Hicks as our target, a potentially decent anchorage tucked behind a cliff face halfway between our start point and destination. Point Hicks was 125 kilometres away. This meant that due to a delayed start to the morning, I'd need to paddle into the night to reach our destination.

Because I needed to start each day in the exact same location I had finished the day before, which on this occasion, was ten kilometres out to sea, we were required to motor into the chop on the catamaran for 90 minutes to get out to the mark.

As we rode the waves, seasickness got the better of me. Matt held my hair back as I vomited over the side of the boat. Alarmingly, at the same time he spotted a large shark pass next to the boat. While dolphins swim in an undulating motion propelling their barrel-shaped bodies up and over the water, sharks swim straight, and their large fins slice through the water, so Matt immediately knew the difference.

I wasn't the only one who was ill throughout the journey to the start line. Blake and Matt were also affected; when not helping me, Matt spent most of the time hanging over the starboard rail retching. The best place to be when sick on a boat is the back deck due to the stability. It is also a good idea to lie flat and stay outside, because keeping your body temperature down is key to quelling nausea. Looking over to see Blake lying flat on his back, arms crossed over his chest like a mummy, I realised that in choosing to paddle in these treacherous conditions, I hadn't considered the crew. Pangs of guilt recurred throughout the paddle as I watched the crew suffer their own difficulties at different times. All I wanted was for everyone to enjoy the experience, and though I was willing to take on the pain and mental load myself, the idea of my crewmates struggling was difficult to deal with.

Any regrets had to be put to the side, however, as we were now just a few kilometres from the start point and the crew had begun zipping up their waterproof sailing dry suits to protect them from the wet conditions. The final step was securing a safety line to each lifejacket, attached via a stainless-steel carabiner to the side railing, which allowed the crew to move back and forth along the deck. Witnessing the thoroughness of the preparation, under the skipper's directions, I realised things had just gone to a whole new level.

As the rain and wind picked up, I knew I needed to be on my game. One wrong move could prove fatal. All I had to attach myself to my ski was the leg rope, which I secured around my ankle with velcro, and though I wasn't sure the leg rope would hold in the gale-force winds, there was no other option. Zipping up my lifejacket, I was handed a two-way radio for communication with the boat. Finally, I secured a personal locator beacon to my lifejacket, a device that would allow the emergency services to find me if I went missing.

Now ten kilometres offshore, the water was a dark grey and the sun was well and truly hidden behind the storm clouds. As the crew lowered my ski into the ocean using the ropes system we had developed, I sat on the back step, watching the breaking swells crash into the boat, trying to convince myself it would be worth it. Blocking out thoughts of family and home comforts, I knew there was no room for weakness out there; I had to get in the zone.

With a brief opening between the waves, it was time to go. Blake held my ski steady, and I squatted down on the back step of the catamaran. I gripped the edge of the ski so it floated in the water, then stepped down into it. I placed my backside in the seat then slid my legs into the footwells. I used my paddle to brace and squeezed my core to avoid being thrown off like a bull rider at a rodeo. Sprinting away from the boat, I narrowly avoided a collision with the catamaran, a threat which provided the biggest risk to my safety outside of sharks and huge swells. Once clear, I focused on the task at hand. Completing the

125 kilometres would require equalling my personal best effort, but I had no choice as there was simply no safe place to land before Point Hicks. It was going to be a long day.

For the next 13 hours, I committed myself to the paddle as if my life depended on it. Seagulls twirled in the sky above me and the rain fell so hard from the sky that I couldn't see a metre in front of my ski, so I relied heavily on feel to know what the ocean was doing. I was frequently launched into wind tunnels that shot me out. Trying to stay within 100 metres of the boat was sometimes impossible and my fastest speed was recorded at 28 kilometres an hour. I realised that I was at the mercy of Mother Nature, the wind and waves carrying me wherever they pleased.

With the wind gusts measuring up to 80 kilometres an hour, the crew didn't need to unfurl a single sail, nor require the use of engines to move forward. The force of the wind alone carried the catamaran the entire way, at an average speed of 13–14 kilometres an hour. I could barely keep up with the boat even though the crew were sailing as slowly as possible.

There is a specific moment from the day that I will never forget, and it involves the Hilltop Hoods, one of my favourite Australian musical acts. I'm a huge fan of rap and hip-hop, and my playlists contain plenty of international and Australian rappers. My waterproof speaker was attached to my ski, but I couldn't reach it to change songs, so instead I embraced the different songs that came on, changing my rating according to the tempo of the beat. Halfway through the day, 90 kilometres into the paddle, the rain was stinging my face and my muscles were beginning to fatigue. I started to fall behind the boat, at first 50 metres and then 200 metres behind. If I fell any further behind, the crew would be unable to see me. Lactic acid was overcoming my muscles and I struggled to lift my rating to increase speed.

And then it happened.

Changing to the next track, the speaker began blasting the familiar tune of 'The Nosebleed Section' by the Hilltop Hoods, the first line ringing out clear above the whistling wind.

The words sparked a fire within me. This was a song about the underdog, about taking the hard road. The words resonated with me, as a middle child, as an athlete who didn't have natural ability but worked hard for everything she got. And now, as a young woman in the middle of the ocean trying against all odds to stay in the fight.

By the end of the hook, I'd clawed back half the distance to the boat. During the first verse, I closed the gap further, and by the end of the chorus I was just 50 metres behind. The bass blasting through my chest, I pushed harder, gripped my paddle tighter and desperately kept my balance in the ski as the wind continued to whip around me. As the final verse began, I knew I was going to make it.

Closing the gap to 20 metres, the faces of my crew were now identifiable. Drenched from the rain but looking resolute, they silently urged me on. One last push in the closing chorus and I was back level, glancing across to see Blake holding the GoPro, documenting the wild scenes. I had done it.

When darkness fell, I was 100 kilometres into the paddle with 25 kilometres still left to Point Hicks. The last few hours of paddling were difficult. Even though the wind had dropped and the ocean had flattened, there was no moon in the sky, meaning my main light source was the dull green starboard light of the catamaran. But though I could barely see my paddle in front of me and my muscles ached from the huge load inflicted on them, my crewmates got me through by telling jokes, sharing stories and rattling off trivia, which kept my mind active and distracted me from my feelings of doubt.

Arriving at Point Hicks that night, I was mentally and physically drained. Though I'd achieved another personal best distance, I didn't feel like celebrating as I had to back it up the next day with 115 kilometres still to be paddled until we reached the sanctuary of Lakes Entrance. Climbing aboard, I savoured the warmth of the bucket bath and prayed my stomach would accept dinner so I could fuel my body with the nutrients it desperately needed. Fortunately, I didn't have a repeat of the night before and I digested the food without the need to run to the back step.

The next day, we enjoyed lighter winds and calm seas. Though the rain hung around, we'd survived the worst of the conditions. Paddling into Lakes Entrance at the end of another huge day, officially crossing into Victoria, I was a different paddler from the one I was just a few days before. Though I was sore, nauseous and mentally needing a break, I somehow felt stronger. Taking a risk and backing ourselves, we'd pulled off the near impossible.

Though I didn't know what was around the corner, the previous two days gave me the confidence to believe that whatever was coming, we were ready.

*

Lakes Entrance was a scenic spot in which to spend a few days off, plotting our route to South Australia. While there, we met local delivery man Paul, who had followed my journey for the past month. A fast-talking man in his sixties, Paul was a paddler himself and had met all four people who had completed the expedition prior to me, including Freya, who had begun her journey a little further along the Victorian coast in the town of Queenscliff. Freya had travelled anti-clockwise, passing through Lakes Entrance during the early stages of her trip. Paul arrived with a copy of Paul Caffyn's memoir of paddling around Australia in 1987. Throughout my own paddle, I would look to Caffyn's book for inspiration, empathising with his blistered hands, and feeling excitement when he spoke of places I was passing by over 30 years later.

On 11 January, I made the first big right-hand turn of the expedition, rounding the southeast corner of Australia. Wilsons Promontory is the southern-most point of mainland Australia, meaning that once I navigated the rugged coastline, I would be in the treacherous waters of the Bass Strait. By now my regular attire consisted of steamer, jacket, beanie, gloves and lifejacket over the top, and I did my best to keep moving to maintain my body temperature, but Wilsons Prom was icy. The crew had spent time tanning in boardshorts just two weeks earlier but were now rugged up in full-length jackets and tracksuits, with hot drinks grasped firmly in cold hands.

The coastline at the bottom of Australia is like nothing I'd ever seen. My closest reference point was *The Lord of the Rings*, which was shot in the rolling hills of New Zealand's North Island. Looking to my right as I paddled, I saw untouched coastline that stretched for hundreds of kilometres, meeting seas that crashed into jagged cliff faces.

As we made the turn, the skipper told me of an upcoming island that would create a fork in the sea, at which point the boat would need to head out to deeper waters so as not to risk running aground. If I was to follow the boat outside the island, it would add two kilometres to my day's paddle compared to taking the inside line, which was shorter but guaranteed I would lose sight of the boat. Deciding on the latter, I knew my inflamed shoulders would appreciate the shorter distance.

And so, in the most southern region of mainland Australia – on a stretch of coast that is largely uninhabited, where the cool waters provide the perfect environment for large seals and even larger sharks – I separated from my support boat. Pushing my right pedal down, I headed for the line between the island and the coast while the catamaran stayed left and slowly disappeared from view.

Paddling on my own in the freezing waters, I wondered if I'd made the right decision. The silence was eerie; I could hear every splash. Penguins fluttered on smooth, dark boulders which stuck up from the sea, and I craned my head to look inside the huge caves that I was passing. My fingers were aching from the cold and my lips were blue in the single-digit air temperature. For two kilometres, I waited to be bumped or bitten, feeling like sitting bait in the sharkiest stretch of coastline.

Approximately 20 minutes after I'd separated from the boat I saw it again. The crew had held a steady ten kilometres an hour to match the speed I had been paddling throughout the day. Matt's and Blake's were the first faces that came into view, and I felt an immediate sense of gratitude. The past two weeks hadn't been easy for me, but as I saw their concern I appreciated again that it hadn't been easy on the others either.

*

One week later, lowering myself into my ski, I knew that in a few hours I would be paddling past the Twelve Apostles. A collection of limestone stacks off the Great Ocean Road, the Apostles stand up to 50 metres high and are an extremely popular tourist destination all year round. Very few people have experienced the perspective from a ski, and I knew I was in for a treat.

The week between the right-hand turn at sharky Wilsons Prom and arriving at the Twelve Apostles had been a tumultuous one, an emotional rollercoaster of relaxation followed by big seas and high stakes. We took a few days off at Apollo Bay, a bustling tourist destination on the Great Ocean Road, popular with surfers and holiday makers. It turned out to be one of the most beautiful places I've ever been. Relieved to have some downtime, the crew made the most of it, partaking in games of Uno, trivia and enjoying fish and chips on the boat.

With a new sense of motivation after the small break, we had set off from Apollo Bay with the goal of completing 60 kilometres for the day. Though we'd been following the weather forecasts closely, it turned out we weren't prepared for the strength of the headwinds. We had decided to keep the catamaran safely anchored up at Apollo Bay, so I was accompanied by Blake and Ben on the jet ski, who would tow me back to the marina at the end of the day's paddle. But I was forced to call it quits after only 20 kilometres because despite a morning's effort I'd barely moved forward. Though frustrated with the lack of progress, I knew I'd been blessed with relatively good conditions so far, having experienced very few headwinds.

The next day, we had to call it quits once again when the seas picked up to eight feet. The boys had driven the jet ski to the start point at Cape Otway and the plan was for me to paddle out and meet them beyond the break. Standing onshore watching the huge walls of white water slam down onto the bank, I was fearful – but not for myself. Ben and Blake weren't experienced in huge seas on the jet ski and were out there in the biggest surf I'd ever seen.

Though keen to see if I could pick a gap between the enormous sets and navigate my ski out the back, I couldn't have the crew risking their lives for the sake of one day's paddling, so I called it. The only way to safety for the boys, though, was back the same way they'd gone out. So they turned around and faced the angry seas once more, ploughing into the huge waves for the ten kilometres back to the boat ramp, proving the lengths they were willing to go for the expedition.

We waited a few more days at Apollo Bay for the conditions to settle, before heading off towards the Twelve Apostles, excitement levels high. For the first month, Jaime had spent his days in the Ranger towing the jet ski, so he was eager to pick up a camera and experience boat life. On his first day aboard the catamaran, the ocean lover was in for a real treat, with the prospect of the Twelve Apostles creating a buzz among the crew. The wind had swung to a pumping tailwind, with huge swells propelling me and the catamaran forward. Within the first few minutes of the day's paddling, a pod of dolphins had surrounded me, riding the waves and kicking off Jaime's boat experience with a bang.

Surfing swells up to 200 metres long, I edged closer to the Apostles. The crew had the headsail up and the boat was cruising in the favourable conditions, with Jaime on cloud nine. His energy was infectious, and I was thrilled for him to have a positive experience after a monotonous month on the road. On New Year's Eve, Jaime and Ben had planned to join us on the boat in Sydney Harbour for the fireworks but at the last minute they'd been informed that no jet skis were allowed in Sydney Harbour. The boys had instead spent the night on land, denied the on-water experience we were fortunate enough to enjoy.

Out in the ocean, the wind in his hair and salt on his skin, Jaime was in his element. Now ten kilometres off the coast, there was no sign of human life around us other than a Lifesaving Victoria helicopter that passed overhead. Amused to think how bizarre we must have looked, I waved enthusiastically as the chopper flew over. The chopper would be the last sign of civilisation we'd see for weeks, apart from the enormous container ships and oil tankers that became a feature as we headed further and further out to sea.

Jaime informed me that the Apostles were just five kilometres up ahead so I asked the skipper to angle the boat towards shore so I could get a closer look. This would be my only opportunity to experience the natural beauty of these landforms from the water, so I wanted to make the most of it. When we were just 800 metres from the Apostles, I could see tourists lining the cliffs to view the spectacle from the safety of land. The enormous waves crashed into the rock structures, creating a loud cracking sound that echoed off the cliffs. The power of the ocean was evident; backwash combined with ground swells lifted me up and down, and the nose of my ski was thrown into the air with each surge.

The Apostles stood tall, huddled together in the ocean. I craned my neck towards the sky to take in the view, the long shadows of these statues of the sea engulfing me. A chill ran up my spine as the sun disappeared temporarily and I envisioned myself as an old woman reliving this moment, recounting it to my grandchildren. The vision was not of an old woman sitting on her couch with regret, as I'd once feared, but of someone who was proud of taking a leap of faith and, as a result, experiencing the world in a way that was incredibly rare.

Turning my head back towards the boat, I saw the crew with their phones out capturing the moment, and Jaime filming on the camera we'd bought before the expedition. Suddenly overcome with joy, I was certain that one day in the future, they too would be telling their grandchildren about this day.

CHAPTER 6

THE OPPORTUNITIES ARE THERE

Paddling into Robe, our first contact with land in South Australia, I felt more than a little guilty.

The week of paddling along the Victorian coastline had been incredible, with the Twelve Apostles, sunsets over the Great Ocean Road and moonrises over the sea making for an unforgettable experience. But though I'd enjoyed every moment, I'd often thought of my land crew, consisting now of Ben and Blake; I wished they could be with us and regretted that they had missed out.

But I needn't have worried. Both keen runners, Ben and Blake had spent the past week exploring the trails of the Great Ocean Road. Never missing an opportunity to immerse themselves in nature, the boys had laced up their joggers, clocking up an impressive number of kilometres while enjoying the view of the coastline from land. Blake had also managed to drive the Ranger back to Melbourne to squeeze in a visit to the Australian Open tennis tournament. It took him three months to tell me that he had watched not only Aussie legend Ash Barty but also all-time great Rafael Nadal – two of my favourite sportspeople in the world. As it turned out, the boys hadn't missed out at all.

Reuniting with the land crew at the Robe marina, we found them in good spirits and I was relieved to see them happy. The short break in Robe was welcome, ahead of our next assignment: the push towards Western Australia, including the perilous Great Australian Bight crossing.

The downtime provided me with a chance to sign into my social-media accounts to engage with the growing community of people following my progress each day. Having accrued over 10,000 followers across Instagram and Facebook, I was receiving dozens of messages and comments daily. I invested an hour or two each day answering them. But there were pros and cons of staying active on social media. I was buoyed by the support sent from around the world, but I also continued to receive messages of criticism in my inbox. Whether it was my poor technique under fatigue or the fact that I had a support boat accompanying me, the opportunities to criticise me and the project seemed endless, with one particularly persistent follower taking the chance to tell me several times that I was going to be eaten by a crocodile in Western Australia.

Not only was I still hesitant to share the extent of my aches and pains with the crew, I was also reluctant to show them the negative messages. They had spent so much time developing my social-media profile, regularly posting edited photos and videos, and I didn't want them to be discouraged. After six weeks of putting my body on the line every day and revealing a side of myself that was far from glamorous, I was also still worried about perceptions. The trolling threatened to tarnish the perfect image of sunshine and rainbows I was determined to paint for the crew, so I figured it best to keep them in the dark.

Looking back, I realise I should have trusted in the crew's ability to deal with some rainclouds among the sun. Like me, they were along for the entire ride, not just the smooth bits. But though part of me wanted to break the wall of defence I had built and share the good, bad and increasingly ugly, I wasn't ready. A lifetime of racing as an individual athlete had created an impulse to want to go it alone and shoulder all the responsibility.

We still needed to guarantee entry into Western Australia but just two weeks from our expected start across the Bight, we received some devastating news. The Western Australian government had decided not to open its borders on 5 February, as originally planned. Since the start of our expedition, Covid case numbers had continued to rise rapidly in the eastern states of New South Wales and Victoria, and as a result the Western Australian premier had grown gun-shy, keeping the state's border closed to avoid an outbreak of the virus in his state.

As a result, we had to apply for an exemption to cross into Western Australia, so Matt liaised with both the local police in Esperance (our first point of land contact in Western Australia) and the Western Australia police. As we weren't Western Australian residents, it was a complex process, requiring dozens of phone calls and piles of paperwork. We were also advised that we'd need to quarantine for two weeks, but thankfully the time at sea crossing the Bight was authorised to count towards quarantine.

Matt's hands were full organising the exemption, but the upcoming stretch of coastline offered limited phone reception, so we made the choice for him to stay on land. The plan was for Matt and Ben to drive across the border into Western Australia and enter quarantine while waiting for us to cross the Bight. It was with a sinking feeling in my stomach that I realised Matt wouldn't be on the boat for the toughest stretch of water I'd face. For the last seven years Matt had been my rock. But in a few weeks' time, I'd have to step up for the biggest test of my athletic career without him.

We made the changeover in Robe: Blake came onto the boat while Matt moved onto land with Ben. Jaime had taken to boat life like a duck to water and would stay aboard, but he would now have to share the tiny front cabin with Blake while I continued in the cabin I had been sharing with Matt.

There were pros and cons to the front and rear cabins. While my front cabin was bigger than the boys' cabin and had an ensuite toilet, marine toilets aren't like typical toilets on land, which flush easily and have minimal problems. Toilets on catamarans commonly get blocked, as the pipe that transports human waste into the ocean has a diameter the size of a 50-

cent coin. When a blockage occurred, the person responsible would need to call the skipper to unblock the pipe, a process I found highly embarrassing. I already felt as though every inch of dignity was slowly being taken from me, and little did I know that the Bight was about to strip away any scraps I had left.

Once Matt had disembarked, Blake took on the role of massaging my knotted muscles at the end of the day. At first hesitant to use full pressure, perhaps for fear of injuring me, he was soon performing deep tissue massage every evening, dedicating two hours of his time to help my broken body. First he applied suction cups to draw blood to the surface to speed up the healing, then he would dig his thumbs into the knots using heated oil, moisturiser and eventually coconut oil when we ran low on supplies. The next morning, my shoulders would be significantly looser and ready for another 100 kilometres of torture. My back had previously been holding significant fluid around the vertebral discs in my spine, but post massage, it would no longer feel inflamed, and I could paddle more efficiently due to the higher amount of shoulder rotation I had when my body was looser.

In South Australia, while paddling up to 140 kilometres a day in 20-knot tailwinds, I'd be in the water for 12 hours at a time. I endured walls of white water smashing into me from the side, my body tensing to balance as the ski tilted and threatened to tip me off. Twelve hours is a lot of thinking time in the ocean, and those long stints often brought back those feelings of loneliness. Paul Caffyn discussed loneliness in his book, and the longer the expedition went on, the more I could relate to his struggles.

Still battling my fear of missing out, I didn't resent my crewmates but grew increasingly frustrated at carrying the burden of paddling alone. In pain all day, every day, I didn't want to complain. Though I wanted nothing more than to be sitting on the bow of the boat with the wind in my hair for just one day while someone else did the paddling, it wasn't an option. The only way we could move forward was if I kept paddling, copping rashes, blisters and sunburn, and continued to fight the feeling of isolation. I needed to keep showing up. Every damn day.

One evening, as Blake placed the suction cups onto my back, simultaneously working his thumbs through the knots in my neck, I decided to be honest.

'You know, the hardest part of this paddle is the isolation.' My words spilled out quickly as I mumbled into the towel laid on the deck beneath me. 'I'm in the water on my own every day and all I want to do is be on the boat. I feel like no one knows what it is like.'

There it was. The first time I'd shown weakness to anyone other than Matt. A chink in my armour finally revealed.

It was close to a full minute before he replied. 'You're right; no one does know how you feel,' he said slowly, choosing his words carefully. 'But no one else could do what you're doing either. No one in the world has ever done what you're doing right now, putting your body through more kilometres than has ever been achieved on a ski. But that's what it takes to get a world record.'

With these words, Blake provided me with what I needed. Understanding. Reassurance. From then on, I knew I could tell

Blake anything. The massages at the end of the day didn't just help me physically. Blake provided a safe space where I could share my deepest concerns.

I finally felt I could open up about the emotional challenges I was experiencing, and from then on I asked Blake's opinion on everything from safety protocols to physical difficulties. It was a relief to know I had someone who understood the challenges, who listened without judgement. Along the way, I also learnt Blake's story. When he took his turn on 'Bonnie Watch', observing me from the side of the boat, we'd share banter and jokes but also speak of our childhoods, failures, lessons and what we hoped to do in the future. Our conversations were often stilted, as I surfed back and forth on the swells, paddling into the boat to ask a question and returning five minutes later to hear the answer, but the interactions kept me sane in a stark environment of dark blue water and grey skies as far as I could see.

Each day I forced myself to put on a shield of confidence to fight on the battleground of wild seas but at the end of the day's paddling, I could take off the shield thanks to Blake's caring and non-judgemental nature. Due to losses and pain in his own life, and through his role as protector in his family, he always seemed to know what to say. The trust I developed in him would be crucial in the Bight, when I fought for two weeks to maintain control of my ski in the wild seas.

South Australians, by their own admission, like to keep a low profile, which is perhaps why the state is rarely advertised through mainstream media channels. While Queensland and

Victoria invest heavily in promoting tourism, you'd be hard pressed in finding much promotion urging people to visit South Australia. The state boasts pristine bays, an abundance of sea life that makes fishing a popular hobby, stunning vineyards and some of Australia's biggest sporting events, and in exploring from the water, I was able to see the state for what it truly is: one of the most visually spectacular regions of Australia.

Taking care of my body was a top priority after a day of punishing it on the water, and at first I hesitated to expend energy to explore the stunning scenery. Arriving at an anchorage before sunset would leave time for snorkelling, spearing and swimming, but unable to switch out of athlete mode, I would stay on the boat while the crew made the most of the crystal-clear water and white sandy beaches.

Each evening I would diligently slide on my compression boots, which worked to flush waste products through my muscles to decrease soreness, before guzzling a protein shake. By the time the boots beeped to let me know the session was finished, it was on to cupping and massage, with dinner consumed somewhere in between. Having been informed that the waters would grow increasingly choppy as we headed further south, I made the most of eating on a settled stomach. If I had reception, I'd reply to the followers who had sent well wishes, and if the boys had edited photos ready for social media, I'd then construct a caption to accurately depict the story behind the photo. By the time I'd finished all this, there wasn't a lot of time left for fun.

My tunnel vision carried from the boat to my ski, and because I'd often forget to look in towards the land while paddling, I missed a lot. Though able to recount the exact number of kilometres we had completed throughout the week, I often failed to remember the names of any of the places we had stopped at due to my intense focus on the task at hand.

This is where eating junk food went beyond providing me with extra calories. The Jatz and Nutella and lollies I was eating before were occasional treats; this was comfort eating on a far bigger scale. After showering and changing following a day of paddling, the cravings would start: chips, lollies, chocolate, nothing was off the cards. An urgent desire for certain tastes and textures dictated my food choices. The rush of salt or sugar provided me with a temporary hit of endorphins after a day of punishment. When denied enjoyment in other areas, I found it within a bag of crisps or a packet of Tim Tams.

Fortunately, a timely reminder to balance work with fun was provided through a missed opportunity while in South Australia. Finishing one paddling day 100 kilometres offshore, the skipper declared the best place to anchor was behind one of the islands that dotted the clear blue ocean all the way to Port Lincoln. Matthew Flinders had added Althorpe Island to his map in 1802, when he circumnavigated the continent. Measuring 1.8 kilometres in diameter, it was home to resident lighthouse keepers until the lighthouse was automated in 1991 and was now uninhabited. Having completed a 72-kilometre day in glassy conditions, we arrived with plenty of daylight left.

There was something about the island that gave off a sense of long-lost treasure. After being stuck onboard for several days, my crewmates were keen to stretch their legs and go exploring, and their excitement was palpable.

As they made their way into the tender to head to shore, I was torn. With little chance I'd ever be coming back to the island, I wanted to join them in climbing the hill to the abandoned lighthouse and viewing the native penguins, mutton birds and wildlife. But though my heart said yes, my body said otherwise. I'd started to experience some pain around my elbow, a clear sign of my limbs being forced to work beyond their means, so I decided to stay behind. I watched from the boat as the crew motored towards the island, cameras around their necks, excitedly chatting about what they would discover. With immediate regret, I pulled on the recovery boots. Entirely alone on the boat, I began to sob.

I was pushing myself beyond what previous record-holders had done, each day entering unknown territory and constantly batting away doubt, and I was distraught at being unable to enjoy the rewards of victory. Victory meant another day of survival, of overcoming all odds to finish incomprehensible distances of paddling. Each day I felt the pressure of knowing that if I backed the pace off even just a little, we wouldn't reach our destination by sunset, meaning the crew wouldn't have the opportunity to get off the boat. But though I'd push myself to near breaking point and reach our destination in time, I still felt unable to enjoy the reward.

The boots beeped to signal the compression cycle had finished, so I took them off, wincing from the inflammation in my back, which was rapidly growing worse. Limping to the front deck, I took my phone out and began scrolling through old photos in my photo gallery, the lack of reception making this the closest thing I had to contact with home. I missed my friends, family and the freedom to fill my days how I liked, and tears began to roll down my cheeks once more.

The sun had started to dip into the ocean when my thoughts were interrupted by the putting of the tender motor and laughter from the crew as they made their way back from their venture. Sitting up, I wiped away any evidence of my sadness but stayed on the front deck for most of the evening, unable to lift myself from my slump.

With less distance to cover, and therefore a late start the following day, the crew jumped into the water to enjoy a quick swim before we set off. Unwilling to get wet before I absolutely had to, I again stayed onboard, making my way to the front of the boat to ponder the day ahead, my mood still low. Sensing a figure in my peripheral vision, I turned to see that Blake had emerged from the water to grab the camera to film content for the morning. In our daily pre-paddle interview, Blake asked questions about everything from my physical condition to my mindset, and since dropping my guard a few weeks prior, my answers had become increasingly honest.

Commencing the interview, Blake first asked how my body was holding up, followed by the plan for the day, and finally my feelings about the upcoming Great Australian Bight crossing. At first straining to keep an upbeat tone to my words, the filter suddenly broke as I told Blake of my anguish. Still feeling isolated, I was feeling regret that grew deeper with every missed swim and island visit.

Studying me closely before responding, Blake's answer was unexpected. 'The opportunities are there,' he pointed out. 'You just need to take them.'

Immediately protesting, I stressed the need to prioritise my body. Extra walking and swimming were distractions from time better spent in the boots or stretching.

Blake held the line. 'The mental side is just as important as the physical,' he urged. 'It's time to find some balance. You're better off slowing down and taking time to enjoy the amazing places you're paddling us to, instead of rushing to get to the next place.'

I knew Blake was right. Recognising the victim mentality that had developed within me, I suddenly understood. While it was my responsibility to continue to put one stroke in front of the other, it was also up to me to find balance. I held a one-month buffer on the previous world record set by Freya, so perhaps I really could stop once in a while to take in the beauty of my surroundings, occasionally jump into the water for a quick swim prior to a paddle or head ashore when time permitted. Making a pact with myself, I pledged that from then on, when the opportunities arose, I'd take them.

Feeling significantly lighter, I thanked Blake for his advice, and we returned to the back deck to begin the paddling day. With

45 kilometres to complete, I put my waterproof headphones in my ears and got to work. The headphones were a blessing, though they had taken a while to be included as an essential item on the expedition. The waterproof speaker that had been suctioned onto my ski at the start of the expedition had corroded thanks to excessive time in salt water, and not even freshwater rinses at the end of each day had prevented malfunction after a few weeks. Thankfully, a crew member had brought a set of wireless headphones onboard and kindly lent them to me one month in. They were completely waterproof, meaning that even when I fell off my ski and gave the headphones a thorough soaking, I'd still be treated to crystal-clear tunes when I remounted.

Wearing the headphones felt like claiming a tiny piece of my privacy back. No one on the boat could hear what I was listening to, so my music became the one thing in my day that wasn't shared with everyone else. Plugging into a whole other world and allowing myself to be carried away by the dulcet tones of Vance Joy, I could, just for a moment, forget the heavy burden of chasing a world record.

Nearing our destination after several hours of paddling, I glanced up to see a smattering of islands ahead, the nearest just a kilometre away. Drawing closer, I squinted to get a better look. *Were they ... caves?* The island in view didn't have grassy slopes like Althorpe but a rocky exterior, and on closer inspection, I saw that at its base sat three decent-sized caves. I was overcome with a feeling that had been missing in the past few weeks: excitement. The caves represented adventure and an opportunity to explore, exactly what I promised myself to embrace following my chat with Blake. The unknown lay within these natural structures, and I suddenly couldn't wait to see inside.

Jaime was on Bonnie Watch, and remembering I had my spare skis onboard, I realised I had an adventure buddy.

'I'm going to paddle to those caves. Wanna come?' I asked, already knowing what the answer would be.

'Absolutely,' came Jaime's swift reply. One of Jaime's best traits is his spontaneity; he is always up for an adventure and brings fun and energy to any situation.

As Jaime headed inside to inform the skipper of our plan, Blake appeared above deck.

'This is my opportunity,' I told him. 'And I'm going to take it.'

His smile gave me a sense of pride greater than on any huge paddle day I'd completed. Blake had told me the opportunities were there if I looked for them, and just a few hours after our conversation that morning, I was grabbing the one that presented itself to me with both hands.

Giggling like school children, Jaime and I slowly paddled away from the safety of the catamaran towards the caves. Grateful for the calm conditions, he took long, careful strokes as he simultaneously recorded on the GoPro he'd brought along for the excursion. Cleverly, the boys had also insisted I strap a second GoPro to my chest, with the documentary we planned to make post paddle always in mind.

With three caves to choose from, we started with the medium-sized one on the left. As we approached the opening, a steady grumbling sound grew louder. Sharing a look of excitement, we urged each other on, taking the last few strokes to enter the cave. Roughly 20 metres in diameter, the space inside was tight, and I estimated there was just enough room for me to turn my ski around to exit. Once inside, the water grew choppier due to backwash off the cave walls, and I strained to maintain balance. As I tapped my way towards the opposite side of the rocky enclosure, the grumbling became a growl. The swirling water created an echo that bounced off the sides of the cave, spilling secrets kept for thousands of years. I glanced across to share a look of wonder with Jaime. We burst out laughing, invigorated by the surreal nature of the situation.

Emerging from the cave, it was as if all my past worries had disappeared. I was aware that very few humans would ever have set foot within those caves in front of us, and I felt a deep sense of gratitude. The cave was like a great-grandmother, full of wisdom that could only be gained through decades of existence. As I left the first cave, I felt my sense of spirituality start to return, something I had all but lost among the grind of hard paddling.

Paddling towards the second cave, we were accompanied by two large dolphins. Their dark grey fins had deep scars and missing flesh revealing their significant age. The dolphins guided us towards our next destination, like tour guides of their island home. Our visit to the second cave was brief, and we both quickly retreated as the outer rock walls whipped the water up into a chop that threatened to knock us off. Not wanting to risk injury or damage to our crafts, we paddled backwards out of the cave, pleased to see the open sky once more.

The third cave was significantly larger than the other two, and we nicknamed it the 'Grand Daddy' due to the deep rumbling sound that vibrated through our bodies as we entered. There was a hole in the cave's rocky roof, and I craned my head to look up at the blue sky above, feeling a complete sense of freedom. With nowhere else to be in that moment other than right there, I began reflecting on the beauty of nature, deciding that a greater power must exist.

While the water was cool, it wasn't unpleasant. Paddling back towards the boat, I felt refreshed in a way that went beyond the physical. I wasn't surprised to see Blake pulling on a wetsuit, snorkel in hand, preparing to swim the 300 metres from the catamaran to the caves. As he plunged into the water and took his first strokes towards the cave from where we'd just come, he was taking his own advice: seeing an opportunity and grabbing it with both hands.

Deciding to cut the paddling short that day, we agreed that Wedge Island, located just around the corner from the caves, would be our anchorage for the evening. As we reached the bay of Wedge Island and prepared to drop anchor, I spotted a pod of dolphins and a single seal in the water. Not thinking twice, I grabbed a snorkel and dived into the water, coming face to face with the juvenile seal as I did so. With a startled look, it took off with a strong kick of its tail. My own fear gave way to laughter, a welcome release from the tension that had previously felt all-consuming. Looking across to the less flighty dolphins, I swam alongside them as they dived and leapt, effortlessly graceful in the water. The dolphins' squeaks were clearly audible, and in that moment I felt part of their family, a shared love of the ocean connecting us and transcending communication barriers.

Some say that the master will appear when the student is ready, and I was ready to learn a few different lessons that day. To learn patience from the caves; to slow down and admire the natural world around me. The value of fun from the seal, which taught me humour can be found in the most unexpected of places. And from the dolphins, the importance of connection; though sometimes we can feel isolated, we are never truly alone.

CHAPTER 7

GUARDIAN ANGELS
IN THE BIGHT

FOLLOWING THE EXPERIENCE IN THE CAVES AT WEDGE Island, we spent the next few days making our way towards Coffin Bay, our last point of contact on the mainland prior to the Great Australian Bight crossing. As it turned out, before we faced what was to be our biggest test to date, there was a little more fun to be had.

Greenly Island is located 40 kilometres off Coffin Bay, and we decided to anchor there and motor in to Coffin Bay, so that Greenly would be our departure point when we were ready to begin the Bight crossing. As we approached the island, I looked up to see Jaime with camera in hand, alternating between shots of me and Greenly. He suddenly yelped in delight and made wild gestures with his hands, alerting me to the presence of 20 seals sunbathing on the smooth rocks at the base of the island.

I could see several large male bull seals positioning themselves at the front, guarding the much smaller cubs and their mothers.

The sight of the seals caused mixed emotions in me. I appreciated our good fortune to encounter these intriguing creatures in the wild; however, the seals reminded me of the terrifying great white sharks that hunt them. As the number of seal sightings increased, the chances of running into that most dangerous predator in the ocean also grew.

Trying to keep my fear inside so as not to detract from the good vibe of the crew, I watched them dive into the water to greet the seals. Jaime dived in first, and he must have seen the dark figures of the seals beneath the surface because he let out a loud shriek.

'Blake, get in the water now!' he demanded, urgently submerging his face to check the shapes were nothing sinister. Needing no further encouragement, Blake leapt over the railing to join him and the seals in the dark water. The distance from boat to island was a decent 200 metres, but the boys covered it quickly, anxious to set foot on dry land. Reaching the island, they scrambled up the rocks, making their way to the top. As I watched their silhouettes fade into small dots, I took out my phone to record the scene, admiring their spontaneity. The rest of the crew also jumped into the water to explore, leaving me alone to think about what lay ahead.

I tried not to consider the dangers of crossing the Bight too deeply. I'd done a lot of research prior to the expedition, and had been exposed to a vast array of opinions on the task ahead. One of Australia's top super yacht captains had suggested to me that it would be virtually impossible to paddle across the Bight east to west, due to winds predominantly running back the other way. A meteorologist I consulted described it as a waiting game, assuring me I would gain assistance if I waited for a favourable weather window. Meanwhile, our skipper had made the crossing by boat over a decade before and had experienced glassy conditions.

I knew I was taking a huge gamble; if I didn't get a favourable weather window, we could be stuck in Coffin Bay for a significant amount of time, eating into my hard-earned buffer on the record. And if the weather turned nasty while we were out there … well, we would be in big trouble.

From all reports, we had luck on our side as the winds were due to turn easterly in a few days' time, providing a tailwind to complete the 1200-kilometre stint. But the crossing would still be risky, as conditions can change quickly and a day that starts favourably in the morning might be very different by lunchtime. Regardless, knowing that the opportunity for me to paddle with a strong tailwind might not arise again for several months, we made plans to spend three days in Coffin Bay and then motor back out to Greenly Island to begin the adventure.

The stay in Coffin Bay was an enjoyable one. Between strolls on the beach, calls to friends and family and several games of Uno, we did chores on the boat and stocked up on provisions for the next few weeks. Not missing the irony, I was highly amused that we would be setting off into the most treacherous waters in Australia from a place whose name conjures images of a funeral.

We valued any opportunity for humour, as the Covid situation continued to ramp up around the country and the rest of the world. Thankfully, after weeks of phone calls and frustration, we had finally been granted an exemption that would allow us to cross the border into Western Australia. We were required to spend a total of 18 days isolated from civilisation, meaning extra days of isolation pre and post crossing would need to be adhered to, but we had received permission to include our time at sea within our isolation period. Matt and Ben, crossing by land, would need to spend the standard 14 days in mandatory isolation.

I spent the final day at Coffin Bay contacting each of my family members and friends, telling them of our intention to cross the Bight in less than two weeks. This gave them an approximate timeframe as to when I would next speak to them because we'd have no reception so far out to sea. I knew my little nephews didn't completely understand what I was about to do, but just hearing their voices was enough to make me eager to get the ordeal over with so I could talk to them once more.

Having organised a final supper for the boat and land crew at the local pub, I went to the tiny cupboard in my cabin to find an outfit for dinner. It was 31 January and the next day we were to begin our Bight adventure. We'd be parting ways with our land crew for two weeks at least, so it was the last time we'd all be together until we reached Western Australian soil. If we made it.

The Coffin Bay tavern served a tasty menu of tender steaks and fresh seafood. When everyone was well fed, the conversation shifted to the Bight, and Matt asked us to provide a word or phrase to sum up our feelings about the next two weeks. Blake said 'heavy duty', to emphasise the enormity of the task ahead, whereas I focused on the adventure aspect with 'once in a lifetime'. There was a palpable excitement in the air, like the evening before a big race when the preparation is done and all that's left is the execution. Taking our time leaving the restaurant, we embraced the luxury of walking on solid ground just a while longer.

After dinner, it was time to say goodbye to Ben and then to Matt. Knowing it wasn't going to be an easy task, Matt and I drove to a local playground for our final conversation before being separated by 500 kilometres of open ocean. An expert at concealing my emotions when I want, I chose to convey a neutral expression as we spoke of what was ahead. Matt, however, was struggling to contain his feelings, and the quiver of his lip almost broke me. I forced back tears, reassuring him everything would be okay, but the strain in my voice threatened to give the act away. I managed to hold a confident tone, reminding him that it would only be two weeks until I'd see him on the other side. Deep down, however, we both knew the truth; there were many things that could go wrong on an open-ocean crossing, with fatal consequences. After one last hug, Matt drove me back to the boat that would be my lifeline for the next few weeks.

Clambering over the port-side chain and stepping onto the back deck, I removed my shoes, beginning the transition back into boat life. Taking one last glance over my shoulder, I watched Matt climbing back into the car, his shoulders slumped. This man had given up his job, entire savings and time to back my project. And now, I was saying goodbye with no guarantee I'd return. Not able to keep a poker face like his wife, the truth was written all over his face. He was terrified of what was ahead. And deep down, beneath the confident front that threatened to dissolve at any moment, so was I.

That evening, we motored out to Misery Bay, the last point of contact with the mainland before we set out for Greenly Island, where I'd finished paddling a few days before. With a good run, I would cross the Bight in 10–12 days, meaning we would need to stay offshore on the boat until our mandatory 18 days' isolation was up and we could land in Western Australia. I figured we could worry about that when we got there. The marina at Coffin Bay was too close to civilisation to count as isolation, so we decided to spend a day in the region of Misery Bay to give us an extra day to count towards our total.

As the sun set over the sand dunes of Misery Bay, Blake grabbed the camera. Heading to the front of the catamaran, we recorded a video in which I asked people to donate to Gotcha4Life through the fundraising portal I had set up. 'For the next two weeks, I'll be pushing my mental and physical limits as I cross the Great Australian Bight,' I told the camera. 'I can't achieve the hundred thousand dollars without you. Can you donate and help me in my mission?'

Sharing the video to social media, we hoped it would help generate momentum for our fundraising efforts. Would it work? As we were soon to be out of reception for two weeks, we'd have to wait until we reached Western Australia to find out.

Motoring out to Greenly Island, the vibe among the crew was high. The speaker blasted John Farnham, and the crew danced as the boat swayed back and forth, bobbing around like a cork in the ocean. The further we headed out to sea, the more the swells picked up, until the familiar early signs of seasickness began to take hold, and I found myself running to the starboard rail to throw up my breakfast. Focusing on the positives, I reminded myself that at least the growing swells would push me along.

Reaching the smooth waters of Greenly Island by lunch, I strapped on my watch and zipped up my lifejacket. I also secured the two-way radio, which I could use to communicate with the crew. Taking one last look at the lush slopes of the island, I batted away last-minute feelings of doubt and climbed down into my ski. A pod of dolphins surfaced five metres to my right, as though wishing me a safe journey. From the rocks at the base of the island, several seals watched us closely, their barks comforting against the backdrop of wind and crashing waves. Bolstered by their presence, I hoped the crossing wouldn't be too bad. But as I continued to paddle, glancing back to see the island fade into the distance, the wind picked up in the open ocean, and the seals and dolphins disappeared, choosing to remain within the safe waters of the island. With headsail at full mast, the catamaran was flying along in the breeze, and I knew the paddling was going to be fast. Putting my head down, I picked up my stroke rate. This was it. The Great Australian Bight.

Twelve hours after beginning the crossing, I'd covered 122 kilometres, marking a successful first stint. Though the paddle was mostly drama-free, the biggest challenge was balancing in the ski at night in the high winds. During the day, I enjoyed surfing breaking swells that were positioned perfectly behind me, but when the sun went down and I was still out there making the day's target number of kilometres, everything changed. I was barely able to see a metre in front of my ski in the darkness. Though I tried my best to maintain my balance and avoid falling out, I was still averaging three fall-outs a day, often because of a lapse in concentration. When this happened, the crewmate on Bonnie Watch became my lifeline: they alerted the sailor at the helm so the boat could come back to pick me up.

In high winds, the catamaran took 500 metres to slow down, so from the time I fell in until the boat returned, I would desperately scramble to get back in my ski, watching the catamaran disappearing into the distance as the crew furled the sails. Falling out of the ski three times on the first night, I struggled to get my bearings in the darkness, with breaking white water slamming into me from the side. By the time I climbed aboard for my bucket bath under the freezing night sky, the familiar queasiness associated with seasickness had well and truly set in.

The skipper and crew used the chart plotter on the boat to record where I was pulled out of the water each time I stopped for a break, so I could be dropped back to exactly the same spot when I resumed paddling. The winds were so strong that sometimes we'd end up as far as 20 kilometres away and would have to motor back to the mark. The crew had a roster so there was always someone at the helm.

The following day I chased small swells for 73 kilometres, averaging ten kilometres an hour. Even in the daytime, the water beneath me was almost black, adding to the ominousness of the situation. The skipper informed me that the bottom of the ocean lay three kilometres below us.

It felt too quiet. I'd seen no evidence of marine life since the dolphins and seals of Greenly Island; the only sound outside of wind and waves was the occasional chatter from the crew and music thumping in my headphones. I turned the volume up and used the music to distract myself from the pain, but when I turned it off, I was shocked by the silence. After a few minutes of hearing nothing but the wind whistling and swells crashing, I'd be desperate for mental stimulation and would paddle towards the boat for a conversation. Hundreds of kilometres out in the open ocean, my mind was often far from paddling as I spoke with Blake and Jaime, letting our conversations carry me back to memories of home, school, local cafes: any place other than the great, big, dark, silent, open ocean.

While there was no sign of life in the water, I was grateful to have some company in the sky. With its three-metre wingspan, the albatross has always been one of my favourite animals, and I love how they soar so gracefully above the ocean. And now I was able to appreciate their beauty first-hand as the birds flew directly over me, swooping so low I could almost touch them, then gliding back up towards the sun with the next strong gust of wind. Unlike mutton birds, who return to land every evening, albatrosses stay at sea for months at a time, only returning to

123

land to nest. Knowing how rare it is to encounter an albatross, I savoured the experience.

On day three, the seasickness ramped up. Over the previous two days, I'd experienced minor episodes of vomiting, but the wind now picked up to 20 knots, throwing the 38-foot catamaran around like a rag doll in the huge swells. Several times, the 5–6-metre swells lifted the catamaran up and then caused it to drop so deeply into the ocean it disappeared out of my sight for a moment, leaving me fearful for those aboard.

Suffering from overwhelming nausea all day, the only place I didn't throw up was when I was sitting in my ski. I was able to cool my temperature by splashing water onto my face, and my stomach was settled by the endorphins naturally released through exercise. Though reflux gradually became more of an issue due to the sheer exertion of paddling all day, my gut was okay while I was in the water. But on the boat it was a different story. I spent most of my time aboard hurling over the starboard railing, the contents of my stomach spilling into the sea. More than once, I glanced over to find Blake hanging over the opposite railing, also vomiting. Jaime's stomach was relatively unaffected, and Blake and I watched on with envy as he made his way around the boat without having to run to the back deck every ten minutes.

By the end of day three, I had scraped and clawed my way through 106 kilometres with nothing left to throw up but gastric acid, which burned as it made its way up my throat.

By day four, I began pulling the drawstring of my tracksuit pants extra tight to keep them from falling down. The last time

I'd held down a full meal was a few days prior, and I was visibly losing weight. Not only was I ravenous, I was starting to feel the effects of dehydration. My lips cracked and bled, and the pawpaw lotion I applied meticulously wasn't enough to repair the damage. There was no chance for the skin to heal because I'd be straight back on the water the next day, my lips once again exposed to the burning sun, cutting wind and sting of the salt water. Dragging my body through 100 aching kilometres on that fourth day, I reminded myself that each stroke was a metre closer to the other side.

I started referring to the Bight as a 'hell hole'. It felt as though we'd been sucked into a vortex of desolation and the only way out was through. Chilled to my core, I attempted to retain body heat by wearing a waterproof jacket over the full-length steamer I wore every day, as well as booties and gloves. The cold affected my coordination and, as a result, I fell out of my ski regularly, each time gritting my teeth as the ten-degree water lapped around my chin, and my weakened arms tried to haul my body back into the ski. There was no time to mess around. Any laughter that had previously accompanied fall-outs was well and truly absent as the stakes continued to climb.

My blood sugars plummeted the more I vomited, and my need for carbohydrate became evident through the shake of my hands. I was craving something sweet, but I was unable to hold down anything sufficient. The crew were now extremely concerned for my wellbeing, and they openly discussed turning around and heading back to Coffin Bay.

We were 300 kilometres into the crossing, so if we kept heading further west, we would be halfway across and there would be no point turning back, so we needed to make an urgent decision. Discussing the pros and cons, we knew that by heading back I could go to hospital and see a doctor, replenish my body and come back out when I was ready, but on the other hand, we might not get another suitable weather window for months. This was possibly our only chance to conquer the Bight.

Blake was on Bonnie Watch and had been watching me for the past hour while occasionally vomiting into the ocean himself. I was keen to get his opinion and as I looked up at his ashen face from the water, I could see he was drained. Like me, he hadn't eaten a proper meal for nearly a week and his muscle mass had started to decline. The small amount of body fat he had previously carried had vanished. It was apparent I wasn't the only one suffering.

'Well, what do you reckon?' Blake asked as I paddled closer, his optimistic tone still present despite his poor physical condition.

Looking out to the ocean, my mind strayed to thoughts of calm water and phone reception, of safety and the sight of land. Cold, scared and starving, I desperately wanted to be warm and dry, eating hot soup with toasted bread and butter. To step off the rollercoaster of pain and isolation and enter peace and tranquility.

But then I remembered the messages I'd received from people following the journey, who'd found inspiration in my ability to overcome the odds. Perhaps if I could find a way to continue putting one stroke in front of the other, no matter how dire the situation, I would continue to inspire hope among them.

Shifting my focus back to Blake, I stifled the urge to vomit. 'Let's finish what we started,' I said. 'We're in this now; let's get it done so we never have to come back out here again.'

I felt guilty knowing this decision would result in more suffering for him. But if Blake was disappointed, he didn't voice it. He simply nodded. Then he settled in for another stint on Bonnie Watch, sipping from his water bottle and trying desperately to replace the fluids he had thrown up in the sea.

On day five I had a revelation about the real purpose of the project. I was 70 kilometres into the day, forcing my arms to keep pushing forward, tasting blood in my mouth as my lips bled, and feeling sick, cold and doubtful. I started to imagine myself in a scene from the well-known film *Interstellar*, where astronauts played by Matthew McConaughey and Anne Hathaway land on a foreign planet to find the lumps in the distance they initially thought to be mountains were in fact tidal waves. My imagination was getting the better of me, and I began freaking out.

And then I heard her.

The unmistakable voice of my grandmother Molly, one of my first role models. Working on her feet in hospitality well into her seventies, Molly was one of the toughest people I've ever known and always had a way of looking at things with a glass-half-full approach. Just like when I was a child, Molly's voice was reassuring and resolute. *It's okay*, she reassured me from beyond the grave. *Just keep going.*

Suddenly questioning my sanity, I wondered whether the spirit of my grandmother was with me or if my brain had conjured up her voice from the long-lost archives of my memory, forming the words I desperately needed to hear. Either way, I no longer felt afraid and doubtful. I felt inspired and empowered. In my moment of need, Molly had arrived. Guardian angel? Maybe. It felt like a higher presence was watching out for me, enveloping me in wings of encouragement and offering a hand to hold while I clawed my way through uncharted territory.

The water was frigid, and the air cut through me like a knife. My hands were blistered and bleeding, and my lips were stinging in the salt. But I knew that Molly was watching over me. As I took the next few painful strokes, I also remembered my pledge to Gotcha4Life, and I knew that if I could find a way to keep showing up and keep moving forward, then maybe someone else going through their own hell hole could find a way forward too.

Later that day, 520 kilometres into the Bight crossing, halfway to our first point of land contact, the wind began to turn. Jaime was on Bonnie Watch and we both observed in amazement as the wind suddenly dropped and, in the space of minutes, turned to hit me head-on. My progress slowed to a stall, and we were forced to call it quits for the day. The quick change in conditions reminded me that we were just spectators at Mother Nature's show.

The headwinds hung around the next day – the sixth day of the crossing – so we were forced to call a lay day. I desperately tried to keep down calories without vomiting. Avoiding my cabin as much as possible, I knew not to tempt fate by heading down to the most unstable part of the boat, and so the back deck became my hangout. Lying on the hard bench built into the deck, I called to Jaime to fetch different things, as the mere thought of standing up made my stomach turn. At first my requests were for food and drink, then pawpaw ointment, massage, extra layers of warm clothing and games of trivia. Never complaining, Jaime kept me fed, warm and entertained.

Blake, meanwhile, was as sick as I was and spent the day flat on his back in bed. It hurt me to see him that sick, and yet there was a part of me that felt somehow less alone, knowing there was someone else who understood how miserable seasickness was making me. The vomiting had stripped us both of every shred of dignity.

As I battled the urge to vomit, the crew took turns at the helm, driving the catamaran into enormous waves that slammed into us, soaking us with water. Scared to move, I remained on the bench until my bladder was about to burst, at which time I was forced to stumble down to the bathroom. Catching sight of my reflection in the mirror for the first time in five days, I was shocked by what I saw.

My skin was like that of an 80-year-old, shrivelled like a prune left in bath water. I was pale but at the same time burnt by the harsh Australian sun that permeated through the clouds even on an overcast day. My fingers were swollen to twice their size, and I wondered if I'd ever fit my wedding ring on my finger again. The only hint of femininity was my long hair, which I continued to blow dry at the end of each paddle, but even that was thinning by the day; clumps were falling out due to inadequate nutrition and relentless exposure to the elements. Turning away from the mirror, I wondered if I'd be able to assimilate back into everyday life after the paddle. A crewmember at the helm called out to warn of a giant wave about to strike, and I grabbed onto the door to steady myself. How could any of us ever be the same?

On day seven, Jaime and Blake made a cake to celebrate reaching halfway. I tried to ignore the shake of my hands as I made my way to the trampoline on the front deck to mark the milestone with my crew. Not having set foot on land for a week, my balance and coordination were almost non-existent and I struggled to put one foot in front of the other. I used every ounce of strength I had remaining to cut the cake and divide the portions evenly, then thanked everyone and climbed back into my ski. Within minutes, I vomited up my portion of the cake.

Though the nausea continued, I was soon distracted. The wind and swells aligned perfectly and I launched into runners that carried me for several hundred metres at a time. I glided over the surface of the water with the assistance of the swells with no need to take one stroke as the ocean and wind did all the work for me. Without the presence of an island or reef to block the wind, the swells were uninterrupted, and the wind was free to whip across the water. Several albatrosses and mutton birds soared on the breeze above me, and I felt exhilarated as I surfed my way through the open ocean. Little did I know, several hours later my legs would be unable to support my body weight and I'd be forced to crawl.

Finishing paddling well past dinnertime, I climbed out of my ski with the usual intention of walking up the back steps of the catamaran to safety. But as I attempted to take the first step, my legs folded under me, and I just managed to grab onto the side railing to stop myself falling back into the ocean. With no other option, I lifted a knee up onto the next step, repeating this action until I reached the top. Crawling along the back deck to the flat bench, I lay down, barely able to move, fatigue and weakness finally overcoming me.

Looking up at the Southern Cross glittering above, I muttered a prayer. Please God, I begged, let my arms still work. The ocean may have taken the use of my lower body but we were still several days from land and I needed my arms to carry me to the finish line.

The next day – day eight – my legs were still too weak to function efficiently. I crawled along the back deck and slid down the steps to enter my ski. Finishing 60 kilometres for the morning, I repeated the same crawling action to climb aboard for lunch, a term we used loosely for a meal that consisted of small amounts of fruit, crackers and water with electrolytes.

Lying flat to give myself every opportunity of holding down the food and fluid, I licked the outer salty coating off a Jatz cracker. Looking up to the dark grey sky, I began to pray once more. I'd been educated in the Catholic school system, but I had been disengaged from any religion since finishing high school. As my body faltered, though, I found myself asking for help from a greater power. I prayed with the sincere desperation that can only come about through fear. The prayer made me feel more at ease. By putting my fate in the hands of a greater power, I felt I could carry on with my role of paddling, knowing there were countless factors beyond my control. As for whether the wind would continue to be at my back, I could do nothing but hope that someone somewhere out there heard my cries for assistance and kept the conditions in my favour.

That evening, back in the water and with the sun hugging the horizon and the afternoon sky boasting glorious streaks of pink and orange, I pulled my wet beanie further down over my forehead as the temperature dropped to single digits. It was going to be a cold one. Blake had just started his shift on Bonnie Watch and we spoke of Broadway and the West End, fighting to hold onto normality in a situation that was far from everyday. The stars and moon appeared overhead. Blake put on his headtorch and lifejacket and sat down to watch me closely, the threat of a fall-out imminent in the big seas and poor light.

Several hours later, after reaching a total distance of 140 kilometres for the day, Jaime joined Blake on the back deck as they prepared to bring me in. As was protocol, one of the men prepared to grab my ski as I approached the boat, while the other stood slightly behind, ready to grab my arm and help me up the stairs. I was manoeuvring my ski towards the boat when a breaking swell smashed into me from the left, throwing me into the water. The shock of the frigid water sent a jolt through my spine, the cold immediately flooding through every part of my body that was submerged, from my neck down to my toes.

Snapping my head up, I saw the crew working hard to turn the boat around. In the 20-knot winds, it felt like forever. Squinting to make out the crew's faces, I saw Jaime and Blake on the back deck.

Their calls came ringing through the night air. 'Bonnie, say something! Do you need us to jump in?'

My lips formed the words that would guarantee my rescue, but nothing came out.

'Help!' I murmured hoarsely. 'I can't get back in the ski.'

In the nine-degree water, my body was rapidly losing energy and I couldn't perform the chin-up style movement required to safely remount my ski. Trying to haul myself up, I slid back into the icy water once again. As I fell, a huge gust of wind ripped across the water and flipped the ski, driving the hard edge into the top of my head. I heard the sickening thud, and after the initial shock wore off I reeled in pain. Jaime and Blake later described the event as one of the scariest moments of their lives. Squinting into the darkness, they could barely make out the silhouette of my ski, and when I didn't answer their calls, they feared the worst.

What they didn't see was the second gust of wind that lifted the ski high out of the water and drove it back down into my cheekbone, making a significant cracking sound as it did so. Lifting a hand to my head to check for blood, I prayed the impact of the ski hadn't broken the surface of the skin. Out there in the middle of the ocean at night with an open wound, I'd be a sitting duck for sharks.

Though there was no evident blood, an immediate lump formed at the spot I'd been hit, and a searing pain made its way up the side of my face. I also noticed a warmth spreading around my body. I would later learn that I was experiencing the early stages of hypothermia.

My legs were barely able to generate a kick, but I started to doggy paddle in the direction of the boat. The safety line was still clipped to my waist, and the ski dragged behind me as I struggled to keep my head above the dark water. As the boat manoeuvred backwards to pick me up, the boys yelled out, willing me to keep going. Just a few more strokes to safety.

Backlit by the deck lights, Jaime and Blake appeared like two figures of hope, their familiar voices providing me with energy. My grandmother Molly had arrived in my time of need, but now I realised that I had two more guardian angels out here in the Bight.

Managing one final surge of effort, I lunged at the boat.

Blake grabbed my wrist and hauled me up onto the back step. Shaking uncontrollably, I managed to crawl up the back steps, still unable to speak. As Jaime rushed inside to get a bucket of warm water, Blake wrapped a towel and jacket around my shoulders and sourced a space blanket. Once I was zipped up inside the blanket, the crew used my hairdryer to blast warm air through the blanket as my hands slowly began to lose their purple colour.

No one wanted to voice what we all were thinking.

That was close.

We were eight days into the crossing and land was still 400 kilometres away. The safety of Coffin Bay was 700 kilometres behind us so turning around was out of the question. The biggest question remained: though my mind was willing, was my body able to finish this near impossible task?

*

On day nine, I got back on the ski in howling winds and breaking chop. Rather than performing the usual step down into my ski as Blake or Jaime helped keep it steady, we instead pushed the ski away from the boat before I leapt out into the ocean after it. It was too dangerous for the boys to hold the ski in these conditions, as one rogue wave could put us all into the ocean. Attached to the ski via the safety line, I was pulled along for several metres before successfully climbing up and into it.

Once in position, I began carving up the water at 12–13 kilometres an hour with assistance from a massive tailwind. It was the conditions that ocean paddlers fantasise about. Feeling like a superhero as I leant left and right to drive my ski down the breaking swells, I tried to put the previous day's events out of my mind.

With the aggressive tones of Eminem's *Toy Soldier* blasting through my earphones, I took note of the lyrics. The rapper spoke about putting on a brave face for his crew, not wanting to worry them with the battles he was facing. Though Eminem and I shared little in common, his words resonated with me.

Launching into another huge runner, I was glad to be the one in the ski. Though at times the pressure felt like an incredible burden, the growth I had seen in myself and those around me made it all worth it.

On day ten, even though I desperately wanted to keep moving forward, we were forced to take another day off. The winds had again swung against us and once more I lay on the hard bench, freezing cold but not able to head inside the boat because I'd immediately start vomiting. With another few kilograms lost to seasickness, I estimated I'd lost nearly ten kilograms of weight since beginning the crossing, only ten days before. My legs were still too weak to support my body, and I continued to crawl around when I needed to move.

To distract me from my pain, Jaime began a new trivia game, and Blake emerged from his cabin to join me in a competition. It came down to the last question and I used my knowledge of ancient history to win. Though I couldn't walk and could barely eat, my competitive streak was still alive and well, and since managing to narrowly beat Blake at trivia that day, I have never let him forget it.

On day 11, the skipper told us that while we had 300 kilometres left to the mainland and the end of the Bight, there was an island a little closer that would provide a safe anchorage. Daw Island was 200 kilometres away and would provide the first still water we'd experienced since leaving Greenly Island. If I could manage two big paddling days, we'd get there by the next evening. Though previous experience informed me that land didn't come into view until it was 20–30 kilometres away, from the start of the next day I began fixing my gaze in the distance, scanning the ocean for any signs of the island. But the horizon remained bleak, with nothing but ocean as far as I could see in every direction.

Every kilometre hurt. My wetsuit was unable to dry in the frigid air between paddling sessions, and because I didn't have a second one I had to pull on the damp suit each morning. The thermals I'd packed were far too thin to offer protection from the icy conditions, and spending all day in a damp wetsuit led to a rash breaking out over my entire body that had no chance to heal.

Knowing we were getting closer to Daw Island, the boys continued the trivia questions, riddles and jokes. My ability to think clearly was somehow still intact despite my poor physical condition.

Several albatrosses followed us, and I wondered what they thought of us. Perhaps they were wondering, *Will they make it?* Sailors far more experienced than us had perished in the Bight, so I wouldn't blame them for doubting our ability to survive.

Working through each song and trivia question, I pushed forward all day and into the night to get us within 100 kilometres of Daw Island.

That evening it was Jaime's turn on Bonnie Watch once more. Aside from writing journal entries and keeping logs throughout the expedition, he'd been busy filming and editing content for the documentary we intended to make, using his years of experience as a cinematographer to capture a variety of angles and scenes. Lying on his belly and extending his arms over the water, camera grasped tightly in his hands, Jaime captured slow-motion shots, close-ups, panning shots and shots from angles I would never have thought of. Even in the middle of the Bight, Jaime's enthusiasm and creativity hadn't waned, and I was grateful to have him on my team. Strapping a GoPro to my chest in certain sections of the paddle, I was also able to capture the expedition from my perspective, and to voice my thoughts in real time.

Now so close to land, I knew that even if the wind turned, I was going to make it. Dehydrated and malnourished, my body falling apart from head to toe, I knew I would be okay.

On the twelfth day, I barely looked left or right. I fixated on the expanse of water ahead, continually scanning the horizon as I searched for any trace of the upcoming island sanctuary. Fantasising about sand between my toes and the feeling of being stationary, I imagined standing upright without vomiting and devouring a hearty bowl of meat and vegetables.

With 30 kilometres until we reached land, a ripple of whispered excitement spread throughout the boat. Peering into the distance, I saw nothing but ocean, so I wasn't sure what the commotion was about, but the smile Jaime tried so desperately to contain gradually spread across his face, confirmation that Daw Island was in range.

Around 15 minutes later, from my lower vantage point, I saw it too. At first it was just a tiny speck in the distance, but the dark shape grew larger until I could make out the two peaks of the island. For the first time in two weeks, I put my paddle down and stopped mid-course. Rather than the feeling of ecstasy I had been anticipating, I was instead overwhelmed with relief. In just a few more hours, we would be in still waters, digging our toes into white sand.

The sunset we experienced a few hours later was spectacular. Just ten kilometres out from the island, I turned my head left and caught sight of a sun that looked like a blazing ball of fire being dowsed in a deep purple ocean. As the last light faded, we continued in darkness and again I was guided by the silvery light of the full moon and the distinct green glow of the starboard light. Approaching the island through a narrow passage between jagged rocks on each side, I focused intently on the task, knowing one mistake could be highly costly in the dark. The skipper informed me he would need to access the island from a different angle, so the catamaran made its way to deeper water. Suddenly my support boat was out of sight.

Just able to make out the sandy shoreline, and with every ounce of strength remaining, I forced my aching shoulders to propel me forward towards the beach, now just 300 metres away.

'You can do it,' I muttered to myself, repeating the mantra I'd leant on so many times over the past two months. And now, just metres from finishing the Bight crossing, I repeated it again and again into the night sky.

Nearing the beach, a rogue wave picked me up and washed me up onto the sand. Attempting to stand, I fell back down into the knee-deep water. I forced myself back up, wincing, and pushed my ski forward so it didn't get washed out to sea. Then I held my arms out on either side of me as I took my first tentative steps up the beach. The crunch of the sand was pure heaven, and I savoured every grain that scraped my softened feet.

Once at a safe distance from the water, I dropped to my knees and turned to see the boat rounding the corner into the bay. Blake's voice blasted through the radio, checking to see I'd got in okay. Holding the radio up to my cheek, I confirmed my safe arrival then I unstrapped it from my chest and sat down. Looking up at the Southern Cross glittering high in the sky above, I was taken aback by the beauty of my surroundings. Thousands of stars glittered brightly in the sky, and though they were trillions of kilometres away, in that moment it felt as though I could have reached out and touched them.

It finally started to sink in. I had done it. Done what many had considered impossible, unthinkable. I'd paddled an ocean ski in a direct line across the Great Australian Bight. By taking a gamble and pulling it off, I'd given myself a healthy buffer on the world record. The record was now mine to lose.

The tide was on the way in, and I let the rising water lap at my feet, thinking over the past few weeks. Instead of to hell and back, I had been to hell and found a way to keep going through. With each surge of water, I willed the trauma of the past two weeks to be washed away into the ocean.

Hearing the crew dropping anchor 100 metres from the shore, I slowly stood up and brushed the sand off my legs, dragging my ski into the water to begin the paddle to the boat. As I climbed aboard, Jaime and Blake enveloped me in a hug as the crew laughed and cheered, everyone drained but ecstatic.

Heading down to my cabin, I closed the door behind me. I double-checked the lock then slumped down onto the hard wooden floor and began to sob. The emotions of the last few weeks poured out of me. It would take two weeks until I could speak about the horrors of the Bight, an experience that would continue to take a toll long after the crossing was finished.

CHAPTER 8

FANTASY ISLAND

THE NEXT DAY, IT WAS TIME TO EXPLORE. AFTER SURVIVING two weeks at sea, we decided to celebrate with a beach walk and hike to the top of Daw Island. Though battered and bruised, my legs weak and my bottom lip still bleeding from sun exposure and windburn, there was no way I was missing the opportunity.

After a brunch of bacon and eggs, enjoyed while basking in the sun on the front deck, we changed into our runners and exercise clothes. Climbing out of the tender and onto the sand, I jokingly fell to my knees to dramatically kiss the sand, reminiscent of a scene with Tom Hanks in *Castaway*.

The crew's laughter suddenly gave way to silence, and I heard Blake instruct me to move back. As I looked up, I came face to face with a death adder, one of many that inhabit the island all year round. They possess a venomous bite that kills a human within 15–20 minutes. The black snake was slithering towards us and ready to strike.

Wielding a piece of driftwood, Blake scared the snake back up into the bush. We had survived the horrifying ordeal of the last two weeks, taking on every element nature could throw at us, yet on a white sandy beach I'd come within 30 centimetres of death. It seemed every time I relaxed, a new challenge popped up. Blake essentially saved my life that day; his quick response prevented a scenario that still makes me shudder.

We were somewhat hesitant to continue with our plan of hiking to the highest peak of the island, but the skipper informed me that noise and numbers were our best bet in keeping the snakes at bay. Pulling my socks up to protect my ankles, I set out across the beach with the group to begin our trek to the top.

Deadly snakes aside, the island was incredibly scenic, like something from a fantasy. Perfect barrelling waves collided with the rocks on either side of the island, seals darted in and out of the break, and unique shells could be found among the grainy white sand. With his camera secured around his neck, Jaime stopped to capture the sight of baby seal cubs chasing after their parents, slipping over the rocks as they did so. On the last section of rocks before the trail started to ascend, Blake stumbled across the skeleton of a seal, which must have perished many months prior. He chipped out a tooth from the skull using a sharp rock and handed it to me. I pocketed it, planning to buff and shine it up, knowing it would forever be a symbol of what we had achieved.

Despite several stumbles over loose stones on the overgrown trail, I was surprised how nimble I felt as I picked my way to the top. Estimating I was by now 15 kilograms lighter than when we'd left the Gold Coast two months prior, I possessed a different physique entirely as excess body fat had given way to lean muscle. My body was continually conditioning to what I was asking of it.

We reached the top of Daw Island one hour before sunset, as the temperature dropped and the sun dipped towards the horizon. Blake took the opportunity to perform an abdominal plank on a rock, an exercise he had done every day since beginning the paddle. He'd often hold the plank for as long as ten minutes, and his favourite place to do it was on the starboard side of the boat, where he would talk, sing and joke to get through it. In a strange way, it helped me to see someone else in physical pain, even if only briefly.

Perched on the rocks at the top of the island, we watched as the first streaks of orange tinted the sky. We only had a few minutes to watch the show because we had to make the descent before nightfall. Our vantage point had a complete 360-degree view; to my left the sun was disappearing into the ocean, and to my right, a bright full moon was making its presence known. In front of us, nestled in the protection of the bay, was the catamaran that had been my lifeline, and as I pivoted around on the spot to look at what lay over my shoulder, I saw the Great Australian Bight stretching onwards, a seemingly never-ending expanse of deep blue ocean.

Never again would I have to take on the relentless beast that is the Bight. In fact, would anyone, ever? If so, I hoped that, like me, they would have a sense of naivety going in, as I doubt anyone would attempt it if they knew the reality.

*

Later that day, I was devastated to learn that the necklace that Jaime had given me back at the start had gone missing; I'd worn it every day in all conditions and after searching my entire cabin for the gold pendant and coming up empty-handed, I knew it must have been lost somewhere in the middle of the ocean. Jaime saw my disappointment and, without a word, he simply unclasped the chain around his own neck and put it around mine. This simple act of generosity warmed my heart. The previous gold pendant had seen me through some of the toughest, ugliest and also most beautiful moments, and to lose it felt like losing a part of me. With Jaime's pendant sitting comfortably on my chest, I felt confident it would keep me safe through whatever we were yet to face.

The next day we set the chart plotter to find the quickest route to a hospital. Though my body had been carried by the euphoria of finishing the Bight crossing, I had lost too much weight and was extremely dehydrated. It had been two weeks since I'd last held down vegetables or meat, and the risk of iron deficiency and electrolyte imbalance was pressing. I needed medical attention as soon as possible. Always a forward thinker, Matt had organised a health check for me as soon as I reached the mainland. He had called to tell us as soon as we had reception that though we were technically still isolating for a couple more days, he had gained permission from the Western Australian government for a hospital visit, so long as I had a police escort with me.

After two weeks at sea, we had to refocus on the seriousness of the pandemic and be grateful for being allowed into Western Australia.

With one final push before we could take time off to recuperate, I continued to go hard, surfing the swells that remained at my back. Jagged rocks lined the remote shoreline of the beaches leading into Esperance, but I wasn't fazed. The sight of land was by this stage a luxury, promising calmer waters than those of the unforgiving open ocean, and a chance to settle my reflux-riddled stomach.

Finishing 20 kilometres off Esperance, we marked our location into the chart plotter and began sailing towards the marina. Blake had been in contact with Matt throughout the morning and had made the local police aware of our impending arrival. Heading down to my cabin to change into dry clothing, I was filled with a strange mix of emotions. Returning to civilisation after a few weeks at sea I felt nervous. Would I be able to adapt back into a fast-paced world of noise, people and cars?

And then there was Matt. For two weeks, he and Ben had been cooped up in the shed of a property near Esperance as part of their mandatory quarantine, with no way of contacting us. They'd kept track of our progress through the tiny yellow dot of the AIS satellite marker on the boat, which updated our position every couple of hours. At any given time, they'd known where we were but not our physical condition or state of mind.

Sailing through the heads of the harbour, we spotted Matt and Ben waiting on top of the rock groin, and I immediately noticed Matt's new haircut. Short back and sides was his signature look, and he'd very obviously had a recent trip to the hairdresser. As he and Ben waved cheerfully on the deck, we waved back, looking more weathered than we allowed ourselves to admit. But rather than excitement, I felt a distinct numbness. Matt and Ben looked eager to hear of our progress, to soak up our recollections of the crossing over a flat white or cold beer. But so much had happened at sea, how could I possibly share what we had experienced? Where would I even start? I wasn't ready to revisit the trauma of the past few weeks and felt weighed down by the perceived pressure to talk about it.

Camera in hand, Blake readied himself to film the highly anticipated reunion, but instead I turned away and retreated down to my cabin, back to the safety of the world I was now more comfortable living in.

Out at sea, there was no Covid, war or money troubles. There was just ocean. The problems on a boat were many and varied and a wrong decision could prove fatal, but they were not the problems of life back on land. Maybe if I stayed on the boat, I wouldn't have to face reality and all the issues that came with it.

When I heard the anchor drop, I knew I had no choice but to return, so I gathered up my driver's licence and Medicare card and scooped my belongings into a bag with my drink bottle. Reluctantly, I walked back up the stairs to greet the government official who would check my identification and provide instructions on how to proceed.

Stepping onto the pontoon, I saw that Matt was looking as nervous as I felt, and I realised it wasn't easy for him either. Both he and Ben had undergone an isolation period of their own, and if I was unsure where to begin in recounting all we had gone through at sea, how could he possibly know what to say either?

As per the requirements of our exemption, the crew was to spend another two days in isolation. But with the smell of fish and chips wafting down towards us, the thought of stepping off the boat must have been incredibly tempting.

Checking my ID, the police officer asked me questions to confirm my identity.

'What's your full name?'

'Birthdate?'

'Place of birth?'

I handled the first few questions without issue, but things soon got more complex.

'What date did you last set foot on land and where was your last point of land contact?'

I suddenly froze. Turning helplessly to the crew, I felt the glare of the officer burning into the side of my face. *Don't you dare ask for help*, his body language seemed to say.

Looked like I was on my own.

Straining to remember, I had flashbacks of rolling five-metre swells and falls-outs into the dark ocean as I retraced our steps. Picturing Daw Island and the seals, I tried to remember what had come before, but it was as though nothing existed prior to the Bight. As though the world as I now knew it lay within the 1200-kilometre stretch of water we'd given everything to conquer.

What did we do before the Bight? And more importantly, who were we?

But that didn't matter to the officer whose job it was to screen those entering Western Australia. I felt like a potential plague-carrier, a threat to everything the Western Australian government had worked to protect.

'We left at the start of February ...' Buying myself time, I tried to work backwards as the officer shifted from one foot to the other. *What is the date today?* I genuinely had no idea. And then I remembered a small piece of information that would save me. Someone had mentioned Valentine's Day recently. But was that yesterday or the day before? I had no idea, but I knew the annual day of lovers fell on 14 February. All I had to do was work backwards. It had taken us 12 days to cross the Bight so working back from the fourteenth I realised we had left on the second.

'The second of February,' I answered, trying to sound confident.

'Okay, and where did you leave from?' replied the officer, looking only half convinced.

'Coffin Bay,' I said without hesitation, the memory of the ominous name flooding back.

'No, the last point you anchored,' the officer demanded.

Inside, I started to panic. Having been at sea for so long, I seemed unable to cope with this kind of thinking.

'Think of the place where you filmed the Gotcha4Life video,' I heard a crewmate mutter, referring to footage we had filmed the day after we left Coffin Bay.

The officer was growing impatient. With no apparent interest in what we had endured, I knew he'd send me back onto the boat without hesitation, ignoring my need to see a doctor.

Finally, I remembered.

'Misery Bay. That was the last time we anchored before we crossed the Bight.'

'Okay, Miss Hancock, come with me.'

Careful not to trip as I stepped off the boat onto the floating pontoon, I was relieved to have passed the officer's test.

Turning to Matt, I was unsure what to say but knew I needed to give him a hug. But as I reached out to him, he firmly shook his head. We needed to maintain the 1.5-metre distance strictly enforced by the authorities. As my 18-day isolation period hadn't yet been served, I was still technically in quarantine, which meant no contact with anyone outside of my crew on the boat. I was directed to head straight to the waiting ambulance on my own. Located in the nearby parking bay, it was surrounded by two police cars that would follow us to the hospital. This was a different world to the one I had known just a few months prior.

Arriving at the hospital, I forced my leaden legs to carry me through the door. Greeted by a nurse in a hazmat suit, I was asked to step on the scales. I wasn't sure what to expect, but the number on the scales was hardly surprising; at 63 kilograms, I was 14 kilos lighter than when I'd left the Gold Coast. Though

I had expected the weight loss, I immediately felt concerned; losing a fifth of my body weight so quickly put stress on all my organs.

I was ushered into another room and a sample of my blood was taken for testing. My small veins had made this process difficult in the past, and I prayed the nurse would locate a vein straightaway, as I wasn't sure how much more physical pain I could take. Thankfully, she used a small butterfly needle to get the job done and before long dark red blood was filling the pathology tubes. The blood oozed out slowly at first, indicating my severe level of dehydration, but eventually the flow increased, providing enough to fill two tubes, which were taken away to be studied. In the meantime, a second nurse began setting up the intravenous fluids that would quickly rehydrate my weakened body.

Two hours and 2.5 litres of intravenous electrolyte solution later, I'd started to regain some strength. The blood pathology had revealed no evident deficiencies in terms of iron, calcium or other trace elements, and I felt I had dodged a bullet. My body had somehow withstood the lack of food to come out the other side unscathed. With that positive news, I was free to go.

The nurse asked if I had a lift arranged, which made me confused. Escorted to the hospital via two police vehicles, I was now allowed to freely walk out of the building and call someone for a lift back to the boat. There seemed to be many contradictions throughout the Covid pandemic, this being the latest.

I rang Matt, who was waiting with Ben in our Ranger outside. When I told him I was free to leave, he sounded hesitant in his reply. Covid protocols had been so stringent that I think he didn't know what to, but he eventually told me I'd see him and Ben the moment I walked out the door. True to his word, there they were. As I stepped into the car and closed the door behind me, we couldn't shake the feeling that we were breaking the law. We decided to make a quick stop on our way back to the boat to get a takeaway pizza, which Matt was able to purchase as he and Ben weren't in quarantine, unlike me. It was my first takeaway meal in over two weeks, and I savoured every bite of the cheesy, salty treat.

We ate the pizza in a deserted park and then Ben wandered away to give Matt and me some privacy. It was our first opportunity to talk without Covid officers or hospital staff around. I didn't bother diving into stories of the Bight because there was simply too much to unpack; I figured it could wait until tomorrow. Instead, Matt told me of his adventures over the past two weeks; how they had found a local farmhouse through Airbnb and ended up staying there for two weeks. Ben had caught up on his uni work, and they'd both managed to keep my social media updated, which was fortunate because by now I had a large community of people following my journey online.

'And,' Matt excitedly informed me, 'you raised just over five thousand dollars crossing the Bight. The donation page was going nuts.'

While we talked, the park slowly became a hive of activity as families arrived to make use of the swings and slides. I felt like a regular person having an evening catch-up after work. I missed my friends and family, but although we were back in reception, I hadn't called them because I didn't know what to say. I was relieved to not have to talk about the Bight just yet. At some stage the media and my close network would demand it of me, but right then I couldn't face it. I felt the sun on my face and reached for another slice of pizza, grateful that my stomach accepted the food easily.

We made our way back to the boat and decided not to mention the pizza; it felt like our little secret. Climbing aboard, I turned back to farewell Matt and Ben, in a scene that was becoming all too familiar. Looking at Matt, I could see the trip was starting to take its toll. Though his haircut and bright shirt attempted to serve as a smoke screen, I could see right through it; the constant separation was getting to him. We had been married for just one year prior to the trip, and now we were again forced apart after a quick reunion. I had a sense that if we could survive the expedition and come out of it together, nothing would ever break us. I just worried we wouldn't get that far.

*

The next day, setting our sights on Albany, we continued to head west, by now well and truly on our way towards turning the southwest corner of Australia, a significant milestone. We were looking forward to the promise of sunsets over the ocean, white sandy beaches, blue water and coral reefs. Planning to stay close to shore and use the jet ski as an escort, we'd be treated to a front-row view of some of the most spectacular coastline in the world.

We reached Albany on 25 February, day 69 of the expedition, a few days after Matt and Ben. Everyone was ready for a few days' rest to recharge for the next stretch. With our mandatory quarantine period now over, I was officially a free woman. Jaime filmed the moment I stepped onto the jetty, capturing the utter relief on my face.

Matt and I headed to an Italian restaurant that evening and, over a bowl of pasta, spoke of everything and yet nothing of the Bight, as I still wasn't ready. The following day, the entire crew enjoyed an outing to a local bowling alley, and my competitive nature returned as I tried unsuccessfully to win the overall point score.

After three days, we were ready to head back to sea. Matt dropped me off at the marina and I boarded the catamaran once more, with the plan to catch up with him and Ben in a few days' time.

Less than a week later, we rounded the southwest tip of the country, passing the stunning white lighthouse at the tip of Cape Naturaliste. It was every bit as awe-inspiring as the images online had suggested. The lighthouse stood in stark contrast to the brown-green slopes below, and I could see the cape from ten kilometres away. Making the second major right-hand turn of the expedition, I was relieved to finally be taking on the west coast. Little did I know that the state would seem to go on forever and give me some close calls.

From Cape Naturaliste, I completed a week with the jet ski as my sole source of support while the catamaran took a break in Fremantle. With Jaime and Ben on the jet ski and Matt and Blake in the Ranger, we made our way up the coast. Staying close to shore in case the jet ski had issues, I paddled big days of 80–100 kilometres, and we camped at night at caravan parks and on beaches.

On day 78 of the trip, I set out from Eagle Bay just south of Perth. Ben was driving the jet ski with Jaime and me on the back, towing the ocean ski to the spot where I'd finished the previous day. We were zipping across the water at 30 kilometres an hour, with Jaime facing backwards, desperately gripping the tail of my ski while doing everything he could not to lose his balance as we were thrown all over the ocean. Reaching the marked location 20 kilometres offshore, I lowered myself into the ski and began paddling. This stretch of coastline was known for its great white sharks, and I couldn't help seeing ominous shadows in the smooth water. With 71 kilometres of paddling ahead, the sun was already high in the sky but I never doubted we'd get to shore before it set.

The glassy conditions gave way to favourable chop as the wind picked up, and I was soon travelling at 11 kilometres an hour, enjoying solid runners as I zipped back and forth to check in with the boys on the jet ski. Other than stopping for a sandwich a few hours in, I didn't slow. My body was honed for the enormous paddling load and I powered through the water with every stroke, eating up the kilometres.

After 58 kilometres, I exited the trance-like state I often entered while paddling and looked up at the sky to see the first tint of orange on the horizon. The sun would be setting soon. Looking back at the jet ski, I could see the boys were deep in conversation as Ben checked the dashboard. What was their concern? We had brought an extra jerry can of fuel so surely we weren't running low? We'd been moving quickly all day, though, so perhaps our speed had churned up the fuel at a higher rate than usual? The thought of running out of fuel in the sharky, isolated waters made me shiver.

At 78 kilometres, I heard the jet ski pull up beside me, and Ben spoke the words I had been dreading. 'We're almost out of fuel. We need to change our path 'cause we won't make the eight kilometres to where Matt is waiting. Head straight to the beach.'

Pushing my right pedal down and angling for the shoreline, I felt uneasy. We were five kilometres offshore and Ben hadn't said if we had enough fuel to make it in. What if we ran out before we got back in? Would I have to paddle in for help in the dark? The sun was well and truly setting now, the last light of the day glowing on the horizon. Paddling as hard as I could towards the beach, every kilometre edged us closer to safety.

Two kilometres offshore, the boys directed me to climb onto the jet ski. By now it was nearly completely dark, and it was far too dangerous to be paddling in these waters with only the jet ski for company. Doing what I was told, I climbed aboard, grateful for another day of paddling to be done but nervous as to what would unfold next.

Slowly putting towards shore, Ben kept the speed low to conserve fuel. After seeing him glancing down at the fuel gauge nervously, I snuck a look over his shoulder. I shouldn't have. The gauge arrow pointed to empty. With basically no fuel and two kilometres to the shore, we were in big trouble. Despite the minimal reception along the isolated stretch of coastline, Ben was able to get a call through to Matt to inform him of our situation and explain that we would be landing eight kilometres further south than the planned meeting point.

The last kilometre seemed to drag on forever and my heart pumped hard as I willed the jet ski forward, metre by metre closer to safety. I started mentally preparing myself to paddle to shore in the dark to get help if we ran out of fuel, but I desperately hoped it wouldn't come to that.

Somehow, we managed to putt our way in until we were 500 metres from the beach. Looking towards land, I saw a big shore dump crashing onto the beach. We would have to navigate it to get to safety. With the jet ski weighing close to a tonne, it wouldn't be easy. Dropping the speed right down, Ben used the onshore breeze to help us in, conserving the remaining fuel until we were within the break zone.

Squinting in the dark to pick a break between the swells, Ben spotted an opportunity and used every last bit of fuel to floor it. Hitting the beach with a thud, Jaime and I were thrown off sideways and the jet ski tipped on top of us. Crawling out from under its huge weight, I saw my ski and paddle being scooped up by the ocean. Stumbling after my craft, I caught up to it

50 metres down the beach. I grabbed the ski and hoisted it up onto the soft sand, tossing my paddle after it. My relief was short-lived, however, as I saw the boys struggling to pull the heavy jet ski up onto the beach.

Running back to help them, I caught sight of another figure stumbling towards the jet ski in the darkness, also intent on giving them a hand. The stranger was a man named Damo, and Damo was highly intoxicated. The comedy of errors was made more humorous by Damo's attempts to help, each push ending with a groan and face plant in the sand. Luckily, Damo's wife, Isha, had consumed fewer beers than her husband and she ran down from their picnic set-up to help. With the extra muscle behind the jet ski, we were able to eventually shift it further up the sand, away from the dangerous shore dump that threatened to carry it back into the ocean.

Suddenly, I heard a chorus of voices carrying from further up the beach. Straining to see with no moon, I clocked a group of 20 or more figures heading towards us. What was happening? We were on a deserted stretch of beach, and only Matt knew we'd put ashore, yet these people had seemingly appeared from nowhere.

Before long, we were surrounded by a crowd of friendly faces who told us they were there to help. Some of the group secured the jet ski onto a trailer, the rest handed out bottles of water. Still confused, I soon learnt that Matt had put the word out about our situation through the local Facebook group and nearly the entire Preston Beach community had answered the call. A woman named Jan asked if I'd like a massage then plonked me down on a blanket and dug her thumbs into my aching shoulders. She then informed me that I would be taken in by one of the locals for a hot bath and dinner. Still struggling to comprehend it all, I was moved by the generosity of the community.

Eventually Matt arrived; the Ranger had had to be lifted out of the sand after getting bogged further up the beach. Once the jet ski was secured, Ben and Jaime headed off in one direction while Matt and I were led in the other. A little over an hour later, I was in a hot bubble bath, soaking in essential oils and then, for the first time since the beginning of the paddle, eating dinner at a proper dining table.

The next day, the same group of generous souls who had helped us gathered on Preston Beach to see us off. Two of them – Lovell and Graham – were heading home to Perth and they invited us to stay with them in their house that night. Lovell is a talented artist and Graham is a successful arbitrator who had been a top middle-distance runner as a young man.

After a 70-kilometre day of paddling that day to get to Perth, I made my way with my crew to Lovell and Graham's art-filled sanctuary. We swam in their backyard pool and enjoyed Lovell's delicious cooking, and ended up staying for five days.

*

A few weeks later, it was time to link back up with our support catamaran to tackle the infamous Zuytdorp Cliffs located

500 kilometres north of Perth. The cliffs are an intimidating 200-kilometre stretch of steep rocky limestone extending from Kalbarri to Steep Point and remain a little-visited segment of the Western Australian coast. The area carries a certain mystique due to the shipwreck that took place several hundred years earlier.

Standing 250 metres above sea level at their highest point, the cliffs are named after the *Zuytorp*, a trading ship of the Dutch East India Company, which was dispatched from the Netherlands in 1711, heading to Indonesia carrying freshly minted coins. The ship never arrived at its destination, and, as no initial search was undertaken, it wasn't known whether the boat was shipwrecked or taken by pirates. In the mid-twentieth century, the wreck of the *Zuytorp* was located in the waters below the enormous cliffs, which were named in its honour. Though the fate of the crew is still unknown, it is widely believed that some survivors of the wreck successfully escaped, assimilating with local Indigenous communities in the area.

Over 300 years later, paddling ten kilometres out to sea, I could feel the backwash off the cliffs. As the water swirled under me, I focused my concentration on the task at hand, willing myself to hold my balance and reflecting on the writings of Paul Caffyn, the pioneer who paddled this stretch 40 years before me. Caffyn had hugged the cliffs and taken breaks on the sand of small bays dotted along this section, often having to negotiate ten-foot waves on his way back out to sea. His expedition was incredibly inspiring, and I was honoured to be following in his steps by completing the treacherous section of coast myself.

Unfortunately for myself and Blake, who was onboard the catamaran as support crew with Jaime, the backwash caused our seasickness to return with a vengeance. It had been a few weeks since I'd experienced it, as the conditions had been far calmer close in to shore when I'd been accompanied by the jet ski, and my stomach was more settled as a result. Now back with the catamaran, the closest distance to shore I paddled was ten kilometres, which meant days spent in rough seas again.

It took us three days to navigate the cliffs, and on board the catamaran I was forced to carry a bucket with me as I made my way around the boat. Again, I spent as much time as I could lying flat on the back deck to limit the nausea. I would wait until my bladder was about to burst then run to the bathroom, holding my head in my hands while I urinated, the rocking of the boat making me dry retch. If I had to empty my bowels, and stay longer in the rocking room, I would end up vomiting into the bucket while I sat on the toilet. The whole process was embarrassing and miserable.

The week of love and care at Lovell and Graham's seemed a world away as I pulled my thermal top over my head and lowered myself back into my ski in the dark. I was now regularly paddling at night because there was nowhere safe to anchor next to the cliffs; the more kilometres I paddled each day, the sooner we would get to calm waters.

By the time we reached Steep Point at the end of the cliffs, I was a mess. Physically drained from the seasickness and the effort it took to balance in the backwash, I had gotten through the last day by blasting Eminem in my headphones as I tried to block out every other sensation.

Reaching the end of the Zuytdorp Cliffs should have been a celebration of successfully navigating one of the toughest stretches of coastline in Australia, but I wasn't in the mood. Feeling weak and drained, I paddled away from the boat towards the cliffs, craving privacy.

The following day, after paddling into Shark Bay on the other side of the cliffs, I suddenly felt overwhelmed by the pain in my body. I climbed aboard the catamaran and rang Matt in tears.

'Please come and get me,' I begged, suddenly desperate to spend time on land to let my body recover.

This was the first time Matt had heard me upset since the start of the expedition, so he leapt into action.

'Ben will come and get you,' he assured me.

And within 30 minutes, Ben had pulled up next to the boat on the jet ski that he and Matt had towed from Kalbarri. He helped me as I climbed on. In my hands I held a small bag of dry clothes. I had every intention of spending the next few days on land.

As Ben manoeuvred the jet ski around the bends of the bay on our way into land, I struggled to maintain my composure. When I reached Matt onshore, I collapsed into his arms and let the emotion pour out of me. Having endured freezing conditions, pain and isolation throughout the trip, I'd had enough. Matt simply held me, sensing that what I needed in that moment was not words but an ear to listen. Ben gave us some privacy, something I'd craved for so long and now finally had.

Eventually I composed myself and wandered over to the car, where Matt told me he had a surprise. A fan of surprises, I wondered what on earth he could have bought for me in such a small town. With only one cafe, chemist and small supermarket in Shark Bay, there were minimal options for buying a gift. Deciding not to ask questions, I buckled up my seatbelt and Matt drove the three of us away from the bay towards town.

Reaching an intersection, we turned right, heading away from civilisation. *What is going on?* I wondered. Five minutes later, we arrived at Shark Bay Airport, and it was apparent we were getting on a flight. But where to?

'It's time for you to gain a different perspective,' Matt said gently and led me towards the office. 'We have a flight booked for 3pm,' he advised the receptionist, who smiled and nodded as though she was expecting us.

'The pilot won't be long,' we were told, and before long a tall man in his mid-thirties, with aviation uniform on, strolled into the room to collect us.

'Are you ready to see the cliffs?' he asked us, and suddenly I understood; we were going to see the cliffs from the sky.

From the moment the helicopter lifted off the ground, I was in my element. Escaping my troubles on land, I pulled my phone out and began snapping selfies in the back of the chopper. The pilot had been informed of the expedition and angled straight for the cliffs to give me a closer look.

'Here they are, the famous Zuytorp Cliffs,' he told us. 'I bet it's a bit easier to fly over them than paddle.'

Hovering directly over a particularly rugged stretch of cliff face, I began to absorb the enormity of what I'd done. *I paddled that*, I thought, smiling to myself as the realisation settled in. Watching the waves crash into the cliffs, the backwash visible as the water bounced out to sea, I allowed myself to feel an emotion that had been lost in my self-pity. Pride. Throwing my head back, I laughed. The type of belly laugh that fills a person up with a sense of warmth all over. The type of laugh that gave me hope that maybe one day life would return to normal.

Thanking Matt as the chopper touched back down, I climbed out a new person. I now felt overwhelming gratitude and my cup was filled. Once again I felt able to put back on the invisible superhero cape that was required every day of the expedition. Driving away from the airport, I reminded myself it was okay if the cape slipped sometimes or even fell to the floor in tatters. No one was perfect. Even Superman had his bad days, but it's the way we handle them that counts.

Would I let the past few days break me, all the hard work going to waste? Or would I, like Superman, dust myself off as I stood up and straightened my cape?

Deciding on the latter, I realised that strength is found not in clear waters but in the choppy seas. The ability to continually fight even when the challenges are seemingly insurmountable is a real superpower.

CHAPTER 9

KING WAVES KILL

On 28 March, I had my first major shark encounter.

We were completing the final stretch of a 41-kilometre day, heading towards the remote coastal town of Carnarvon. The chopper flight still fresh in my mind, I blasted my headphones loud. But this wasn't like taking a walk after work with air pods in, the only dangers an over-zealous bike rider passing a little too closely on the right. This was the ocean. And in the ocean, you can't block out your surroundings because one wrong move can be fatal.

The surface of the water was smooth, the type of conditions in which your reflection shines back at you. Jaime was on Bonnie Watch, and I could see his relaxed posture give way to visible concern as he shifted from leaning against the side railing to standing upright, frantically gesturing at me to come closer to the boat. Thinking the signal was to alert me to come in for a snack, I signalled that I was coming, but I was in no rush as I rapped along enthusiastically.

As Jaime's gesturing grew more frantic, I suddenly had a sinking feeling in the pit of my stomach. He wasn't calling me in to the boat for food. Like a bolt of lightning, I remembered that I was in Shark Bay, an area known for the feared great white. Increasing my paddling rate dramatically, I sprinted my way up to the boat, ripping my headphones out, which allowed me to hear the crew's instructions for me to climb aboard. I pulled myself onto the back deck without diving out of the ski to stretch my legs as I usually did, and demanded to know what the fuss was about. But I knew the answer before it was spoken.

'Big shark,' Jaime began. 'It popped up on your right and did a deep dive back under your ski. The fin was massive. I think it was a great white.'

I felt the blood draining from my face.

Without knowing it, I had been clocked by the ocean's most fearsome predator, an experience which many horror movies are based on. The great white shark is the type of creature that keeps some people away from the beach their whole lives. Just a few kilometres from the safety of shore, I'd narrowly escaped an attack.

We made the call to end the day's paddling and motored into the safety of the marina, and as we did so, I couldn't help but scan left to right across the bay, searching for traces of the beast that had chosen to spare me.

My lack of concentration had almost cost me. Forgetting where I was, I had become complacent and had not respected the crew's calls to come in to the boat. Though part of me wanted to block out the dangers, I now appreciated that fear was an asset, keeping me on my toes in an environment with countless threats. In the ocean, being fearful could be the difference between surviving or not.

While the incident rattled me, I knew it was important to get back on the water as soon as possible. After a day off, I nervously restarted at the same location where Jaime had spotted the shark, and we continued the trek north towards Broome, another 1800 kilometres up the coast. According to locals, Broome was home to another fearsome ocean predator: saltwater crocodiles. The presence of crocodiles would be a danger all the way across the top of the country and down the east coast as far as Townsville in Queensland, meaning 5000 kilometres of coastline was crocodile territory. The idea of great white sharks wasn't nearly as terrifying as the thought of these prehistoric reptiles that can grow to over six metres long. My ocean ski was six metres, so it was shorter than the largest male crocodiles up in the warm waters of Western Australia.

The catamaran had to return to Queensland for a scheduled appointment at the Great Barrier Reef, so on 30 March, we said goodbye and began using our jet ski as the primary support vessel. A few days later, in a tiny town called Seabird, I would meet an Australian legend, who would help us out by joining the expedition with his fishing boat, but more on that later.

Among our group, Ben was the sole owner of a jet-ski licence, and on our first stint together from Carnarvon, he smashed out 75 kilometres of driving in the hot, flat conditions. Holding the throttle down for that long and keeping the vessel tracking steadily next to me at 11 kilometres an hour was no mean feat, requiring an enormous amount of concentration. From the very first day of our endeavour, Ben had stepped up to every task asked of him and now, over three months later, I was asking him to rise to his biggest challenge yet. Little did we know, he would soon save my life.

Quobba Station coastline, or Red Bluff, is an extremely isolated stretch of coast. Established in 1898, Quobba is a family-run pastoral station stretching over 180 kilometres along the Ningaloo coastline. When the sea grows to a certain size, the swells roll in from the Indian Ocean and crash into sea caves, pushing the water up and out of blow holes within the rocks. The blow holes are a popular tourist destination, but we were particularly lucky to be getting a first-hand view of the caves from the water.

The Quobba area is also known for its surfing breaks, though surfers are urged to be careful. Sharks are a danger, but the main hazard comes in the form of giant waves that creep up seemingly out of nowhere and surge over the rocks and cliffs. Driving along the coastal road, tourists will encounter the famous 'King Waves Kill' sign, which is a popular spot for a selfie but also a serious warning. Injuries and fatalities have occurred in the area over the years and visitors are warned never to turn their back to the ocean.

Ben and I spent the better part of the day slowly grinding our way along the Quobba Station coastline. After 72 kilometres, or seven hours, of paddling in the flat, negotiating the famous cliffs, our next challenge involved heading into the beach safely to meet up with the rest of the team on land. Matt, Jaime and Blake had stopped frequently along the roadway, spotting us in the swirling waters below. They had arranged a campsite for us that night and would take us there once we were safe and dry.

My hands were aching, the joints continuing to swell with each day of paddling, and I gritted my teeth as I pushed through the pain. Completing two more arduous kilometres, I knew we were close to the finish location but there seemed to be no sign of a beach or the others. We were sitting 100 metres out from a bay with headlands on either end that consisted of jagged cliff faces that dropped steeply into the ocean. The cliffs created a backwash so strong it made sitting on the ski a difficult task and I knew our journey to shore could be rough. After calling Matt to check what had happened, Ben informed me that the others were in fact another kilometre further along, waiting around the corner on the next stretch of beach.

Just one more kilometre, I urged my aching body, adjusting my grip on the paddle to relieve the pressure on my knuckles. But this made the paddle slip from my hands, and I realised an adjusted position wouldn't work. Returning to the regular grip, I winced as I took the next stroke. The paddling action made it feel like needles were jabbing into my fingers.

One kilometre further north, we spotted the others on the shoreline and prepared to head in. I was keen to get to dry land and on to our campsite for the evening. Our accommodation on this stretch of coast was to be swags in caravan parks and on beaches.

But a phone call from Matt soon put a halt to any thought of finishing for the day.

'It's too shallow to come in,' Matt informed Ben from his position onshore. 'You'll run aground on the reef.'

Ben started to stress. The fuel capacity of the jet ski was limited to 90 kilometres, so we had to make a decision soon or waste fuel and risk a repeat of Preston Beach. Thinking quickly under pressure, Matt soon crafted a plan for us to return to a beach we had passed ten kilometres further back and exit safely there. Taking off my gloves, I saw that my fingers had swollen to twice their usual size and I knew I didn't have it in me to paddle the ten kilometres. I would have to jump on the jet ski with Ben. But there was a catch. Jaime wasn't with us, so Ben or I would be required to hold the ocean ski while the other drove the jet ski. Taking a few minutes to decide on the best course of action, we concluded that with the poor condition of my hands, I'd have little chance of holding the surf ski securely in the growing chop and swell. I'd only ever driven the jet ski once before – and in calm conditions – but I'd just have to figure it out as I went.

Ben marked my finish location on the chart plotter and I climbed out of my ski and into the driver's seat of the jet ski. He turned around so we were back-to-back and, after grabbing hold of the tail of my ski, he instructed me to get going. Pulling back the throttle, I threw the jet ski into a bunny hop and lunged forward over the large swells. I was unable to apply the pressure required to hold an even speed. As Ben desperately clung to my ski, squeezing his legs against the jet ski's seat to stay on, I apologised each time I caused us to lunge forward over the large swells. Rogue waves were a threat, so Ben urged me to guide the jet ski further away from the cliffs. I tried to be gentle on the throttle as I turned to the right, steering us further out to sea.

Five kilometres into the journey, I grew impatient. After a day of hard paddling, my hands were increasingly sore, and I was desperate to be dry and fed. Without realising it, I put more pressure on the throttle and the jet ski picked up speed as we crashed into the incoming swell. Ben had instructed me to hold ten kilometres an hour as a maximum, and I was shocked to look down at the speedometer and see 18 kilometres an hour. Realising my error, I quickly pulled upwards on the throttle, but as I did so, a large swell collided into us and the jet ski was launched into the air, crashing back down into the water with force. I turned back to Ben to apologise, but instead I heard him yell above the wind, 'STOP!'

Ben had lost his grip on my ski in the commotion, and it was now floating towards the cliffs.

As a surf lifesaver, it is ingrained within me to react swiftly to danger in the ocean, and instead of pausing to make a plan, I jumped. I had faith that the loud hum of the jet ski would deter any sharks. Leaping off the side, I swam after my ski, my sole focus on stopping the craft crashing into the cliffs, which we were quickly approaching. But the strong winds caused the ski to roll away from me, like a hat lost in the breeze, twisting and turning to evade recapture by the owner. The cliffs, rather than a spectacle, were now a death trap. With no beach for five kilometres either side, I realised my mistake. Powerless against the pull of the ocean, I was now reliant on Ben rescuing me, and the gap to the cliffs was closing all the time.

Just 100 metres from the cliffs, I desperately lunged at my ski. With one final stroke, I reached it and grabbed the foot strap, knowing I would be okay so long as Ben got to me straightaway. Turning back, I was shocked to see the jet ski still 100 metres away, with Ben scrabbling around as though searching for something he'd lost.

It was then I realised that by diving into the water after my ski, I'd had taken with me the single most valuable item on a jet ski. The key. It was attached to my lifejacket and when I jumped, it had come with me, instantly cutting the engine. Ben was left with a floating jet ski and no way to start it. He'd looked on helplessly as I swam away to my craft, but then he suddenly remembered something crucial.

The learner key.

Used to limit learner drivers from reaching high speeds, the green learner key accompanies the regular key in a jet-ski driver's toolkit. And now it would save both our lives.

Retrieving it from under the dash, Ben jammed it in the ignition and fired up the engine. Now just 70 metres from the cliffs, I was in trouble. I was kicking hard against the current, but the swells were sucking me in with no mercy and the fatigue from the day's paddling was setting in.

Ben came careening towards me, the urgency of the situation not lost on him. White water sprayed up from either side of the jet ski, and he whipped the tail around so that I could climb aboard. Ensuring I was safe, he reached down and grabbed my ski, using what appeared to be superhuman strength to lift it out of the water and balance it across his lap.

As he drove us back out to sea and away from the immediate danger, I scolded myself for my stupidity. By now I had no doubt about the presence of guardian angels, and it was becoming obvious they didn't just exist in a spiritual sense. That day, floating towards the cliffs of Quobba Station, which had claimed the lives of many, I'd been saved by a guardian angel with long blond hair and a green learner's key.

*

We took a few days off after the incident to recover and got back to work on 3 April, which marked day 106 of the expedition. We'd tested a few different combinations on the jet ski, but my preferred set-up was having just one person to accompany me for the day. Even then, I still periodically wished for the privacy that I'd craved since the Bight.

Since the start of the trip, I'd had minimal time to myself. Breakfast was made for me in the morning and I would be handed a smoothie while I prepared for a pre-paddle interview. Post interview, I would be helped into my paddling clothes because my aching hands or seasickness often rendered me incapable of doing this on my own. The crew would assist me into my ski, and for the next 10–14 hours, I would be observed. From my first stroke to the last, my movements were tracked; everyone knew where I was and what I was doing at all times. As a 31-year-old who had known independence for a decade, the lack of anonymity was overwhelming.

I'm often asked about toilet breaks throughout a paddling day, and let's just say that while sitting in a ski in wet paddling gear, I became elite at multi-tasking. But even as I subtly slowed my pace so that I could drop behind the boat for a minute of privacy to urinate, I would be questioned as to why I had slowed down and whether the pace of the boat was too fast. Every one of my actions was accounted for.

Once a month, when I had my period, I developed creative ways to prevent the crew from knowing.

'You stay up on deck,' a crewmate would inform me, trying to protect me from seasickness. 'I'll get your dry clothes from downstairs so you don't have to head to the cabin.'

Needing to change my tampon, I'd fumble my words as I unsuccessfully searched for an excuse to head inside.

'No, I've got to head down there,' I'd mumble, leaving the other party confused. Why would someone go down to the stuffy cabin when they had been vomiting all day? Sure enough, halfway through changing my tampon, I'd feel the vomit rise in my throat as nausea overcame me. I'd do my best to empty the contents of my stomach into the sink or toilet as opposed to the cabin floor. Early into the Bight crossing, I had been sitting on my bed when the nausea came on quickly and all I could do was project the vomit outwards onto the floor so it didn't soak the sheets. As if I didn't feel dehumanised already from the lack of privacy, seasickness took things to a whole new level. I was reduced to a primitive state: scared, hungry and desperate to reach a safe sanctuary.

Part of me knew I should have just told the crew the truth. I had my period, a natural occurrence for a woman. Most of them had sisters and all of them had female friends. It wouldn't have come as a shock, but I couldn't bring myself to do so. It felt like the one skerrick of privacy I had left and I wasn't willing to give it up. As the only woman in my team, it seemed easier to grit my teeth through the pain of menstrual cramps and suffer in silence than to simply tell the men around me what was going on. Having grown up with sisters and a tight female friendship group, I still felt far more comfortable sharing intimate details with women.

Eventually, after months of hiding my periods and urinating secretly, I'd had enough; I wanted to spend a day without worrying about others. Willing to risk my safety to do so, I informed Matt that I wanted to do some paddling alone. We were in one of the most remote sections of Australia, and behind the scenes I was begging my husband to let me head out to sea without the jet ski.

We ended up fighting about it – he emphasised the importance of safety and I pushed back on behalf of my emotional wellbeing – and eventually I won the battle. Knowing my stubborn nature, Matt shifted his focus onto making sure I had everything I needed to be self-sufficient. Food, fluids and electrolytes, headphones, radio, sunscreen and flares were among the equipment packed into the bum bag I would wear for the excursion.

On day 108, the sun high in the sky and an endless expanse of crystal blue water stretching in front of me, I set out from the pristine waters of Coral Bay to take on my first paddling day solo. Throughout the excursion, I would be navigating my way past Ningaloo Reef, a coral system that spans 250 kilometres along Western Australia's northwest coast and is considered the jewel in the crown of Western Australian tourist attractions. The largest fringing reef in the world, parts of it lie just metres from shore, making it a popular spot for snorkelling, diving and fishing, helped in no small part by the 26-degree water temperature. If visitors are lucky, they'll spot any number of local marine life, including dolphins, manta rays, dugongs, turtles, even humpback whales and whale sharks. The great white sighting in Carnarvon was still fresh in my mind and I knew that the abundance of sea creatures would also draw reef sharks, as well as creatures much bigger. But I didn't dwell on those thoughts too long. I would be hugging the coast for the day, keeping the shoreline no more than 500 metres to my right for safety.

Glancing back over my shoulder, I saw the crew waving me off and I could hear the buzz of Blake's drone as he captured the moment. With the winds so prevalent, there had been minimal opportunity to launch the drone until Western Australia, but now Blake was making the most of the calmer conditions, putting the drone up to capture a different view of the scenery. The distance to the planned exit point was 59 kilometres and for the first ten kilometres of the day, I revelled in my newfound independence. With no one to answer to, I was totally free. Free to sing aloud without fear of being judged, free to slow or stop as I pleased, and perhaps most delightful of all, free to urinate while sitting in my ski without having to explain my slowed speed.

Just 20 kilometres into the paddle, I noticed how parched my throat was. Caught up in the beauty of white sandy bays and shallow reefs, I'd clocked 15 sea turtles on my journey so far, but the number of times I'd taken a sip from my water bladder could have been counted on one hand. Aware of the negative effects of dehydration on performance, I reached forward and pulled my 2.5-litre bladder towards me, guzzling it greedily as the sun beat down on me. A layer of sweat coated my forehead as I reapplied zinc to my nose and lips. Squinting into the distance, I spotted the white lighthouse, which was just a few kilometres short of my destination for that day.

Turning my head to the left, I noticed the reef curving back out to sea. Now floating on dark water, I paddled in between turquoise blue ocean and the deserted white sandy beach to my right. With the offshore breeze starting to build, I felt the water rushing back out to sea, attempting to take me with it. Planting my foot firmly on the right pedal, I resisted the temptation to head towards the outer reef, a prospect that was incredibly dangerous without a support vessel.

Another ten kilometres in, my concentration started to wane. I estimated the ambient temperature to be around 35 degrees, and there seemed to be a blurry haze off the water that made me disoriented. Without the jet ski, I had no one to turn to for reassurance or to double-check the distance to the finish. It was just me and my headphones, and these had started to malfunction and repeat the same song over and over.

Somewhere around the 30-kilometre mark, I was sucked out towards the outer reef. The moving water was strong, and I was quickly pulled from the dark blue gutter to the turquoise water further out to sea. With a sudden shock, I realised where I was. The shore was now 800 metres away, and I was paddling directly over the reef I had been warned by local skippers to avoid at all costs.

Pushing down on the right pedal, my rudder turned sharply, and I urged my ski towards shore, but it was too late. A large surge of water lifted the nose of my ski as a solid five-foot wave formed to my left just ten metres away. As the wave sucked up all the water from the shallow reef, I was overcome with a feeling of dread as I realised it was going to break.

Two seconds before the wave hit me, I threw my paddle to the side and put my arms over my head to curl myself up into a ball, aware of the potential damage from a scrape with the sharp coral below. The wave picked me up and threw me from my ski and I began tumbling over and over, all the time praying that if I was going to collide with the reef it would be with my body rather than my face. But the impact never came, and when I eventually popped up in deep water, I was relieved to have escaped unscathed.

The battle was far from over. Desperately scanning 360 degrees around me, I spotted my paddle floating 30 metres further out to sea and my ski another 50 metres towards shore. Making a split-second decision, I took off swimming after my ski. The ski was my lifeline that would keep me afloat; the paddle could wait. As I stroked hard through the water, I passed objects that had been lost in the commotion. Lollies, biscuits, sunglasses, hat, headphones, everything had been thrown from my ski, but there was no time to scoop them up. My priority was to get to my ski as fast as possible. A hundred dollars of gear was gone with one wave and a lapse in concentration.

With ten metres left to swim, my mind flicked to a scene in the horror film *Jaws* where a young woman swims across the water and is dragged underneath the surface by a monster that is later revealed to be a great white shark. Peering into the water below, I could see darker patches of reef clearly contrasted against light blue, which created shapes that my mind imagined as monsters. Pulling my head up above the water, I swam like a water polo player, unwilling to peer below the surface. Grabbing hold of my ski, I had flashbacks to the Quobba cliffs, except this time Ben wasn't coming. If I was going to get out of this alive, it was up to me.

Since beginning learn-to-swim classes at the age of five and over my years as a professional athlete, I had swum hundreds of kilometres using a kickboard. I would now lean on that experience as I held the ski in front of me and kicked as hard as I could, churning up the water behind me. Throwing every ounce of anger, pain and regret I'd ever known into the action, I kicked as though my life depended on it because my life truly did depend on it. With the knowledge that I was entirely on my own, I was lifted to a new level of athleticism. A power coursed through my body, a channel previously untapped. Perhaps it is only in the face of danger, or death, that we find out what we're capable of. Perhaps it is only when every single safety net is taken away and we are entirely responsible for our own fate that we find a whole new realm of possibility.

Kicking my way towards my paddle, I prayed the new set of waves rolling through didn't reach me. Thankfully, the power of the first wave had pushed me and the paddle a long way into shore; with one big punch, I had been blasted into safer waters. Finally, I reached my paddle and grabbed hold of it. I remounted the ski and, pressing the right pedal down, navigated my way 100 metres further in. Having lost my hair tie, my knotted hair lay over my face as I sat in the calm water thinking through what had happened. My mind immediately thought of the boys, waiting for me at the other end. What if I had never turned up? With 30 kilometres until civilisation, chances are no one would ever know what had happened.

My desperate thirst returned, but when I reached for my water bladder I realised it too had been lost, meaning I was facing 30 kilometres of paddling in the searing sun with no hydration.

I was going to have to put the perfectionist elite athlete within me aside and accept that I would have to perform while extremely dehydrated and with no food to fuel my body. There was no other way.

By the time I passed the lighthouse, I was delirious. The past three hours of paddling had been horrific, and with no food, water, hat, sunscreen or sunglasses, I was not only sunburnt but shaking from low blood sugar levels. Ben was the first to see me, having run several kilometres down the beach from where the car was parked, and I was grateful for his company as he kept pace with me, his feet sinking into the wet sand.

I stumbled up onto shore, barely able to speak as the boys grabbed my paddle and ski. They noted the missing items but I couldn't explain what had happened. I made it to the car where Matt handed me a Powerade and a packet of biscuits, and I sat in silence on the way to the campsite. I wasn't able to fully recount the story of what had happened until later that afternoon.

Now realising that being alone on the water was unrealistic, I was happy to have company on the jet ski for the next week as we hopped between white sandy beaches, stopping to see turtles, dugongs and rays. All the while, we made sure to stay well inside the dangerous waters of the outer reef.

After ten days of jet-ski support, we made it to Exmouth. It was here we had to face up to one of our biggest hurdles. Our original plan of using the catamaran as our support vessel for the entirety of the circumnavigation had changed so we needed a new boat. Broome was now just 1000 kilometres ahead, and jet-ski support would not suffice in crocodile-infested waters. In addition, there was a 100-kilometre gulf to cross from Exmouth to Onslow, a distance the jet ski was not capable of covering due to fuel constraints. We needed to find another option.

Little did we know, a chance encounter we'd had in the tiny town of Seabird three weeks earlier would change the trajectory of our expedition, bringing an increased sense of adventure and excitement. The master will appear when the student is ready, so the saying goes, and for the next two weeks we would be treated to a masterclass in Indigenous culture and boating in the wild west.

Enter the gold diggers.

I was competitive even as an eight-year-old, diving for the beach flags as a Sawtell nipper.

My sister Courtney and I were stoked to be young ironwomen. She was 19 years old and I was 18, and we were racing against the best in the world.

Game day. I set off from Mermaid Beach, Queensland, on 19 December 2021. Ocean swimmers and paddlers kept me company for a few kilometres and then it was just me, my support crew and the big blue. (Blake Bradford)

White sandy beaches turned into cliff faces as I reached Jervis Bay, on the south coast of New South Wales. 2 January 2022. (Blake Bradford)

In Victoria, the temperature was 12 degrees and I wore three layers of clothing to stay alive. I was falling out of my ski into the ocean about three times a day. (Blake Bradford)

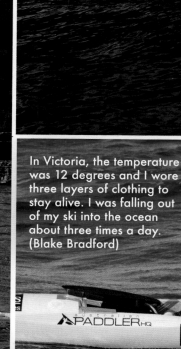

I covered 240 kilometres in two days from Eden, New South Wales, to Lakes Entrance, Victoria — and paddled alongside a storm in the middle of the ocean. 7 January 2022. (@sheabell.images)

Approaching the Twelve Apostles, Victoria. Unlike most people, I got to see these 'statues of the sea' from the water. 16 January 2022. (Jaime Sallows)

Deep at the bottom of Australia, off the South Australian coast in great white shark territory, I was forced to paddle through the night to get to safety. 20 January 2022. (Blake Bradford)

In order to break the world record, I decided to cut straight across the Great Australian Bight rather than hug the coastline, which meant I'd be 500 kilometres out to sea. I used the wild winds to my advantage on day three of the 12-day crossing. 3 February 2022. (Blake Bradford)

Albatrosses kept me company on the Bight crossing. They can stay at sea for months at a time. South Australia, February 2022. (Jaime Sallows)

I made it! After 12 days at sea, I was on dry land at Daw Island, Western Australia, where we were treated to spectacular views. (Blake Bradford)

Steep Point is the most western point of the Australian mainland and marks the northern end of the intimidating Zuytdorp Cliffs. I was suffering from intense seasickness as I navigated this 200-kilometre stretch of Western Australian coastline. 24 March 2022. (Blake Bradford)

It's little wonder tourists flock to the paradise of Western Australia's Ningaloo Reef. After spending a day paddling alone, I was glad to be accompanied by Jaime Sallows and Ben on the jet ski. 6 April 2022. (Blake Bradford)

Out in the ocean, at the base of the cliffs below Quobba Station, a split-second decision almost cost me my life. Ben Lavery was my guardian angel that day. Here we are, safely back on dry land, hooking up the jet ski to the support car. 30 March 2022. (Jaime Sallows)

The Kimberley region of Western Australia is picture-postcard perfect. May 2022. (Ben Lavery)

Compression therapy helped to remove lactic acid from my body and reduce soreness after a day of tackling fierce headwinds in the Kimberley. 10 May 2022. (Ben Lavery)

A bucket-list experience! Visiting the King George Falls in the Kimberley was a beautiful reprieve from paddling in crocodile-infested waters. 15 May 2022. (Ben Lavery)

The Hamill family, aka the Cruising Kiwis, safely shepherded me across the top of Australia and we were overjoyed to arrive in Darwin on 19 May 2022. (L–R): Rob, Rachel, me, Ivan and Declan. (Blake Bradford)

It was a challenge to find a support boat to take us across the Gulf of Carpentaria, and once out there we battled relentless swells, gusting headwinds and seasickness. My ski didn't have a back rest, which made it very uncomfortable; in this photo, you can see the back brace that my husband, Matt, bought for me to wear. His knowledge of sports science was invaluable. June 2022. (Jaime Sallows)

Jaime played a key role in capturing the journey. Gove, Northern Territory. 14 June 2022. (Blake Bradford)

Jaime had to pull me out of the water in the middle of the Gulf of Carpentaria. Later that day, our skipper, Josh, made the decision to bail on the crossing and we motored to the safety of Weipa. 20 June 2022. (Blake Bradford)

I set a new personal best for distance paddled in 24 hours (172 kilometres into headwinds) during my second leg of crossing the Gulf of Carpentaria. 30 June 2022. (Blake Bradford)

Windburnt and sunburnt after completing a huge week of paddling along Queensland's far north coast. 5 July 2022. (Blake Bradford)

Heading back down the east coast of Queensland, I was treated to a front-row view of the many beautiful islands, such as the Percy Group near Mackay. (Blake Bradford)

Mike Janes, my coach at Mermaid Beach Surf Club, joined the crew in Queensland and helped me take on the women's world record for longest distance paddled in a 24-hour period. Airlie Beach, Queensland, 12 September 2022. (Blake Bradford)

Blake Bradford (left) and Mike were on Bonnie Watch as I set the new world record, covering 235 kilometres in 24 hours, from Airlie Beach to Townsville. (Jaime Sallows)

I'd done it! Just over eight months after setting off, I crossed the tape at Mermaid Beach on the Gold Coast as the new world record holder, beating the previous mark by over two months. 28 August 2022. (Karlee Nurthen)

Top right: The Gold Diggers – Goatee and Ryan – were our support boat crew up the Western Australian coastline, and they came to Queensland to surprise me at the finish. 28 August 2022. (Karlee Nurthen)

Below: Together again. Matt and I back on Gold Coast sand. 28 August 2022. (Karlee Nurthen)

Bottom: It was an honour to raise $100,000 for mental health charity Gotcha4Life. Here I am with CEO Gus Worland. September 2022. (Gotcha4Life)

Wearing a crown of native Australian flowers, I was thrilled to be the youngest and fastest-ever paddler – and first Australian woman in recorded history – to circumnavigate Australia. (Karlee Nurthen)

In my 12,700-kilometre journey around Australia, I encountered the cruelty and majesty of Mother Nature.

Taming an angry ocean off Eden, New South Wales. 7 January 2022. (@sheabell.images)

Gliding in a glassy sunset off Port Hedland, Western Australia. 17 April 2022. (Jaime Sallows)

CHAPTER 10

THE GOLD DIGGERS

SEABIRD IS A COASTAL TOWN JUST NORTH OF PERTH, WITH A minuscule population of 107, meaning the chance we would find our next crew in such a place was next to none. Regardless of the odds, it was at Seabird that we met the man who would guide us through 1000 kilometres of king tides and the huge currents of Western Australia's rugged Pilbara region.

One week before the Quobba cliffs, I was finishing a 45-kilometre day that had started just north of Perth. I was paddling with Jaime and Ben alongside me on the jet ski. The colour of the water made it feel like we were in *Pirates of the Caribbean*, bright turquoise blending with aqua, and the paddling was far from a chore. Landing on the beach, I watched the boys hook the jet ski up to the Ranger, but the powdery white sand wasn't ideal for towing such a heavy load, and the car soon became bogged. The wheels spun without forward progress. After a few heated exchanges among themselves, the boys managed to release the car and jet ski from the clutches of Seabird Beach.

By the time we made our way up the boat ramp, we were ready for a cool drink at our campsite out of the relentless sun. We were packing up our gear, when we spotted a figure climbing out of his car and wandering over.

'G'day, how youse going?' he inquired. He was in his late forties and a wide toothy grin was visible beneath an enormous beard and moustache. The other distinctive thing about him was his t-shirt: black with white lettering, the shirt read: 'It's f*** this shit o'clock'. The man's name was Goatee, and Goatee was an Aussie legend.

We introduced ourselves and Goatee asked what we were doing in Seabird. He'd noticed the branding on our Ranger and jet ski and concluded we weren't just any regular out-of-towners on holiday. As we told him of the expedition, Goatee's smile grew wider, his excitement barely contained as he jumped from left foot to right.

'Yeah, man, that's siiiiiiiiick,' was his highly animated reply. 'You guys are next level crazy, hey. That's epic, man.'

Blake grabbed the camera from the Ranger and quickly set up an interview with Goatee. It was a masterpiece. Blake's north Queensland accent combined with Goatee's Western Australian drawl provides a perfect example of the Aussie slang that people from overseas love. We soon discovered Goatee was a gold prospector and worked up north near Broome. The Pilbara is a dry, thinly populated region in the north of Western Australia, known for its rich Indigenous history, and it happened to be where Goatee had lived his whole life. He knew the area like the back of his hand.

We snapped a few photos and promised to give him a call to catch up if we had time, then after a quick goodbye, he skipped off down the boat ramp. What I didn't know at the time was that Goatee had been battling with poor mental health since separating from his partner a few months earlier and had come to the beach after a particularly low morning. That day he had hopped into his car after finishing work, reached an intersection that would take him right to Seabird or left to the river-based town of Guilderton and chosen the former. It was this decision to turn right that would bring him into our lives. During our brief encounter, Goatee mentioned that he had a fishing boat and joked that he'd love to come along for a day of paddling. One month later this jest became reality as I set out from Exmouth with Goatee and his friend Ryan in their fishing boat, *Good Times.*

It wasn't before some exhaustive searches elsewhere, however. The crew and I had made nearly a hundred unsuccessful phone calls to contacts in the sailing world trying to find a boat to accompany me for the rest of the journey.

Then Matt had a lightbulb moment. 'Why don't we give Goatee a call?'

Within the first 30 seconds of the phone call, Goatee was in. Exmouth to Broome was the assignment, and he and Ryan would step up and deliver so far above and beyond, I would be left with a permanent memory of what selflessness and strong work ethic looked like in the purest form. Thrown together in bizarre circumstances, all of us were aware that our paths would never have crossed otherwise. We formed a bond that would see us through uncharted waters and past deserted islands, big sharks and dangerous whirlpools. As I had done with the crew who had been there from the start, I would several times put my life in the hands of these two men.

The town of Exmouth marked the end of the Ningaloo Reef and the start of our second encounter with Goatee, a meeting that was no less eventful than the first. Our crew had taken up residence in the front yard of the Exmouth Yacht Club, and as Goatee and Ryan drove into the car park, their six-metre aluminium-plate fishing boat, *Good Times*, attached, the heavy burden our crew carried – financially, physically and mentally – seemed to dissipate.

Goatee was wearing his Akubra hat, which would be permanently affixed to his head for the next two weeks. He introduced us to Ryan, a softly spoken man of much wisdom, whose passion for the land and Indigenous culture ran deep. Without realising it, we had linked up with television royalty, as the two men, we discovered, were stars of the Discovery Channel show *Aussie Gold Hunters*. The show was broadcast to millions around the world, and over the coming weeks, the men would regularly be stopped in the street by strangers asking for photos. Their easy-going nature and larrikin humour made them crowd favourites.

Goatee and Ryan were also tough. Several prospectors have gone missing or been murdered over the years while fossicking, and the men told us of how they would arm themselves while on a job, working as a team to protect each other. From our first meeting, I could sense their unbreakable bond, which had been formed in childhood and strengthened in the 40 years since.

Ryan was the yin to Goatee's yang, and he brought a calm energy that balanced Goatee's enthusiasm and excitable nature. Together they were the ultimate team. They were also sticklers for safety. Gold prospecting is not for the faint-hearted, and when working in remote locations in the outback, preparation is crucial. Equipment such as satellite phones and personal locator beacons, and adequate water and supplies is essential. If any element of safety is missed or overlooked, the consequences can be fatal. I would double-check my lifejacket, head torch, LED lights and whistle before I hopped in for a stint of night paddling, and I will forever be grateful for their dedication to my safety as I took on one of the most remote parts of coastline in the country.

Though Goatee and Ryan loved a laugh and a cold beer at the end of a big day, when it came time to work their effort was unmatched. While grinding out 14 hours of paddling, I would look up to see Goatee in the driver's seat of his six-metre vessel, sweat dripping from his forehead, his vision remaining locked firmly on the speedometer as he strained to keep an even pace for me.

Meanwhile, Ryan would prepare healthy wraps for lunch and rinse my paddling gear with fresh water to protect me from chafe the next time I wore it. On the first night of our meeting at Exmouth, my crew was heading out to dinner and I apologised to Goatee and Ryan as I wouldn't be coming. The next day would be a 100-kilometre paddle and I prioritised stretching over a trip to the pub.

'We aren't going either,' Ryan was quick to reply. 'We're going to make sure the boat is ready to go.'

If there was ever a doubt, I knew in that moment we had the right men for the job.

On 9 April, day 112 of the expedition, I paddled 105 kilometres with Goatee, Ryan and Blake in the fishing boat beside me. Starting the day early, by lunchtime the wind had picked up to 20 knots and I surfed the small wind swells back and forth, keeping Ryan's Hawaiian shirt and Goatee's Akubra in my peripheral vison.

Climbing aboard for lunch was tricker than getting onto the jet ski but after a few attempts, we had it nailed. While I paddled alongside the boat, the boys would fasten my ski with a rope, trailing it behind as I climbed up the back steps and aboard. With an Esky stocked full of protein shakes, Powerade and my favourite jelly snakes, thanks to Ryan, my blood sugars were never at risk of running low. Finally able to hold down food without the risk of vomiting, I powered through the kilometres in the glassy conditions.

One of the biggest challenges of the Pilbara was the heat. With the ambient temperature around 40 degrees, we had also been warned by locals of the warm water temperature, which commonly reached 32 degrees. I soon found there was no relief from the heat while paddling; splashing my face wasn't refreshing and would do nothing more than provide a coating of salt on my skin, therefore Ryan used the hose to cool me down. As I pulled up alongside *Good Times*, Ryan would spray me with the hose, the sprinkler-like pressure taking me back to a childhood of sliding belly-first on plastic tarps in the backyard while Dad hosed it down to keep it slippery. Only allowing myself to dive back into past memories for a moment, I would soon return to the tunnel-visioned athlete mentality I now slipped into easily.

Blake had been highly energetic all day. His positivity was always welcome, and his support had gotten me across the Bight and was now a crucial part of my success. But in the last five kilometres of our very first day with *Good Times*, we had a clash. As I paddled up behind the boat, we shared some banter and personal jokes, which were by now a standard part of our interaction.

But then Blake replied to a question I had asked by saying, 'What's that, shagger?'

I saw red.

'What did you call me?' I quickly shot back but was met with a blank stare, the loud engine of the boat interfering with clear communication. Perhaps 100 kilometres of paddling in the scorching sun had gotten the best of me. Either way, spending all day, every day with Blake had allowed any filters to be completely removed.

'If you ever call me that again, you're off the boat,' I snapped.

Blake's startled look informed me that no malice had been meant in the comment. The word was simply a part of the slang he had used his whole life. Irritable after paddling all day in the sun, I'd reacted more aggressively than intended and immediately regretted it.

Outside the boat ramp of Onslow, I was hauled aboard, and Ryan was quick to begin rinsing my paddling gear in fresh water in preparation for the following day. As we motored in to meet the rest of the crew waiting on the ramp, I watched as a golden sun dipped below the horizon. Turning to see Blake capturing the moment on camera, I wondered what he was thinking. Almost four months away from home and any sort of routine, he'd now been snapped at by the person he spent all day, every day supporting. Did he, like me, ever want to throw it all in? Though he'd never said otherwise, I could only take him at his word when he insisted he'd never leave the project. I hoped he meant it. We'd found a new support vessel and navigated our way through remote areas of coastline, but the one thing that remained the same was my core support crew. Having come so far together, I couldn't imagine finishing the expedition without each of them beside me.

The following day, we smashed out 101 kilometres in strong tailwinds. Racing alongside *Good Times*, I was cruising at a decent 11.6 kilometres an hour when I glanced over to see the boat get knocked sideways by a large swell. It looked as though she might tip. Goatee's squeal was audible above the wind and the waves, but to our shared relief, the boat quickly bounced upright and the crew was able to let go of the side railings they'd grabbed onto. Thinking back to the Bight, I remembered the power of the ocean over a ten-tonne catamaran and felt grateful for the calmer conditions of the west. If the swells grew any bigger, the fishing boat wouldn't be able to handle it. Matt was making phone calls left, right and centre to line up a new catamaran from Broome, and I prayed Mother Nature would play the game until then.

Cruising 20–30 kilometres offshore, we decided that instead of coming back to the mainland, we would set up our swags on one of the many islands dotted along this stretch of remote coastline. Reaching our destination island at sunset, Blake unfolded the swags while I ran up to pee behind the dunes. A lifetime of changing with a towel on pool decks and in surf club car parks had removed any prima donna within me, so the prospect of camping without access to a toilet or shower left me unfazed, as did living off dehydrated meals for the next two weeks. With limited access to fresh fruit and vegetables, we found use for the dozens of powdered meals we'd kept stored in our Ranger since the start of the trip. A single meal could contain a massive 1000 calories, more than what some people consume in a day, and the options included everything from butter chicken and lamb rogan josh to apple crumble and crème brulee for dessert. One cup of boiling water would transform a bag of powdered nutrition into a palatable meal, which would sustain me for the long days of paddling.

After three days with Blake onboard, it was time to head into the mainland to pick up Ben for his turn on *Good Times.* It also provided the opportunity to take a well-earned day off after I'd completed over 300 kilometres of paddling over three days. Accommodation at the nearby Karratha International Hotel was kindly provided by local marine pilot Steve, who also paddled ocean skis in his spare time. Steve had been following my journey online and reached out over Facebook, offering to put us all up at the hotel. It was a welcome relief from the soaring Western Australian temperatures.

The day off was also an opportunity for Goatee and Ryan to teach us about the oldest surviving culture in the world. Having grown up in the Pilbara region, both men had spent their childhoods surrounded by Indigenous families and elders, absorbing teachings and stories that had been passed down over tens of thousands of years. Ryan's family had long provided guided tours of the region to tourists, in particular of the sacred rock art, or petroglyph engravings, at Murujuga National Park (on the Burrup Peninsula). Murujuga National Park is 35 kilometres from Karratha, so it was the perfect opportunity to visit a site that is thought to have the highest concentration of rock engravings anywhere in the world. Some experts believe the petroglyphs, with an estimated 500,000 to one million engravings, date back 40,000 years.

I took the opportunity to remain in the cool hotel room and ice my aching finger joints, knowing I had a two-week stint of 100 kilometre-odd days ahead of me, while the crew accompanied Ryan and Goatee to the petroglyphs. They returned that afternoon much more informed about Indigenous culture, thanks to Ryan, and with an understanding of the deep meaning of rock art to Indigenous people, with the carvings providing a link to stories, customs and knowledge of the land and resources. The carvings show human figures and hunting methods, marine life and extinct creatures, and provide a first-hand insight into ancient times. Though I was unable to attend, I was pleased the crew had such a unique experience.

The next day, it was time to get back to business. Since beginning the expedition, Ben had spent most of the time on land and only a handful of days on the jet ski, and I was looking forward to his company. Climbing aboard the boat with Ben, I readied myself for a big day of paddling ahead. Goatee hopped into the driver's seat and, with Ryan next to him, turned the key in the ignition. Immediately he knew something was wrong. The sound of the engine was off. Jumping out to assess the problem, Goatee concluded that we needed an oil change. The men had worked overtime leading into the trip to get the boat into a seaworthy condition, but motoring 300 kilometres in three days had taken its toll. Not wanting to sacrifice a day's paddling, we decided we'd use the jet ski to escort me to our destination in Point Samson.

The rest of the crew drove off to find a fuel station, leaving Ben and me in the shade at the boat ramp. I kept myself in the relaxed state needed for ultra-endurance performance. Since the beginning of the expedition, I'd practised compartmentalising my emotions, trying to bring a sense of professionalism and calm to my paddling. Adaptability had gotten me this far, and

I used the same strategy to deal with the last-minute change in support vessel. Sure enough, within 30 minutes, the jet ski was in the water with me paddling alongside as though it was always the plan.

As I rounded the port of Dampier, I was joined by Steve and fellow marine pilot Gilly for the last ten kilometres of the day, and their company was appreciated by the entire crew. Extended interactions with new people were few and far between in the remote west, so we soaked up every opportunity we got. No one appreciated their presence more than me. Not long after they began paddling beside me, I made my way past some enormous iron ore carriers, and a huge tiger shark darted in front of my ski. The flash of the shark's grey body was unmistakable against the ocean's deep blue. Gilly had seen it too, but his nonchalant reaction was quickly explained. 'Happens all the time around these parts,' he said with a smile, observing the shock on my face.

Common occurrence or not, a shark sighting was enough to make the hairs on the back of my neck stand up. I maneouvred my ski to position myself in between Steve and Gilly for the rest of the afternoon's paddle and I wondered how many sharks I'd shared the water with in the past few months. A glimpse of a tail, the tip of a fin or a hint of dark grey was all you were likely to view of the elusive creatures, as most of the time they stayed well below the surface, viewing their prey from underneath.

*

The following day, *Good Times* was back in action. We headed towards Point Samson, careful to pick our way through the iron-ore carriers because these huge vessels create big swells as they motor towards the port to be loaded. With the ocean flattening out, I was now hosed down regularly to keep my body temperature cooler. The heat was seemingly approaching from all angles, so Ben and I took to playing charades to keep me focused. I was still falling out of my ski every now and then, but mostly only towards the end of big days when I lost concentration. Now just a few hundred kilometres from Broome, it was a habit I needed to break. The patience of a crocodile is terrifying, their ability to stalk well documented, and staying atop my ski would be my best chance of survival.

Jaime came aboard for his turn on the boat on 17 April, for an Easter Sunday that ended up being one of the most memorable days of the expedition. Ryan had spoken about the 'staircase to the moon', a natural phenomenon that occurs when the full moon rises over the exposed tidal flats of the Pilbara coastline. An optical illusion is created when the silvery glow of the moon on the water looks like a set of stairs leading to the sky above. Though we were passing through at the right time of year, the chances of us witnessing the spectacle depended on the weather, sunset and tides, all of which affected visibility. Not holding out hope, I had all but forgotten about the natural wonder when I began the paddling day from Port Hedland towards Cape Keraudren.

Always aiming to take the shortest route wherever possible, we knew hundreds, even thousands, of kilometres could be saved by paddling further out to sea as opposed to hugging the coast. With only the fishing boat for support, paddling extremely far out to sea wasn't an option, and hugging the coastline meant we could camp. But this method came with a risk because the huge tides of the Pilbara meant running aground was a very real threat. The tides also affected the ease and speed of paddling; when the tides were at their strongest and running against me, my speed would drop to a snail-like two kilometres an hour. On the contrary, with tidal assistance, I could reach 18 kilometres an hour with less effort. The tides were at different times a foe or friend, and significantly influenced our planning.

Throughout the day, we stayed 100 metres from shore, making our way from point to point as we tracked up the coast. The landscape changed and white sandy beaches gave way to red soil. The contrast of dark soil against the blue ocean was one of the most beautiful things I'd ever seen, and I couldn't believe I'd never heard of the beaches we were passing. It was as though I had been given access to a new world and I made a promise to myself that when I returned home, I would get out and explore whenever I could.

Halfway through the day, the tide started to turn, and I sensed an emotion in Goatee and Ryan that was previously unseen: concern. The depth of the water was now only 1.3 metres and the motor of the boat was unable to function in less than 0.3 metres; if we kept going, we'd risk being left high and dry. Paddling hard, I aimed to cover the final 15 kilometres before we ran aground.

A few kilometres later, Goatee lifted up the huge 90-horsepower motor to give us a better chance at making it through the shallow water without scraping the bottom. The depth was now 0.5 metres and the waters seemed like they'd get the better of us, but we pushed on. Paddling ahead of the boat, I looked around for the deeper channels, manoeuvring my ski into the darker patches, squeezing out as many metres as possible. If we could just get to the cape up ahead, we'd be okay.

Crunch.

My paddle scooped up sand as I took a stroke on my left side. *Not good.* If I was touching the bottom, how was the boat still moving forward?

Turns out, it wasn't. Shallow waters had claimed *Good Times* several hundred metres behind me. I stopped my watch to ensure the kilometres I'd completed were recorded and paddled back to the boat to find the engine spluttering, caused by the silt that had been sucked up off the bottom.

'You bloody bastard,' Goatee cursed as he climbed down off the boat and stood in the ankle-deep water to check out the damage. 'This might take a while.'

A handy mechanic, Goatee began the process of cleaning the motor so we could get moving once more, at the same time informing us that we weren't going anywhere until the tide turned. Knowing we'd be stuck for a few hours minimum, I changed out of my wet paddling gear and into dry clothes.

Within 30 minutes, Goatee had cleaned the silt from the motor and the boat was ready for action but by now we were well and truly beached. There was no trace of the water that had floated us just one hour prior. We weren't going anywhere for a while. Jaime retrieved the suction cups from my bag as I rolled out a towel in preparation for a massage. For the next two hours, he pushed and prodded the knots in my muscles while Goatee and Ryan enjoyed a beer on the front of the boat. As the sun set, it created an orange glow on the horizon to our left, amid shades of colour impossible to replicate in a painting and hardly done justice in a photograph. For this reason, only a few photos were taken that afternoon, all of us realising the power of the moment lay in the present and taking in the scene while it lasted.

And then it happened.

As the sky turned black, the stars came out, but the moon was the real showstopper. Rising over the horizon to our right, the moon gradually grew to a giant silvery ball, which cast a glow over the ocean surrounding us. But that was just the opening scene. A few minutes later, I found out why people flocked from all over the world to the main show – *the staircase to the moon*.

With Goatee and Ryan yahooing at the front of the boat, Jaime and I sat speechless as we took in the shimmery illusion of a staircase climbing up a silky black sky to a round glowing moon. In that moment, I felt like I was exactly where I was meant to be. On Easter Sunday, a day of celebration, I'd been taken to church by two gold diggers in the mud flats of the Pilbara.

When the tide came in and the water rose to one metre in depth, we motored towards the nearest island to set up camp. Arriving in the dark but guided by the light of the moon, Jaime and I carried the swags up the beach, searching for a clear spot of sand not overrun by termites or rocks. When we arrived, the water was running a long way up the beach due to the high tide but by the time we left the next morning, it had rushed back out, leaving 300 metres of dry sand. Still struggling to comprehend the effect of tidal movement in the Pilbara, I was incredibly grateful to have Goatee and Ryan guiding us through the remote waters. And when Ryan handed us warm pancakes for breakfast, my gratitude went to a whole new level.

Matt came aboard for the final three days with *Good Times*, as we made our way towards Broome. It was the first time we'd spent a day together on the water since Adelaide and to mark the occasion I racked up 88 kilometres of paddling, starting around lunchtime to work with the afternoon winds. A distinct wind pattern could be discerned in the northwest, with smooth morning conditions giving way to favourable ocean chop in the afternoon. An added benefit to starting later was missing some of the extremely humid conditions experienced mid-morning. Grinding out a few hours under a burning sun, I knew a slightly cooler change was coming, and by the time the sun set around 6.30pm each day, the couple of hours I had left was far easier in the more civil conditions.

Hanging a speaker off the back of the boat, we blasted hits from the 90s and 2000s that we'd all sing along to. Listening to music with the crew helped me fight the feeling of isolation, which was always knocking at the door, begging to be let back in. I knew I needed to overpower the darkness with light, and music was one way to keep my mood high. We decided the songs; we chose the tempo of the beat. Though we couldn't control the tides, sun, wind or risk of sharks, I saw the music as a way of taking back control. We would have to suffer to succeed, but we controlled the backdrop to our suffering.

My birthday is 23 April, and I requested a well-earned day off. Based at Port Campbell for the day, all I wanted to do to celebrate turning 32 was to watch movies in a room on my own. Time alone allowed me to reflect and regroup after the hundreds of kilometres of pain I forced my body through each day, and I craved it. Not leaving the room once on my birthday, I didn't even head out to get food. When the crew fired up the barbecue for dinner, frying up fish they'd caught that day, I asked Matt to bring me some leftovers in a napkin. Using movies as a form of escape, I connected to wifi for the first time in weeks. As I ate the leftover fish, I binged on Netflix as a way to distract myself from the fact that in a few days, I would be sharing the water with crocodiles.

Sure enough, as we approached Broome two days later, I had my first crocodile encounter. Peering five kilometres into the distance, I could see the red sand of Cable Beach, the location famous for its sunset camel rides. Since entering Western Australia five weeks earlier, I'd been teeing the crew up for a group camel ride and was excited to see the plan through. I was also keen to go sky diving. A fear of heights had prevented me from making a booking in the years leading into the expedition, but in the presence of my crew I felt invincible. Blake and Jaime were keen on sky diving, but Matt and Ben baulked at the idea. The divide was an easy way of distinguishing the cautious members of our group and those with a more spontaneous nature. I wondered if the excessive time spent battling huge seas had made Jaime, Blake and me more prone to risk taking. Perhaps the time spent outside our comfort zone in the ocean had made us more fearless in other areas of our lives.

While paddling towards Broome, my mind on camel rides and sky diving, I saw Matt motion me into the boat. The gesture reminded me of Jaime beckoning me into the catamaran near Carnarvon, and I suddenly felt nervous. Ryan and Matt were speaking in low tones, their gaze cast over my left shoulder, and I immediately knew it was a crocodile. Paddling up towards the boat, I focused straight ahead. If I was in fact being chased by a croc, the last thing I wanted to do was fall off while I was in its sights, so I squeezed my core and concentrated carefully on my balance. Fortunately, as I was later informed, the crocodile got within 50 metres of my ski and then swam off in the other direction, hence the crew's decision not to get me back onboard.

Throughout the final five kilometres of paddling into Broome, I was paranoid. Glancing left and right, I started jumping at sticks floating in the water and at shadows cast by the clouds. When it was finally time to come aboard, I was terrified. With no option of a dry exit, I firstly had to plunge into the water and then climb up the ladder. As I entered the warm, brown water, my heart was in my mouth, and I quickly scrambled up the three steps of the ladder before lying on the back step. Looking up at Matt, his slight nod was all it took to confirm my fear; he'd spotted one. Sharks were no longer the biggest threat to my safety. From now on, we were in crocodile country.

The following day, my idea of a group camel ride on the famous Cable Beach came to life. From atop the camel's hump, the full length of Cable Beach was in clear view, and as I looked out at the expanse of water that stretched ahead, I wondered what was around the corner. Turning back to see Goatee and Ryan laughing atop their individual camels, I was thankful to enjoy time out as a team. We'd survived 1000 kilometres of crazy tides, deserted islands and 40-degree heat, and it was nice to celebrate together. A group of tourists recognised Goatee and Ryan and hurried up for an autograph. For the past two weeks they'd been my heroes of the Pilbara, and it was evident others saw them as heroes too.

Our stint in Broome was an extended one, broken up by a quick trip back to the Gold Coast for a wedding. My sister Georgia's wedding to Chris had been planned a year earlier, and I refused to miss it, so while our crew made Broome their home for the week, Matt and I jetted back to the east coast. Thankfully, the borders were now open across Australia. Back on the Gold Coast, I made a quick visit to the shops the day before the wedding to pick up some jewellery and I hid behind dark glasses to avoid any awkward encounters with people I knew. Other than family, nobody else knew I was making the brief trip home, and I intended to keep it that way.

At the reception the next day, my feet barely survived two hours in heels; the soles had softened from constant exposure to salt water. But it was all worth it. As I walked my little nephew Mason down the aisle and my sisters held the hands of Georgia's other sons, I turned back to see a beautiful, glowing bride who looked perfectly fulfilled. Matt and I spent the reception fielding questions about the trip. As we boarded the plane the following day to head back to Broome, the whirlwind weekend was already a distant memory and we set our sights on the push towards Darwin.

Back in Broome, we had to say goodbye to our golden Aussie heroes. Their work done, Goatee and Ryan were heading back to Karratha where they lived and worked. As we embraced, few words were spoken, but I was left with a strong feeling that our paths would cross again.

'It's time for us to pass you on to your next mob,' Ryan muttered softly. And indeed, we had found a new mob. Matt's phone calls had led to success and, as it turned out, we had the perfect team to take us through the crocodile-infested waters of the Kimberley.

Our new boat crew weren't gold prospectors, nor were they locals. But they knew the ocean like the back of their hands after a lifetime of living on it.

They were the Cruising Kiwis.

CHAPTER 11

KIWIS IN CROCODILE COUNTRY

CASTING THE NET FAR AND WIDE, WE WERE DETERMINED TO find a vessel to escort us home. We were roughly two thirds of the way through the journey by the time we got to Broome, and we'd come too far to call it quits. Traces of a golf-elbow injury had been bothering me on and off since the Bight, but other than slight discomfort, it wasn't enough to stop me. I decided I would paddle to the line with one arm if I had to; quitting was no longer an option.

We had taken to celebrating every 1000 kilometres, and Red Bull shots had given way to champagne showers and homemade cakes. When we'd reached 6000 kilometres, I'd turned my head towards the boat to find the crew dancing, their bellies decorated with '6000 km' scrawled in permanent marker. I'd overheard an earlier discussion about whether we should let our safety flares off to mark the occasion, so I was glad they had settled for something legal.

While I was ticking off milestones, Matt was busy screening options for our next support boat. We released a video on social media asking for help, and while we found that there were dozens of experienced skippers and crew ready and willing, the majority didn't own their own boat. Catamarans and yachts don't come cheap, and many sailors settle for crewing on someone else's boat until they can afford their own.

After a week of stress and hundreds of unsuccessful phone calls, we managed to strike gold. Rob and Rachel Hamill were a couple from New Zealand who had lived aboard their 44-foot catamaran for ten years. The pair had three sons, the eldest of whom, Finn, was overseas chasing his goal of competing at the Olympics in rowing, like his father had done decades before. The younger two, Ivan and Declan, who were 16 and 18 respectively, had lived at sea most of their lives. Ivan had never been to a mainstream school and was remarkably switched on and witty. Declan also possessed the Hamill sense of humour and had a laid-back nature that immediately put everyone at ease.

A quick search of the name 'Rob Hamill' on the internet will prove he isn't your run-of-the-mill recreational sailor. Rob is a world-class athlete, having competed in rowing on the world stage for an extended period of time. But though he'd achieved the extraordinary, Rob is also incredibly down to earth, and in his 59 years he had seen more suffering and loss than many would experience in a lifetime. As a true testament to Rob's resilience, he'd come out the other side of tragedy as someone who positively influences everyone he encounters.

Rob's first love was still-water rowing. In 1994, he won a silver medal at the world championships, and a few years later lined up to represent New Zealand at the Atlanta Summer Olympics. What Rob is most well known for, however, is open-ocean rowing and, in 1997, searching for a new challenge after the Olympics, he took part in the inaugural 3000-mile Atlantic Rowing Race with teammate Phil Stubbs. After 41 days at sea, facing seasickness, blisters, big winds and swells, the two Kiwis crossed the line as winners, a true story of the underdog standing tall against the odds and well-established crews with significantly more money and experience.

The following year, Stubbs died in a plane crash. He was 36 years old.

And this wasn't the first tragedy in Rob's life. In 1978, when Rob was just 14, his elder brother Kerry was sailing on his yacht from Singapore to Bangkok. After drifting off course into Cambodian waters, he was captured, tortured, interrogated and killed by the Khmer Rouge. He was just 28.

Rob had a second brother John, who committed suicide after learning of his brother's fate. Two brothers dying close together is enough to break the strongest of souls, but refusing to be a victim, Rob spent his life searching for what had happened to Kerry. When we connected with the family, they were on their way up the Western Australian coast towards Cambodia to retrace Kerry's steps.

Rob produced a film, *Brother Number One*, about Kerry, the Khmer Rouge and the two million Cambodians who had lost their lives under the repressive regime. I would come to feed off Rob's inner strength as I lowered myself into my ski at night, well aware of the risks I was facing in the crocodile-infested waters of the remote Kimberley region. It felt as though he was always meant to guide me. Watching Rob at the helm, pushing his floating home through kilometre after kilometre in devastatingly hot conditions, I realised that grief doesn't dictate someone's future. It's how a person chooses to move forward that matters. And Rob would inspire me to keep moving forward through near-unbearable pain.

Rob's British wife, Rachel, doesn't just lift the vibe in a room, she positively glows. An elite athlete in her own right, Rach took up triathlon in her later years with much success. A mother figure for me in the Kimberley, Rach would provide the female connection I'd craved for so long. When Rach saw I was struggling while paddling in the heat, she would play trivia with me, sitting in the scorching sun and reading question after question, knowing it was distracting me from the physical pain and helping to relieve my feelings of isolation.

We linked up with the Hamills in Broome. As we began ferrying our gear back and forth between the boat and shore by tender, I noticed the extra width of the Hamills' catamaran compared to our first boat. Climbing aboard, I immediately felt comfortable. A net of fresh fruit hung above the door, which created an instant feeling of domesticity, and the plastic kayaks tied down on the side railings and the stack of board games on the dining-room table told me the Hamills prioritised fun. The galley carried a constant scent of freshly baked brownies and muffins, and for the first time in five months, I felt at home.

Nominating who to bring aboard from my core crew wasn't easy, but in the end I decided on Ben. It had been five months since Blake and Jaime had spent extended amounts of time on land, and I knew a break would be good for them. Matt, meanwhile, had the unenviable task of managing logistics and continuing to find extra sponsorship to fund the paddle. Ben's wide grin told me I'd made the right choice, but I needed a second person onboard to help with support.

With 1000 kilometres to cover in ten days, I had my work cut out for me. I'd been thinking for a while about bringing a coach onboard to help manage the physical load on my body, and I finally decided it was time. Mike Janes was my coach at Mermaid Surf Club on the Gold Coast, and after just one phone call, he was packing his bags and heading to Broome. With Mike, Ben and the Cruising Kiwis, my Kimberley family was complete.

On 5 May, my first day with the Kiwis, I paddled 104 kilometres with the only tailwind I would receive for the next two weeks. Little did I know, the best of the winds were now behind us and after this first day, I wouldn't receive another tailwind until I reached Noosa on Queensland's east coast.

On day two, I grinded out 98 kilometres in the flat in temperatures topping 40 degrees. Though there was no wind assistance, the glassy conditions meant that we were at least able to stop for lunch without drifting off the mark. Sitting 5–20 kilometres out to sea, we could drop the anchor and enjoy a calm lunch in conditions polar opposite to those of the Bight. Lunches with the Kiwis involved fresh smoothies or wraps prepared by different members of the family, and often finished with a quick dip in the ocean. The Hamills had an active YouTube channel (the Cruising Kiwis) and a large following, so they recorded daily happenings in and around the boat, with Rach taking on the role of editing post filming.

If I'd thought the days leading into Broome with Goatee and Ryan were hot, the Kimberley took things to a whole new level. Ben and Mike did their best to keep me sun safe in rash shirt, hat and sunglasses, and by smothering sunscreen on any exposed part of my body. But then on the third day, I decided to leave my rash shirt in the cupboard and go for a tan on my stomach. I arrived on the back deck at 6am ready to paddle in my two-piece swimmers.

Not one to mince words, Ben's response was immediate. 'Where's your rash shirt?' he demanded.

'It's rashing me. I'm going without it for the first stint,' I replied. I could feel his judgement from the other side of the boat, but he let the argument go, perhaps knowing I was about to learn a valuable lesson.

By the time I came aboard for lunch, my stomach was red raw. Though I'd applied sunscreen in the morning, it had long ago washed off in the salt water, leaving my skin exposed to the sun in the hottest part of the day and, as a result, I was left with severe blistering and peeling for two weeks. No matter how much pawpaw I put on, the burns continued to weep. By putting vanity before safety, I was now paying the price. Embarrassed by the mistake, I was hesitant to reveal the extent of the self-inflicted injury, but by day five, I was wincing from the pain of putting my rash shirt on. Pulling my shirt up to show Rach the damage, I hoped she had something more potent than pawpaw ointment in her medicine cabinet. With a look of concern, she raced to get an antiseptic cream. She smeared it on the burns and then covered my stomach with a waterproof bandage. Ben had little to say when he found out, but I knew what he was thinking: *I told you so.*

*

On day three, suffering the effects of the sunburn, the most terrifying moment of the entire trip occurred. Though I'd experienced great white sharks, five-metre swells, near hypothermia, heat stroke and seasickness, an encounter with a crocodile sits on a whole new level of scary.

I was nearing 100 kilometres of paddling for the day. Night had fallen and there was no moon, so the water and sky were unusually dark. This meant I had near zero visibility, and the glow of my head torch lit up a path just 30 centimetres wide. Trying not to think what lay outside my range of sight, I kept the pace high, clocking up kilometre after kilometre in the still conditions. Due to our close proximity to the surrounding islands, the water was riddled with sticks and seaweed. By day I could pick my way through the floating debris, but at night that wasn't possible. Each time my rudder hit a log it would make a resounding *thud* and my heart would be in my mouth until I realised it didn't have teeth and a tail.

The currents that had been plaguing us all day were growing stronger. In the northern parts of Western Australia, circular currents known as eddies are common, and strong eddies are able to create a whirlpool significant enough to pull a ten-tonne catamaran in easily. Rob had warned me of this phenomenon, but I'd all but forgotten about them until we came across one. A really strong one.

Paddling off to its starboard side, I suddenly lost sight of the catamaran. Hearing a yell, I looked over to see the catamaran taking a sharp left turn. *What were they doing?* I wondered, as Mike appeared on the back deck.

'Bon, we're caught in a current. We can't break it until we get enough speed up. Stay close,' he said.

Not needing to be told twice, I sprinted my way up to the boat, settling in as we started to be pulled around in circles. Around and around the current took us, and though my arms were heavy with lactic acid from a huge day of paddling, I didn't dare fall too far behind. The glow of the back deck lights extended just five metres behind the boat, and if I fell outside of that range, I'd be in darkness. Knowing what was in the water, I stayed close.

Mike and Ben had taken to doing crocodile checks with a torch during Bonnie Watch, scanning the water from left to right. As they shifted the torch back and forth, I kept my gaze firmly fixed in front; if the torch light illuminated the silvery back of a crocodile, I didn't want to know about it. Though I knew the risks, I was determined to stay in my bubble. By now I had a system: keep the music loud, gaze fixed in front, don't dare look around. In my peripheral vision, I noticed Mike's torch had stopped on a particular spot over my right shoulder. *What has he seen?* Right at that moment, we broke the current. Released from the grip of the eddy, the boat shot out of the whirlpool and began moving forward once more.

The water now smooth, I prayed the worst of the currents were behind us. Focusing on pulling as much water as I could with the paddle, I willed my ski to go faster, knowing we'd lost valuable time moving in circles. But the paddling felt hard. Harder than ever before. I figured the lactic acid was slowing me down; maybe the sprint up to the boat had been too much. *Why did I feel so slow?*

Grinding away for 20 minutes, the paddling wasn't getting any easier. Finally, Rob appeared under the glow of the back deck lights, nothing but his dark silhouette visible from my position in the water.

'Bonnie, how fast do you think you're going right now?' he inquired.

I was confused. Maybe I was powering along after all, my judgement muddled up in the moving water.

'Ten kilometres an hour?' I replied hesitantly, considering a higher guess.

'You're going two kilometres an hour,' Rob answered. 'The tide has turned and is now super strong. We'd better bring you in.'

Realising there was no point continuing to push against the roaring tide, I didn't argue.

The day had been eventful. Logs that looked like reptiles, whirlpools in the middle of the ocean and now a monster tide that slowed us almost to a halt. Climbing aboard, I'd already forgotten about the incident with the torch and Mike's look of concern. As he retrieved the suction cups from their bag to be placed on my aching muscles, I took the first sip from my protein shake, glad to have finished earlier than anticipated.

A week later, I stared in horror as Mike told me what he'd seen that night. Focusing the torch out to the starboard side of the boat, he'd shone it straight onto the back of a male crocodile, which was sitting just outside the whirlpool, watching me. Breaking the current just after the sighting, the boat and I had been flung forward into smooth waters, and the crocodile had disappeared. When I had climbed safely aboard 20 minutes later, however, Mike had heard water crashing against the boat. Grabbing the torch, he'd shone it into the water to catch the giant tail of a crocodile swimming away. If it was the same one from the whirlpool, it had stalked me for 20 minutes.

What would have happened if I hadn't come onto the boat when I did? Crocodiles were known as observers. They can watch patterns for days while waiting to strike. How long would the predator have waited? Would one more minute of paddling have proved fatal? These were questions I was glad not to have the answer to.

By the time Mike told me of the crocodile sighting, we had almost finished our stint in the Kimberley but had 3000 more kilometres of crocodile-infested waters to go, including along North Queensland. What if I caught sight of one in the glow of my headtorch? How would I react? The situation was too scary to consider. Instead, I decided to stay somewhat in denial. *My ski is six metres long,* I reasoned with myself. *They won't bother attacking me. Plus, I'm moving quickly most of the time; that will be my best defence.*

I resorted to what I'd done since beginning the expedition. I turned up the volume on my headphones to maximum and paddled as quickly as I could, as if my life depended on it. Because now, maybe, it did.

*

On day ten, we called a break, as nine days of pushing myself to the limit in the blistering heat had led to a rash developing over my entire body. Starting under my armpits, spreading down my belly and continuing to the crease of my elbows, the rash had become infected as a result of constant inflammation and exposure to the salt water. Smothering the last of the antiseptic ointment over the areas most infected, I longed for the day I'd be able to live in dry clothes and be out of the direct beams of the relentless sun. This hope got me through, and as I gritted my teeth and pulled my swimmers up over the weeping wounds on my stomach, I reminded myself that pain is only ever temporary.

In perfect timing, the day off was spent among spectacular scenery. King George Falls are the highest twin waterfalls in Western Australia with a descent of 100 metres. They are only accessible by boat or helicopter, and with the falls in full force from late December to early May, we were just in time. Rob and Rach had spoken of the King George River as a bucket-list experience, and I was soon to learn why.

At the end of a 60-kilometre paddling day on 14 May, my priority was to get dry. The heat rash was so bad by now that simply putting a t-shirt on was painful, the cotton lightly dragging over my skin enough to make me whimper.

Heading down to the bathroom to change out of my paddling gear, I was grateful to Rob for encouraging the lay day. A fear of crocodiles had driven me to complete ten consecutive days of huge kilometres, but my body was starting to tell me what my mind refused to believe: I needed a break. My fingers were significantly swollen. And if I didn't take the break now, I was going to pay the price. Stepping into the shower, I was also grateful for the private bathroom facilities onboard the Kiwis' catamaran. It was a luxury to close the door behind me and let the water run over my body. Even though we had to keep showers to a few minutes maximum to save precious water, that two minutes was in complete privacy, where I was safe, comfortable and didn't have to think about how I'd survive just one more kilometre.

In my cabin, I closed the door and pulled out my phone. Though we hadn't had reception for two weeks, I'd managed to download several TV series prior to leaving Broome and selected a thriller series about a psychopathic serial killer who murdered the women he fell for, jealousy and unrequited love not a good mix. The show, filmed in New York, was about as far removed from my current situation as possible, which was exactly what I needed. I started watching that day in my cabin, and by the time we got to Darwin, five days later, I had managed to binge all 12 episodes. In fact, the show helped get me through endless kilometres grinding away in my ski; I'd think of the plotline and try to figure out the twist.

I was halfway through the first episode when I heard Ben's voice booming down to my cabin from the front of the boat.

'Bon, you're going to want to see this,' he called, his excitement barely contained.

Reluctantly I stood up, groaning as I did so, and looked out my cabin window. I was stopped in my tracks. *What is this place?*

I let out a squeal of delight and raced outside to the back deck. I clocked 360-degree views of a deep red gorge. The ancient sandstone cliffs were straight out of *The Lion King*, stretching for hundreds of metres. Craning my neck to the top of the gorge, I tried to soak it all in, then joined the rest of the crew in playing a game of 'spot the crocodile', with some suspicious-looking logs and rocks causing us to point in excitement before realising our mistake. Safely seated on the bow of the boat, I now felt hopeful at the prospect of spotting one of the prehistoric reptiles who'd stalked me just one week prior.

We motored ten kilometres up the river and saw no crocs, but this was no time for disappointment. The gushing sound of the waterfalls was faint at first but quickly grew louder, and as we eased around a right-hand bend, we found what we'd come for, a sight tourists travelled across the world to experience. The King George Falls.

Rob was an adrenaline junkie like me. He drove the catamaran towards the waterfalls, within ten metres of the cliff face, so we could feel the spray of the water off the rocks, and I was so grateful for our fearless skipper. Having helped me through the most dangerous waters in the country, Rob had now brought us to the most beautiful place I'd ever seen.

I glanced around to see the joy on the faces of all those around me. Though we'd pushed ourselves to the absolute limit, one afternoon with VIP access to Mother Nature's greatest show made all the sacrifices worth it. I may have been over 5000 kilometres from my house on the Gold Coast, but that afternoon with the Cruising Kiwis in the middle of the Kimberley, I felt no need to rush home.

It was too glorious a place to leave in a hurry so we extended our stay. The following day, we climbed a winding track to the top of the gorge. At the summit, we were able to look out over the top of one of the waterfalls. Having not used my lower body for two weeks, it took me several hundred metres before

I felt coordinated enough to walk in a straight line. My calves were weak from underuse and my muscle mass had also visibly diminished in my quadriceps as a result of being limited to the tight footwells of the ski day after day. But the climb to the top was worth any discomfort, and as I stood tall on top of the waterfall, looking out over the river below, I saw the vast distance we had covered and felt an immense sense of pride. Though I had endured hardships both in and out of the water, I'd nearly conquered the Kimberley. Darwin was just around the corner. It was our next safe zone and would provide a chance to recover.

Back down at the bottom, we were preparing to climb into the tender to go back to the catamaran but were stopped by a couple walking past. The pair informed us that their friends had been rammed by an angry crocodile while they were making their way up the river in a small dinghy that morning, so they urged us to take care. The sick feeling in my stomach instantly returned and I was forced to face reality. Waving goodbye, we didn't bother telling them that I would be back in my ski the next day, paddling in these very waters.

*

After a full day off, I felt invincible. The angry rash had settled and my body felt like that of a 32-year-old once more so I decided to see what it was capable of. My daily record was still the 123 kilometres I'd paddled on the first day of the Bight; it had been incredibly rewarding, but the big seas had forced me to call it quits after 18 hours, and I knew I could better that effort. Up on the Top End I didn't have the assistance of the significant tailwinds of the Bight, but I believed that if I kept my food and fluids up, I could hit the 150-kilometre mark.

Over the first 14 hours of paddling on 17 May, I managed 103 kilometres. I completed the first 50 kilometres easily, feeling as though I was floating over the top of the water, but the second 50 kilometres was a struggle as my fingers slowly began filling with fluid and my back seized up from being forced into the brutal seated position with no lumbar support. When I climbed aboard for dinner, I headed straight to my cabin to change into dry clothes for the second stint, anxious to avoid another rash by staying in wet paddling gear.

Declan had cooked a spaghetti carbonara for dinner, with homemade brownies on the menu for dessert, which I devoured. Both he and Ivan were capable in the kitchen, and I'd come to crave the berry smoothies Ivan would whip up with assistance from Ben. The boys made me guess the ingredients in the smoothie, and as Ivan and Ben were prone to sneaking absurd foods like jelly snakes and Powerade into the blender, the game was hilariously rigged in their favour. Ten minutes spent guessing, however, was ten minutes of distraction from the life-threatening situation I was in, so I was happy to lose to them.

During the second stint of the day, I completed 57 kilometres, bringing my 24-hour total of kilometres up to 160. Paddling from afternoon through to the evening, I tried to stop myself imagining giant crocodiles watching me, waiting to attack. With the crew taking turns at the helm, every few hours I was kept company by someone new, which helped break up the monotony. Rach started the evening shift and updated me regularly as to our progress; she was followed by Mike who offered words of wisdom from a coaching perspective. Ivan was out of action due to illness, so Declan took the next turn, stepping up onto the front of the boat to appreciate the night sky before handing over to Ben, who loved calculating how far to the next border or milestone. By now the rapport between Ben and me was like that of siblings and we spoke honestly to each other, unafraid to disagree yet respectful of the other's opinion.

Finally, it was Rob's turn at the helm. Hearing of the back troubles I'd been having, Rob had been quick to offer me the use of his rowing suit, which was equipped with extra-thick padding for support. Pulling the suit on before climbing into my ski, it was as though I was equipping myself with Rob's courage and bravery.

Thinking about how lucky I was with my current crew, I sensed a flash up ahead. I jerked my head up to look for the source of the light and all I saw was the dark night sky. *Am I imagining things? Am I dehydrated and hallucinating?* I continued paddling but kept my gaze focused firmly ahead. Precisely ten seconds later, the light flashed again, and I struggled to take in what I'd seen. A dome-shaped, golden light had appeared in the sky for five seconds and then disappeared, leaving no trace among the blanket of stars. Shaking my head, I turned to Rob, who was standing on the front deck looking towards where the flash had appeared.

'What was that?' I asked, as a third flash lit up the sky. Three flashes in a row had occurred now, each one popping up to the left of the last, as though making their way across the sky. It was impossible to estimate the size of the flashes and we couldn't tell how far away they were, but we continued heading towards them. There was no sound to be heard but the motors of the catamaran. In the end there were five flashes in total, with the same ten-second gap between each.

When the display had finished, Rob and I turned to each other.

'I have no reasonable explanation for what just happened,' he informed me.

'Do you possibly think … Did we just see a UFO?' I stuttered, barely comprehending the words coming out of my mouth.

'I don't know. I just don't know,' he replied softly. As he stepped back inside the boat to talk on camera about what we'd witnessed, the sceptic within me searched for an explanation, but I came up short.

To this day, I still don't know what I saw that night in the middle of the Kimberley. What were large domes of flashing light doing out there at the very top of the country, hundreds of kilometres away from civilisation?

Climbing aboard the catamaran several hours later, having completed 160 kilometres in the past 24 hours, I felt validated. Two months on from the rigours of the Bight, my body was now honed for these long distances. I'd paddled further than I'd ever previously done in a single day, but I didn't drop to the floor like in the past; rather I stood strongly, thanking my crew for escorting me safely to heights I never imagined reaching. Having set a new record for myself, my mind started to conceptualise the ultimate challenge: *Is it possible to paddle 200 kilometres in a single day? And if so, could I be the one to do it?*

One of my favourite sayings goes as follows: 'Alone we go fast; together we go far', and I would soon find this to be true. My average paddling speed throughout the Kimberley, besides the night of the whirlpool, had been quick. Rarely dropping below ten kilometres an hour, I'd kept my cadence up, in no small part due to the strong presence of fear, but now just 240 kilometres from the big city lights of Darwin, I needed a little help to make it. For the past two weeks, Mike had spoken of joining me on the water. A competent ski paddler, he'd accompanied me for 20 kilometres on the day we headed into King George River but was saving himself for a big stint when I needed help. And in the days following my 160-kilometre effort, I certainly needed help.

The next day, I managed 90 kilometres at an average speed of 8.1 kilometres an hour, but it was tough. I didn't have the low blood sugar levels I'd experienced in the Bight, but the blistering heat lessened my appetite, making it impossible to consume enough protein to reduce muscle soreness. By the time I finished the day of paddling, my back muscles remained locked in the position I'd forced them to hold all day and I couldn't stand up straight. Sitting all day was unnatural as it was but without a back rest, it was nearly unbearable.

It was over ten days since I had seen Matt and the other boys on land. My boat crew had taken to passing me Hydralyte icy poles every ten kilometres to keep me hydrated and replenish the electrolytes I had lost through sweat. Slurping every last drop of fluid from my water bladder, we'd changed the two-litre bladder for a fresh one every few hours, yet I was still barely urinating due to dehydration. The ice blocks provided another form of hydration and also gave me a goal: ten kilometres, one ice block. Ten more kilometres, one more. The combined cold temperature and sweet taste of the ice blocks make them the ultimate treat.

After a quick break for a dinner of butter chicken made by Rach, I pulled some dry paddling gear on to prepare for the last 50 kilometres of the day. Except this time, I'd have company. Mike and Ben had alternated shifts in watching me throughout the day, sitting on the back step or side of the catamaran to keep me company and check the water for danger. Having seen my pace and mood drop, Mike knew it was time for him to dust off his paddle. He put on his boardshorts and rash shirt and stretched his back in preparation for the slog ahead. Though the stint would be further than he'd ever paddled in his life, he looked excited about the challenge.

The Kiwis cheered as we lowered ourselves into our skis, careful not to fall into the dark water below. Sticking a waterproof speaker to the front of my ski, I began a playlist full of house music that Jaime had uploaded for me. With roots in disco but adding electronic elements, house music typically has a danceable tempo of 120–130 beats a minute, which can slow or quicken according to the style of the DJ. As the songs Jaime had chosen had a chill vibe, the playlist was perfect for long paddling stints, allowing me to zone out for dozens of kilometres as I paddled to the beat.

For ten kilometres, Mike and I chatted away happily, letting the music set the pace and enjoying the drop in temperature that came after sundown. Mike was now almost 40, and I was concerned for his back. I remembered the intense ache of my muscles for the first few weeks of the expedition as I conditioned to the huge physical load. Part of me felt guilty over the pain soon to be inflicted upon Mike as a result of his willingness to help me.

The water was far too dangerous to fall into, so I tried to keep Mike focused by making conversation, covering topics from sport to politics, recent events and the weather. For the first few hours, he conversed fluently, showing no signs of the fatigue that was inevitable when holding a fast paddling speed over a long time. At the 30-kilometre point, however, Mike's replies grew shorter and he started responding through gritted teeth. I didn't say what I knew to be the truth; the pain in his back was only going to get worse. Once the muscles in the lower back tightened, there was very little to be done while still in the ski, locked in the seated position with no back support. Along the east coast, I had taken to diving out of my ski and doing back flips in the water to arch my body back the other way. The exercise had provided temporary relief, but out here in crocodile territory, we didn't have that luxury.

Crocodiles weren't the only threat in the water. Since Broome, I had noticed the frequency of sea snakes increasing and now just one day out from reaching Darwin, they were everywhere. During the stint of paddling with Mike, we saw 20 sea snakes; their yellow bodies with black markings were unmistakable in the clear water. Prior to the trip, I had been told of these ocean-dwelling snakes by experienced fishermen but had shrugged off their warning; my worries were focused on marine animals that were far bigger. But now, as Mike and I dodged the curled-up creatures, some of them the size of a large python, I wasn't laughing. A sea snake's venom is fatal. Even though I'd been reassured that their fangs can only pierce the skin of a human if they bite you between the toes or fingers, I didn't want to test it. As an enormous sea snake passed between Mike and me, both of us missing a stroke to avoid hitting it, I shuddered at the thought of a bite. We'd come so far and the lights of Darwin were now almost within sight, but it was like the end of the Bight crossing once again: I was in the middle of nowhere, face to face with snakes.

For the last 20 kilometres of Mike's paddle, Rob came onto the helm. I'd barely had time to sit and have a chat with Rob about his experience rowing the Atlantic all those years ago. I had so many questions: What did he learn about himself? Did he ever want to quit? And like me, had he experienced the deep, dark depths of the isolation that came with extended periods away from civilisation?

I decided it was now or never.

'Rob, what did you use to prevent chafe in your Atlantic row?' I asked, beginning with a relatively trivial topic as I didn't want to launch in too deep too quickly. What eventuated was 30 minutes of conversation that not only inspired me but got me through the last part of the Kimberley. Under a pitch-black sky, surrounded by sea snakes and possibly crocodiles, and with my skin stinging from the constant exposure to the salt water, I was hurting with every stroke. But as I listened to Rob speak of his adventures, I was carried 30 years back in time to when he had stood up against all odds and succeeded. Rob told me how he and Phil Stubbs had found it incredibly difficult to find sponsorship and were up against teams with significant financial backing. They ended up beating the other powerhouse nations – and they avoided chafing by rowing with no clothes on.

With Rob at the helm and Mike beside me, I felt invincible and their company filled me with the courage I needed to continue.

By the time Mike finished his 50-kilometre stint, he could barely move. He climbed onto the boat, grabbing his back, and hobbled to the back deck to lie flat. For the last ten kilometres, he'd fallen completely silent, and I'd stopped engaging him in conversation, knowing he was taking his mind and body to another place to get through. With Ben on hand to help, I directed him to massage Mike first.

I headed into the galley to grab a snack, another 100-kilometre day under my belt, which brought my total to 351 kilometres in three days. I allowed myself to smile. The next day I would be in

Darwin, having paddled one of the most dangerous stretches of coastline in the world. The crocodile-infested Kimberley would be ticked off the list, taking me one step closer to home.

The following day started slowly. With just 50 kilometres to paddle, it would take me only half a day, and Rob insisted there was no rush. We enjoyed a veggie-filled omelette for breakfast and I took my time in climbing into my ski. Big proponents of food as medicine, the Kiwis had served up two weeks of delicious and highly nutritious meals packed with organic vegetables and fruits, herbs, spices and lean proteins. It was near impossible to get supplies but the Kiwis had stocked up their freezer with fruit and veggies, and halfway through our time together we had asked a research boat and cruise ship for some fresh produce, which they had generously provided. It was two months since I'd lost so much muscle mass crossing the Bight, and I felt much stronger. Without seasickness, my body had been able to better withstand paddling huge kilometres at a high pace.

I completed 40 kilometres from lunch through to the afternoon then climbed aboard for a snack before the final stint. The buildings of Darwin were now within view, and we began seeking phone reception with various degrees of success. Mike and I had a different service provider to the others and weren't as lucky; our phones still showed nil bars of reception, so we were unable to send a message or make a call. Much to the entertainment of the rest of us, Mike had spent the better part of the day perched up on the roof of the boat, the highest possible point on the boat short of climbing the mast, holding his phone skywards to pick up a signal, his attempts so far fruitless.

As I climbed back into the water with just ten kilometres to go, Rob informed me the tide was at its strongest, meaning I'd soon be flying with its assistance. I couldn't believe my luck; just one hour of paddling with a ripping tide, towards a city I'd never visited, with a guaranteed few days off. It was my idea of heaven. Rach filmed me as I slid my gloves over my swollen fingers, and uploaded the content on the family's popular YouTube channel. Looking back over the footage later, the excitement among us all is palpable. We'd finished the Kimberley; this was our victory leg.

Beginning the familiar motion of stroking left side and then right, I felt the water begin to move under me, pushing me along. My level of effort minimal, I turned my head to the right to see trees on the shoreline flying past.

'How fast do you think you're going?' Rob called from the back deck, the second time I'd been asked that question in the past week.

'Hopefully faster than two kilometres,' I quipped.

'Bonnie, you're going 18 kilometres an hour.'

Eighteen kilometres an hour was equivalent to the speed of a car cruising around a car park. Shaking my head, I let out a belly laugh. The variability of conditions in Australia was nothing short of bizarre; temperatures varying 40 degrees in difference, rolling swells giving way to flat seas, we'd been through it all. Reflecting on the past two weeks, I began to feel emotional knowing it would soon be time to say goodbye to the family who now felt like my own. For two weeks, the Cruising Kiwis had thrown themselves into the task of guiding me through 1000 kilometres of pain, fear and everything in between. As a unit we were now unbreakable. Thankfully, I wouldn't have to think about parting hugs just yet. It was time to enjoy our last stint as a partnership, cruising along at 18 kilometres an hour, the Kiwis barely needing to run the engines of the catamaran thanks to the roaring current.

Several hours later, anchored in Darwin marina, with a takeaway pizza on the table and a glass of champagne in hand, we made a toast to the Kimberley: the sacrifices and suffering required to conquer her but more importantly what she gave us: a lifetime of memories wrapped up in two unforgettable weeks that could never be replicated.

CHAPTER 12

'YOU'LL NEVER MAKE IT'

THE STAY IN DARWIN WAS A LONG ONE. MIKE HAD FLOWN
back to continue his coaching commitments on the Gold Coast
and the Hamills were still intent on heading up to Cambodia to
retrace the footsteps of Rob's brother Kerry. They planned to sail
back the way we had come before heading up towards Indonesia
and Cambodia. And so once again, we began the hunt for a
boat, this time to escort us back to the Gold Coast.

The first step was securing accommodation for the week
in Darwin, a difficult task given our shoestring budget. Prior
experience informed us that a skipper and boat wouldn't come
cheap, so we were hesitant to spend our small amount of money
on anything outside of the basics. Fortunately, Matt had a chance
conversation with Michael Anthony, the owner of the Zen Hotel
on Darwin's waterfront, and once again worked his magic.
Michael agreed to provide us with accommodation for the week
while we continued our search for a vessel. In return, the crew

were required to help with various tasks around the hotel. And so at various occasions over the following week, much to my amusement, I'd look out the window of my room to see Blake, Ben and Jaime guerneying the balcony or helping to prepare cob loaf for hotel guests. Things escalated to a comical level when I found Matt dressed in a bartender's apron one night, preparing for the evening shift of serving drinks. If they hadn't proved it already, I was again reminded of the crew's willingness to do anything to ensure the circumnavigation was successful, even if it required faking it until they made it as hotel staff members.

Darwin's population size made the prospect of finding a vessel theoretically more favourable than when we did the same in Exmouth, but there was one problem. It was now May, and the southeasterly trade winds had begun. Commercial boats used these favourable winds to whip up the coast of Queensland and around to Darwin, and no one was heading back the other way. The prospect of bashing into 15–25-knot headwinds each day was not for the faint-hearted, and we knew we'd need some luck to find a skipper willing to take a chance on me completing the task against the odds. At the local marina, we were either laughed at or told in no uncertain terms that we were not only foolish but would be risking our lives if the conditions were as rough as those expected. I was aiming to be the first to circumnavigate Australia in a clockwise direction, and I was also aiming to be the first to paddle into southeasterly trade winds while they were at their strongest. The challenge excited me, however, and I was raring to go, but each meeting led to a dead end, with skippers not willing to risk their boat or their lives in the worsening conditions.

The consensus of the locals was voiced midway through our week in Darwin. Michael organised a function for us on the rooftop of the Zen Hotel on Friday night, and I addressed the group with the intention of finding someone to assist us. Following my brief talk, Michael encouraged me to make my way around the room to pitch for a support boat. After several conversations, which all ended with a vague promise to let me know if anything popped up, I found myself face to face with a middle-aged man who had a lot to say about my trip but nothing of a productive nature.

'You're mad taking on the southeasterlies this time of year,' he shouted above the two-piece band, which had piped up in the corner. 'It can't be done on your little surf ski. You'll never make it.'

Annoyed, I struggled to find the words to reply. Though I'd developed a thick skin after all the messages I had received on social media, hearing criticism in person was a whole other story. The man's words were reminiscent of the self-doubt I fought with every time I hopped into my ski and pitted myself against the odds. I began to wonder if maybe he was right. Maybe it couldn't be done.

As the critic turned away, I had a thought: if I was six feet tall and male, would his view have been different? I debriefed with my crew afterwards, and Rob was quick to lift my spirits once more.

'Don't worry about the doubters,' he reassured me. 'They haven't seen what you're capable of. You're going to find a boat, and you're going to get this thing done.'

That night, I made a promise to myself. Whenever the negative thoughts crept in, I vowed to think of Rob's words and to remind myself that no big success is achieved without doubt, no history-making feat completed without naysayers. What matters is which voices we choose to listen to.

Over the course of the evening, the crew and I made our way through the crowd, sharing our story in the hope of finding someone who could help us. It was Blake who had the most success. He met a Darwin local by the name of Steve who told him that the local marina was currently home to several skippers who might be able to help.

The following day, Steve swung by the Zen Hotel to pick up Blake and Matt and take them to the marina. As Steve began telling the bartender of our plight, a patron walked by the bar and overheard the conversation. The man's name was Josh, and he told Steve he'd heard locals talking about this woman who was circumnavigating Australia on an ocean ski. The manager of the marina had actually already suggested to Josh that he should accompany us, but he'd rejected the idea; now he had a sudden change of heart.

'I've got a big boat,' Josh said. 'Tell me more about it.'

With no other offers on the table, the boys tried to play it cool, hiding their desperation. We'd had a week of stalled progress and each day ate into the buffer over the previous record I'd worked so hard to build. But luck was on our side. One hour after meeting Josh, the boys had secured a handshake deal for him to escort us to Cairns.

Waiting back at the hotel, I had butterflies in my stomach. I tried to avoid thinking about what would happen if the boys came back from the marina empty-handed. In just six days' time, I would be required to head back out to the spot I'd last finished at, regardless of whether I had a support boat. If I didn't do so, my record attempt would be finished as per the rules of Guinness World Records, which stipulates that the paddler cannot remain stationary for longer than two weeks at a time. If no support boat could be sourced, I was facing the very real possibility of taking on the rest of the Northern Territory – in waters riddled with crocodiles – with a jet ski as my only support. And in the sections that were inaccessible by car, we wouldn't be able to use the jet ski because there would be no option for refuelling, so there was the very real chance I'd have to go it alone.

The following afternoon, Matt and I met Josh and his partner, Tina, at the marina bar. Both parties were aware of the huge challenge just around the corner: the Gulf of Carpentaria. The 1000-kilometre stretch between Nhulunbuy (Gove) in the Northern Territory and Cape York at the very tip of Queensland was, like the Bight, an open-water crossing. When I'd looked at the map on my phone two years before, it was the Bight and the Gulf that had stood out like a sore thumb. Though I wasn't aware back then just how challenging open-water paddling is, I knew if I was to be successful that I would be forced to remain at sea for weeks at a time. Across the Gulf there'd be no land in sight for two weeks, no phone reception and, worst of all, a high chance of debilitating seasickness.

But Josh was no shrinking violet, and I could see him light up when I spoke of the challenges that lay ahead.

'I've come so far,' I told him. 'I know I can do it. I just need someone to get me home.'

Fixing me with an intense stare from behind his clear-rimmed glasses, Josh spoke slowly. 'It's not going to be easy,' he insisted, in his unmistakable Queensland accent. 'In fact it's going to be bloody hard. But if we get the right weather window, I think we can do it.' Glancing at Tina, who nodded her approval, Josh confirmed his decision. 'Let's introduce you to *Isabella*.'

Josh had spent his childhood and much of his adult life in the Sunshine State. A 39-year-old mechanic who had quit his job in the mines, he lived aboard his 65-foot sailing ketch, *Isabella*, with Tina, a 35-year-old carpenter from Finland who had a love of the great outdoors. *Isabella* was a beauty. She was the same width as my previous support boats but nearly twice as long, and I immediately noticed the spaciousness of the yacht as I stepped aboard. I also took note of how tidy things were, with not one object or piece of equipment out of place.

Heading down below via the near-vertical stairs that connected the top deck to the lower floors, I was shocked to find a galley equipped with microwave, stove, oven and a full-sized fridge comparable to the one in our Mermaid Beach unit.

'We like our food on *Isabella*,' Josh boomed over my shoulder. 'We make our own bread and like to do a roast once a week, so you won't go hungry. I've spent ten years doing this boat up so that it feels like a home. You'll find a shower just like that in a house and, though we usually keep showers to a two-minute maximum, we might have to make an exception for you.'

It seemed we'd struck gold once more.

We developed a plan to head off in two days' time, giving Josh and Tina a day to clean *Isabella* and stock up with enough food and fuel for the stint ahead. Having asked Jaime and Blake to come back on as crew until we reached Queensland, I felt excited at the prospect of taking on the Gulf. I had a boat, a skipper and full trust in my crew. We'd tackled the Bight in freezing conditions and huge swells, so surely the warm waters of the Gulf would be a piece of cake in comparison? Little did I know how wrong that assumption was.

On 28 May, we set out from Darwin to begin the push towards Nhulunbuy, praying Mother Nature would be kind. She was, and on the first day with *Isabella*, I managed 78 kilometres in a ten-knot southerly. To successfully lower myself into my ski from the yacht, we had to develop a different system to that used on the catamarans. With the distance from boat to water a significant 2.5 metres, we hooked a ladder over the side of the boat and dropped it into the water, allowing me to climb down and slide into my ski, which was lowered into the water using a rope system. Though the process involved a minimum of two to three people, it was far safer than Blake or Jaime holding my ski off the back deck of a catamaran while I climbed into the ski in breaks between five-metre swells.

In the first week with Josh, I averaged 70 kilometres a day, bouncing up and down in chop that smashed into me from every direction as *Isabella* rocked from side to side, testing the stomachs of all those onboard. Tina and Blake were busy emptying the contents of their stomachs over the side railing most days. Jaime was also often forced to lie down on the back deck, suffering nausea he'd previously managed to avoid. This time I didn't get ill, and I was relieved to learn that due to our close proximity to land (we were only 20 kilometres offshore) we were able to anchor each evening and get some relief from the rock of the waves. I finished mid-afternoon most days due to starting around 5am in an attempt to get as much paddling in before the winds ramped up mid-morning. Then I'd climb aboard and wash away the pain of the day under a warm shower, with a protein shake and a massage waiting for me when I emerged.

We reached Nhulunbuy (Gove) after two weeks. The small coastal town was to be our final point of contact with the mainland before taking on the Gulf of Carpentaria. By this stage I'd learnt two things about Josh. Firstly, he spoke in a direct manner – a hangover from countless hours spent in male-dominated environments in the mines – and that I shouldn't take any offence when he grew impatient. Secondly, Josh was extremely practical and could fix nearly anything. If someone was willing to learn, Josh had a wealth of wisdom to impart on everything from politics to tying knots. Teaching Jaime and

Blake how to hoist the spinnaker and tie complex knots, Josh also educated us on the significance of the tides and currents in the Northern Territory, and showed us how we could avoid areas of high crocodile activity. Having sailed in the remote waters of the north many times, Josh brought unparalleled knowledge to the project.

On 16 June, we spent our last day ashore before taking on the Gulf. The two-day break was spent provisioning the boat with food to last us up to two weeks. Josh had previously used *Isabella* for charters, so he and Tina were more than competent in calculating the amount of fresh fruit and vegetables, meat, bread and frozen goods we would need to see us across.

Having studied the weather forecasts over the past week, he was keen to get going. Recent winds in the Gulf had averaged 25 knots, and we had a small weather window in which the winds would be dropping to 10 knots. Unlike in the Bight, the wind here would be blasting me straight in the face, so we needed to attack the 630-kilometre crossing while the wind was at its lowest. Even so, the headwinds were predicted to reduce my speed from 12 kilometres an hour to 7 kilometres an hour, so I began mentally preparing myself for long days of grinding away with no reprieve. Looking around the boat, I saw others preparing in different ways. Josh, for instance, had taken on the task of preparing nutritious casseroles to keep the galley free throughout the crossing, knowing it would be too dangerous to be using knives and other utensils, which would slide off the bench as the boat got thrown around in the wild seas.

For our last supper before taking on the Gulf, we anchored up in the harbour of the Gove Sailing Club. The previous night we'd bought a meal at the club, and I'd savoured the tender rump steak with mushroom sauce, cooked medium-rare as I liked it. By now aware of the importance of loading up on calories during my days off, I'd eaten heartily, placing a particular emphasis on lean meats and green vegetables, the two types of food that I couldn't stomach when seasickness hit.

Now just hours before we began the open-water crossing, we made a toast: to crossing the Gulf of Carpentaria west to east against the odds. But instead of sharing our expectations as we did prior to the Bight, we instead watched on with interest as the television in the corner of the room flashed with advertisements for reality shows soon to be broadcast. It had been two months since I'd sat down and watched TV, and it now felt like a novelty. It conjured up distant memories of being on the couch at home in dry clothes.

The next morning, we set sail. I zipped up the blue lycra stinger suit that reached from wrist to ankle. It had become part of my daily wardrobe to protect me from the threat of potentially fatal stings of box jellyfish and irikanji, which live in the warmer waters at the top of Australia. Then I sat down to answer questions asked by a camera-wielding Blake. We'd managed to raise $5000 for Gotcha4Life during the Bight crossing, and we hoped this crossing would be just as successful. Our overall goal was to raise $100,000, and we were nearly a third of the way there. Confident the fundraising would pick up as we entered the home straight, I wasn't focusing too much on the overall tally but hoped my efforts over the coming week would be considered worthy of some decent donations.

Blake blended some carrots into my berry smoothie to bump up the nutritional value, and I went through my stretching routine before strapping the back brace around my waist. Finally I pulled on Jaime's thick spearing gloves over my callused hands. The gloves fit my hands perfectly, and I hadn't paddled a day without them since Victoria. However, I still couldn't help wondering if even the thick neoprene material of the gloves was going to be enough to withstand my tight grip on the paddle as I battled the headwinds.

And indeed, from the moment I climbed down the ladder and into my ski the following day to begin the Gulf crossing, I knew we were facing a whole different beast. Though the winds had dropped to 15 knots according to the radar, their force felt like a punch to the face, creating a wall of resistance against every stroke. In the Bight, as mentioned, I had been lucky in receiving a favourable weather window, which allowed me to surf my way through the days with the wind at my back. The conditions in the Gulf, however, caused every muscle in my body to tense as I forced my way through one painful kilometre after another. Two open stretches of water – polar opposite experiences.

It was just past midnight by the time I came aboard at the end of the first day of the crossing, after banking the hardest 100 kilometres of the expedition so far. My original plan was to better the 160 kilometres in 24 hours, which I'd achieved in the

Kimberley. But I knew now that would be impossible. With the winds picking up to 20 knots despite the favourable forecast, the ladder swung out dangerously from the boat as I climbed up, and I was careful not to wrap my fingers around the rungs for fear of them being crushed when the ladder fell back against the boat. As Jaime gently slid his spearing gloves from my hands, I winced. The gentle touch of the material was nearly unbearable on my fingers, which had swollen to the size of mini sausages.

Just one sixth of the way through the crossing, I dared not think about the vast distance remaining. With nowhere to anchor in the open ocean, Josh prepared the sails to perform the heave-to manoeuvre that would slow *Isabella*'s backwards progress, reducing the distance we'd need to motor back to the starting point after taking a break. We had only a skeleton crew onboard, so everyone would need to take a turn at the helm, and I felt grateful for the sailing experience Blake and Jaime had gained during our Bight crossing.

As I sat down to Josh's heated casserole and a warm bun made by Tina the day before, I gripped the sides of the dining table to prevent myself from sliding onto the floor. By this stage, the boat was rocking so dramatically, it was unsafe to leave heavy objects untied, and as Josh had predicted, the only safe way of preparing food in the galley was to heat up a meal in the microwave. From the first cautious bite into the lamb and vegetable dish, my body began to reject the food and I became aware of my salivary glands working overtime before the dry retching started. I was soon sprinting to the back deck to vomit. *Here we go again.*

I was in good company, however, as Blake was by now suffering greatly and had been forced to lie flat on his back up the front of the boat throughout the day to hold off the nausea. Glancing up towards the boat from my position in the ski, I'd often noted the only visible part of Blake was his feet, which stuck out from behind the base of the mast.

With Blake unable to stand upright for long periods of time without vomiting, the onus was on Jaime to work overtime in looking after me. Knowing better than to continue trying to force food down, I limped back inside from the back deck and drank two cups of water, the growls of protest from my stomach growing increasingly louder. *You can do this*, I told myself. The sound of Blake's retching was audible above the wind. *It's just a bit of seasickness. You've done it before and you can do it again.*

It was still dark when I lowered myself into my ski the next morning. My empty stomach craved the food my body needed but refused to tolerate. Reaching down to click the start button on my smart watch to record my distance, I thought back to a message I'd received leading into the Gulf crossing. My inbox was filled with notes of encouragement and wishes for a safe voyage, but a particular message had captured my attention. A parent of a teenage boy had got in touch to inform me that she was taking inspiration from the journey. Her son had tried to commit suicide earlier in the year and she was encouraged by our mission to raise funds for mental fitness.

The purpose of the project ran much deeper than how far and fast I could paddle. I was starting to see that the paddle was just a vessel through which I could communicate a clear message: sometimes life is hard and we don't feel great, but things will get better if you lean on the people around you to help you through. I was aware that rates of poor mental health and suicide had been increasing throughout Covid. The desire to break down the stigma around vulnerability and speaking about mental-health issues had been the driving force behind me choosing Gotcha4Life as a charity. This message from a parent who had almost lost a child not only strengthened my resolve to continue the quest I was on, it sparked an ongoing desire to continue advocating for Gotcha4Life once I finished.

By the time I hit stop on my watch at the end of day two of the Gulf, I'd banked 90 kilometres in 15 hours, half the distance I'd usually complete in that timeframe with the assistance of tailwinds. Gripping the ladder to climb aboard as the sun began to set, I wrapped my fingers around the rungs, too drained to care if they got jammed between the ladder and the boat. Reaching the top, I extended my right hand to grab onto Blake's and he pulled me aboard as Josh worked desperately at the helm to steady the boat. *Isabella* was being smashed by wave after wave with no land to shield the onslaught of swells crashing into her. I lay down on the bench on the back deck as Jaime slid my gloves off, and the pain in my fingers was so intense I had to stop myself screaming. Maybe I shouldn't have resisted; maybe a long bloodcurdling scream would have released the agony I fought to forget, the fear I tried to quell through humour, and the overwhelming feeling of doubt that trying to do something that had never been done before was actually now going to prove a stretch too far.

On day three, I clawed back 110 kilometres on the Gulf. Three days at sea with no land in sight, the only way I could tell we were moving forward was by watching my watch slowly ticking over the distance. Blake and I hadn't held food down in three days, and Tina was curled up in a ball inside, migraines pounding in her head like a sledgehammer. Josh was visibly stressed and though the seasickness hadn't impacted him and Jaime, all I'd seen him eat since we set off was a couple of muesli bars. The skipper's job was to keep the boat in order and the crew safe. Tina's deteriorating condition was significantly affecting Josh, as was the fact that the supporting metal chains that attached the aluminium tender to the yacht had snapped, unable to withstand the enormous pressure they were placed under as *Isabella* bashed her way through the frothy seas.

'I think this boat will be ten inches shorter by the time this trip is done,' Josh muttered, checking the chart plotter to ensure we were on track for our targeted destination of Seisia.

On day four, the winds picked up even further. Still not holding down any solids, I was solely consuming Hydralyte ice blocks and finely sliced pieces of apple. Midway through paddling, I'd call to Jaime or Blake for some apple, and they'd race down to the galley to quickly prepare the food, occasionally adding some lollies or sweet biscuits into my food bag in hope that I'd be able to stomach the treats.

On day two, I'd noticed a slight tremor in my hand as my gloves were pulled off and now four days in, I was shaking from head to toe, my nervous system out of balance from extreme physical exertion and lack of sustenance. In my mind, I saw only one solution: paddle faster. The quicker I could get the kilometres done, I figured, the sooner we'd be out of hell hole 2.0. But there was one major problem. I was moving at a maximum of seven kilometres an hour in the strong headwinds, and no matter how hard I forced my arms through each stroke and ignored the pain in my aching fingers, I couldn't paddle any quicker than walking pace.

By the end of the fourth day, I could barely lift myself up the ladder. It usually only took ten seconds, but it was well over two minutes by the time I stepped up out of my ski and hauled myself up, one painful rung at a time. At the top of the ladder, I had just enough energy to whisper my thanks to the crew, before stumbling to the bench on the back deck where I lay straight down. *How did I get here?* I wondered. Feeling emotional, I didn't even have the energy to cry. Instead, I turned over to face the wall to block out the scene before me: a stressed skipper, one crewmate lying debilitated on the floor, another wrapped over the railing vomiting, with the last one patiently waiting to take my gloves off.

Staring at the blank wall, shivers coursing through me like electric shocks, I considered my options. If I were to quit, I knew no one would judge me. By pulling the pin, we could motor to safety and recover until we were ready to come back out. But on the flip side, who knew when another suitable weather window would present itself? Currently at sea in 15 knots of wind, the conditions were possibly as good as they were going to get. Several minutes passed before I slowly rolled back over to face reality, finding Jaime standing before me with an empathetic half-smile.

'We're halfway across,' he said, sensing the doubt within me. 'Just half more to go.'

As Jaime began patiently removing my gloves, one painful centimetre at a time, I wondered if my body had another half left.

On day five I begged for my mum. The previous night, I'd called out for Jaime from my cabin, seeking a bucket urgently as the apple and Hydralyte began to make its way back up my oesophagus. Jaime had run towards my cabin from the back deck when he heard my calls, but he hadn't made it in time. Instead he was met with the sight of me mopping up the vomit from the doona. Without a word, Jaime left to grab a bucket and towels to clean up the rest of the mess. Bucket baths in the Bight had felt dehumanising, but the Gulf had taken things to a whole new level. At rock bottom, I felt more animal than woman. Unable to sit up without vomiting, I had been forced to change in and out of my paddling gear while lying flat on my back and I was now receiving assistance to clean up the watery vomit I'd covered myself in.

It was Blake's turn on Bonnie Watch on the morning of day five. He came down to my cabin to inform me we had 20 minutes motor left until we were at the precise spot I'd finished paddling the previous day; in other words, it was time to get moving. Once Blake left, I reached down and pulled my swimmers up and over my body while still lying flat on my back, repeating the process with my paddling tights and rash shirt until I was completely dressed. Appearing at the door once more, Blake helped me to my feet.

'I want my mum,' I whispered hoarsely. 'I just want my mum.'

I wanted Mum to tell me it was going to be okay. But Mum wasn't coming, and the only way I would hear her voice again soon was to keep moving forward.

'Come on, Bon,' Blake encouraged quietly. 'I'll help you to the back deck.'

Using his arm to support me, I made my way slowly to the helm. Vomiting five times as Josh motored *Isabella* towards our starting mark, I was still dry retching by the time I got in my ski.

*

'Strand, Fleet Street, Trafalgar Square. I've got the red ones. Now time to move on to the green.' Shifting in my seat in a futile attempt to relieve the pins and needles that shot all the way down my right leg, I proudly informed Blake of my progress in recalling the locations of the Monopoly board game. Not in the mood for trivia, I'd thought up this most recent game to distract myself with, and it had kept me occupied for most of the morning as Josh grew steadily more anxious with the increasing winds, our progress stalling to just five kilometres an hour. Watching him pacing the back deck, checking the chart plotter against the forecast, I knew Tina remained glued to the floor of the galley. She had vomited up the migraine tablets she usually relied on. Once again, I felt pangs of guilt from seeing others hurting in their attempt to help me, and I was frustrated I couldn't get us to calm, safe waters any quicker.

Throughout the morning, the wind continued to increase and following a lapse in concentration, I was thrown out of my ski into the swirling water. Still clipped to the ski via a safety line, I allowed myself a moment to regather my thoughts before heaving my body up and into the craft, but this time I didn't have the energy and I fell back into the ocean. Kicking desperately, I tried once more, furiously beating my legs to propel my body upwards but was once again unsuccessful. Five times I attempted to climb into my ski, after which time I was so drained I could barely tread water as I waited for the boat crew to collect me. When Josh saw me, he decided to call it.

'Alright, that's it. We're not going anywhere,' his shout rang out above the roaring wind. 'We're borderline going backwards. We've gotta get out of here.'

Grateful for his decision, I realised that for the first time since beginning the trip, I truly had nothing left to give. No longer able to stand or sit unsupported, I'd pushed my body to near breaking point and if I continued, my physical health would deteriorate to the point where a fall-out could be fatal.

After another agonising climb to the top of the ladder, I staggered to the back deck and rolled over to face the wall, this time not bothering to turn back the other way. Above the roar of the engines, I could just make out Josh's words as he informed the crew he was setting a direct line to Weipa, located closer to our current location than Seisia, which was further north. No longer wanting to block out reality, on the contrary I craved to re-enter the real world where people laughed, dogs barked and you could speak to a family member at the push of a button. Done with taking on the ocean, I was sick of seasickness and being brave. I wanted to be like every other 32-year-old woman, whose worries didn't involve sharks, crocodiles or huge wind gusts that ripped chains off boats. I just wanted to be … normal. As Jaime rolled the gloves off my fingers, I wanted it to be the last time he did so. I never wanted to put the gloves or my paddling gear on again.

CHAPTER 13

THE LAST RIGHT-HAND TURN

THE 300-KILOMETRE MOTOR TO WEIPA LASTED 18 HORRIFIC hours. *Isabella* was only capable of holding a maximum speed of eight kilometres an hour against the relentless headwinds, and it was unsafe to stand up without holding onto something secure. Several times I was caught out while scurrying from the back deck to the toilet, my body thrown against a wall as another wave smashed into *Isabella*, attempting to knock her over. Josh had visibly lost weight and his face was ghostly white as he ran from the galley where Tina was lying, back up to the helm to ensure the autopilot was holding us on the correct line.

Evening fell as we drew within 12 hours of our destination, and I could no longer hold onto my bladder. Lying flat on the floor of the back deck, I'd been holding on all evening, knowing a trip below would result in an episode of vomiting. Above deck, my body temperature remained low with the assistance of the sea breeze and I was able to control the vomiting, but below deck, my temperature rose, leading to nausea and dry retching.

For the first time since beginning the expedition, I considered peeing over the side of the boat. With everyone inside, I could crouch down low, aiming the stream into the ocean, and the crew would be none the wiser. But after taking a closer look at the huge swells, I realised that it would only take one slip and I'd be thrown overboard. Our first skipper had informed us that many male sailors who had been lost overboard were found with their fly down, having slipped and toppled over the railing while relieving themselves. I wasn't keen on joining them as a statistic. And so, using every bit of my strength remaining, I propped myself up onto my elbows and forced myself to my feet, grabbing onto a pole as I did so. Whimpering with pain, I hobbled down the stairs towards the living room and toilet. The boat was rocking violently as I grabbed onto the side of the dining table. Objects were being thrown left to right with the force of the ocean, as I inched my way towards the bathroom.

The nausea was quick to return once I was below deck, and a coating of sweat began to develop over my forehead before my stomach churned and the burn of acid reflux in my throat became unbearable. *Lie flat*, I reminded myself, and dropped down onto the middle of the hardwood floor, desperately attempting to hold down the vomit. I braced my feet against the wall and held onto the base of the table to anchor myself as once more we were pounded by the relentless swells.

'Please stop,' I begged in vain, as Mother Nature showed her true power. A tear rolling down my cheek, I prayed once more, this time for the ocean to calm down long enough so I could make it to the bathroom to empty my bladder with dignity. Just making it in time, I managed to urinate and flush the button before turning around and vomiting an acid-like substance into the bowl.

Motoring into the harbour of Weipa on 21 June, we were shells of the humans who'd left Nhulunbuy. During the last five hours, we had barely uttered a word to each other and everyone's energy batteries were at an all-time low. Though it had been five days since I'd seen Matt, I was far from excited about our reunion. It had taken two weeks for me to speak openly about the horrors of the Bight, and similarly, I was hesitant to open up about what we'd been exposed to in the Gulf.

Not yet having had the time to process how I was feeling about bailing out halfway across, I had little chance of finding the words to describe what we'd been through. Poor Matt. Having followed his wife three quarters of the way around the country, he'd patiently waited on land each time I headed out to sea, and instead of greeting him with a romantic kiss, I was a near-mute vibe killer. In fact, for the past six months, I'd barely been invested in our relationship. From the day we'd left the Gold Coast, it had been all about me: how I felt isolated, how my hands were sore, how I doubted if I could continue. I couldn't remember the last time I'd inquired into his wellbeing.

Anchoring up at Weipa, Josh ran the tinny in to pick up Matt and Ben from shore. Twenty minutes later, I could hear the boys greeting Blake and Jaime on the back deck, but I chose to remain in my cabin, feeling far from social. Despite recognising how little love I'd shown Matt, I couldn't bring myself to walk the 20 steps up to the top deck to see him. Instead I pulled out my phone to check social media, overwhelmed by the hundreds of messages received since we'd set out from Nhulunbuy. Swiftly crafting replies to my followers, I realised I was communicating with strangers before greeting my own husband. *What is wrong with me?*

Five minutes later, I heard the shuffle of Matt's footsteps as he made his way towards the cabin.

'Hello?' he called warily, unsure of the condition he'd find me in. Not shifting from my prone position, I smiled weakly as I offered a hoarse hello.

Concern washing over his face, Matt asked the one question I wasn't ready to answer, 'Are you okay?'

Unsure how to respond, I turned back to my phone, continuing an online conversation with a paddler from France who had been following the journey. It was easy to interact from behind a keyboard. What was far more difficult was sitting face to face with the person who knew me best. *Was I okay?* Truth was, I didn't know. Physically, other than an intense soreness in my muscles that seemed to be worsening, I was relatively intact. I was malnourished but had managed to avoid serious injury in the huge seas. But as for my mental state, I wasn't so sure. In giving everything I had to the Gulf, it felt as though part of me could never be replaced, as though whatever fragments of innocence I'd had within me were now gone, lost somewhere on the bottom of the ocean. *What does that leave? Who am I now?* I simply didn't have the answers.

And while I was hurting, I managed to hurt the person who'd been there for me for the better part of a decade.

'I want to take a break,' I muttered in Matt's direction, my voice barely audible above the generator that was cranking at the front of the boat. Not thinking before speaking, the words tumbled out as though spoken by someone else. Except they weren't.

'What?' Matt's reply was one of shock, and I could see his heart breaking in front of me.

'I can't be a wife; I can't tap into that side of me. I have nothing left to give.' A sick feeling formed in my gut as I spoke. I wasn't convinced I was doing the right thing, but I felt I had no choice.

'You don't have to be any certain type of person. I know you can't give me love at the moment, but that's okay. I don't expect it.' Matt's reply was typical of the person he was. Selfless.

But even though I hated myself for it, I couldn't give him the reply he so desperately needed to hear.

'I just need some time. I want to be alone,' I whispered, turning away once more.

Leaving my husband of 18 months and partner of seven years standing at the door, I focused my attention on my phone, checking the latest news stories to see what I'd missed while I'd been at sea. Shutting out Matt, I now looked to block out reality altogether; anything to escape the fact that, at some stage, if I was going to break the record, I was going to have to go back out into the swirling, evil mess of water known as the Gulf of Carpentaria.

A whole week passed without Matt and me addressing the conversation; in fact, we barely spoke at all. Reading the cues, he gave me space, and for the first few days, I spent most of my time alone, watching movies and playing chess against the computer program on my phone.

Having lost weight in the Gulf, I put my body into a caloric surplus, supplementing my diet with chips and sweet biscuits to put the weight back on, knowing I'd be vomiting my way through the second stint. But I was also eating as a coping mechanism. Stuck on land, my buffer on the record was being reduced the longer we stayed put, and with my marriage hanging in the balance, it felt like the only way to get any joy was through the comedy movies I was devouring on my own and the endorphins that flooded my body with every bite of a biscuit.

Contributing to my low emotions was the fact that Josh was determined not to go back out into the Gulf. The past week had shaken him to his core and he was reluctant to put himself, his boat and the crew back into the life-threatening conditions out there. I, however, had no choice; though the winds kept coming, I'd have to face them if I was to complete the crossing.

Growing increasingly desperate, I took the trip into shore to seek out contacts in the Weipa community who could possibly help. Tege, a local boat captain, was up for the challenge. She was small in stature but a force to be reckoned with as one of the few women in her field. Tege informed me of an upcoming weather window.

'It's Sunday today; Thursday is your shot.' Tege spoke calmly but with conviction. 'If you don't go Thursday, you'll be stuck for months. These are the worst southeasterlies we've had in years, and they aren't stopping. I can take you on my boat but she's not that big and we'd get rolled around out there. Ask your skipper one last time.'

Armed with my newfound local insight, I arranged to meet with Josh and the crew to give it one last shot. Sitting around the dining table, the boys and I pleaded our case; we needed to get back out there, to complete the last 300 kilometres of the Gulf, and if it wasn't *Isabella* who accompanied me, I'd be forced to take a smaller boat that might not handle the conditions.

'I've been following the forecasts too,' Josh replied slowly. 'I agree that this Thursday is your only shot. I don't want to put the boat or crew back into that again, but I understand you've got no choice.'

Silently praying, I hung on his words, hoping he'd have a change of heart.

Finally, the skipper uttered the words that kept the expedition alive. 'I'll take you, but under one condition. When you get back out there, I need you to paddle harder than you ever have. We need to cover the distance as fast as possible, or we could be facing 30 knots of wind straight in the face.'

Josh's challenge made the hairs on the back of my neck bristle and I sat up straighter in my chair. Though one week before

I'd never wanted to look at my ocean ski again, something now shifted inside of me, as though I was answering a call to arms. Over 15 years as a professional athlete had readied me for moments like this one. The overall circumnavigation was a marathon, and it was important to pace myself to avoid injury, but what Josh was proposing was an all-out sprint. Rather than being intimidated, I was excited by the prospect. Having paddled 160 kilometres in 24 hours while in the Kimberley, with a fear of crocodiles driving me on, I wondered what was I capable of now. Perhaps I could push the limit once more, maybe even crack the seemingly impossible 200-kilometre mark within one day?

It was time to find out.

After a final shop to provision the boat, *Isabella* was fuelled in preparation for the voyage, but this time no stews or casseroles were prepared. We all knew what was coming; Blake and I were undoubtedly about to spend the next few days at sea hurling up the contents of our stomachs, and Josh would be too stressed to eat. Tina, meanwhile, would be staying on land and making her way to Seisia by car with Matt and Ben; suffering from severe migraines and seasickness at the same time on the first half of the crossing had been so awful that she didn't want to risk joining us for the second half.

*

On Wednesday 29 June, ten days after we'd anchored in Weipa, we headed back out to sea to finish what we'd started.

The farewell between Matt and I had been brief, both of us unsure what to say, but instead of sadness at the thought of our relationship ending, I felt numb. My mind focused on the task ahead; it was as though I had no emotion left for anything else. Athletes are notoriously selfish, a product of being told to prioritise our training and competition over everything else, and my actions over the week in Weipa confirmed it. As Matt, Ben and Tina stood on the jetty to watch us leave, little did anyone else know that Matt's worries went beyond the physical dangers we would soon be facing in the Gulf of Carpentaria.

Beginning our motor out to the starting mark at 10am, it was 11pm by the time Josh cued me to get ready.

'Twenty minutes from the mark,' the skipper shouted above the wind, as *Isabella* bobbed around like a cork in the angry seas. All four of us had spent most of the day lying flat on our backs trying to quell the feeling of nausea. Now just three kilometres from the mark, Jaime called Blake up from below deck to massage my shoulders in preparation for the paddle ahead. But when Blake arrived, his face was as white as a sheet. Kneeling to begin the massage, he fought to hold back the dry retching that had begun several hours prior.

'Where would you rather be?' I joked, as the boat slammed down hard against a huge wave, sending me sliding across the floor.

'This is what you call heavy duty,' Blake replied, in reference to his description of the Bight.

Blake wasn't wrong; this *was* heavy duty. But, I reminded myself, so were we. After loosening up my right bicep, Blake moved onto my left side, driving his thumb into my deltoid. At the same time, we were belted by breaking swell, which threw buckets of water over the deck. Blake released my arm and sprinted to the side of the boat to vomit. He stayed there for the next ten minutes. Returning even paler than before, he picked my arm up to continue, but I quickly told him not to worry about the rest of the massage.

Clambering into my ski just after midnight, it was with the steely sense of determination I'd had in the Bight. My stomach was swirling but my body was loose from the week off, and I felt capable of producing something special. Cranking my headphones up full blast, I began paddling to the aggressive sounds of UK rapper Stormzy. Not the time for the dulcet tones of Vance Joy, I needed some hardcore rap to give me a sense of invincibility. No matter what the next 24 hours were going to throw at me, I would be ready. Though my body was bruised and my spirits near broken, I would keep moving forward. This was my one chance, and I was going to make the most of it. Hitting start on my watch, I took my first few strokes into the 15-knot headwind, the swells resolute in their attempts to push me back to Darwin.

Twenty-three hours and 50 minutes later, I sobbed as Jaime sat on Bonnie Watch asking me trivia questions, urging me through the last part of what had been a torturous ordeal. Now 172 kilometres deep, my fingers were no longer capable of straightening, and my back screamed in protest with every rotation.

'What is the largest city in Turkey?' Jaime shouted over the wind, his presence over the last 24 hours crucial in getting me through. Halfway through the day, I had confirmed I was going to attempt a 24-hour stint to see if I could better the 160-kilometre mark set in the Kimberley. Unwavering in his support, Jaime had sat on the side of the boat in the huge seas, providing encouragement, updates and nutrition as I grinded through the final kilometres of the Gulf, motivated by the fact I would never have to do it again.

'Istanbul,' I finally answered, tears rolling down my cheeks as I remembered the city from the iconic James Bond movie *Skyfall*. Surprisingly, out of dozens of questions, I had answered just a few incorrectly. On high alert to the threat of falling out in the massive swells at night, after nearly 24 hours of paddling, I was recalling facts I'd struggle to remember on a good day. The power of the mind never ceases to amaze me, and I forced myself to focus on the next question as the pain threatened to overwhelm me at any moment.

Thankfully, I soon heard the words I'd waited all day to hear.

'Twenty-four hours, 173 kilometres. That's the furthest any woman has ever recorded paddling in open ocean. Congratulations!'

Jaime and Blake lit sparklers to mark the occasion. Offering a weak smile, it was not a sense of joy that overwhelmed me but relief. We were going to make it.

Now just 107 kilometres out from the smooth waters of Seisia, I knew I had the remaining distance in me, but I still had to execute it. Slowly making my way up to the safety of the boat, I didn't feel like a world beater but a young woman who had been given no choice. If I didn't finish off the Gulf within the one window presented, I could have been stuck on land for the next eight weeks waiting for a break in the wind that wouldn't come. I couldn't have remained idle for longer than two weeks, as per Guinness World Records rules, but there were no skippers willing to go out in those conditions other than Josh, and I couldn't have headed back out to the spot on my own as I would have had no way to navigate. The world record attempt would have been over. Instead, we were just one day from reaching mainland Queensland at Seisia to make the final right-hand turn of the expedition. Climbing aboard to see Josh struggling to hold *Isabella* steady, I felt incredibly grateful that he had dug deep and agreed to re-enter the hell hole of the Gulf so we could conquer it for good.

After another day's paddling, we made it to Seisia and allowed ourselves a day off. With a population just shy of 300, the pretty coastal town relies on a weekly drop of fresh food delivered to shore via a barge, but when conditions are rough, as was the case when we arrived, the barge cannot access the ramp and the town is left without many fresh-food items. Heading to shore, my first trip to the local cafe was to seek out an ice cream but I was disappointed to find the freezer empty, not even the less popular icy poles remaining. The only option was a fish burger or pizza for lunch, and we could forget washing it down with a soft drink because those were well and truly out of stock. Happy to be back on dry land with a settled stomach, the limited choices didn't bother me. I savoured my fish burger, watching on with amusement as each tourist who entered the shop was informed of the same thing: the barge still hadn't come.

Later in the afternoon, Josh, Tina, Matt and I piled into the Ranger to take the 40-kilometre drive up to Cape York. The northernmost point of Australia, the Cape would mark the last right-hand turn on my trip, after which I'd officially be on my way home. The prospect filled me with mixed emotions; I would have just 2500 kilometres of the expedition remaining, but with the southeasterly trade winds still ripping up the coast for the next few months, I'd be facing headwinds that rivalled those of the Gulf. This meant that, far from a victory stretch, my home state of Queensland would present one of the toughest slogs yet.

Something else was concerning me. I'd been able to manage my back throughout the trip so far with a combination of stretching and massage helping to relieve the tension, but I'd recently noticed a nasty pain in my spine. The spine is made up of a series of interlocking bones called vertebrae and between each one is soft tissue known as a spinal disc, with the discs essentially working as shock absorbers for the spine. Each disc contains a tough outer layer with gel in the middle. A bulging disc occurs when the spongey centre of the disc pushes out through a tear in the outer portion of the disc. A bulging disc can occur if too much pressure is applied to the disc, and if left untreated, it can rupture, causing spinal nerve impingement, which is extremely painful and takes a long time to heal.

I estimated the pain to be located around the lumbar vertebrae, towards the base of my spine, and the area was incredibly sore to touch. The pain had worsened halfway through the second stint of the Gulf, and I'd tried to ignore what I knew to be true: the symptoms pointed to a bulging disc. I hadn't experienced pain in my back so severe since the time I'd fractured two lumbar discs at the age of 21 when I was hit from behind by a rogue surf ski at training. Knowing how important my back was for lifelong healthy mobility, I found myself asking the question: *If this paddle leaves me with long-term physical ailments, will it be worth it?*

Grunting with pain as I slid into the passenger seat for the drive up to Cape York, I no longer felt certain of the answer. The next day I would slide back into the seat of my surf ski with no back support other than the back brace, the pressure on my lumbar spine continuing to increase. I could see a doctor or physio, but what was the point when I wouldn't be able to follow a treatment plant that would undoubtedly involve stopping the activity that was causing the trouble? With one fifth of the trip remaining, I was about to enter a whole new level of pain.

The only land access to Cape York was via a red-dirt road that pierced through tropical rainforest. I stuck my head out the window to take in the scenery, the varying shades of green providing a welcome change to the blues of the sea. Arriving at the Cape, we followed a dirt track around the headland until we reached a sign that officially marked the 'northernmost tip of the Australian continent'.

Laughing with Tina as I struggled to regain my balance after so much time spent at sea, I listened as she told stories of her life back home in Finland. When I'd first met her, Tina's strong accent had been difficult to understand, but by now I'd grown used to it. I empathised with her as she stated her intentions to return home as and when border restrictions allowed, not having seen her family in over two years. The conversation with Tina was a reminder of the world that existed outside the expedition. I'd been protected from the issues plaguing the world and, though my back was in an incredible amount of pain, I knew that once the expedition was over I'd miss the simplicity of life on the ocean.

Waiting until those before me had taken a photo next to the sign at the tip of the Cape, I slowly moved up to take my place as the northernmost human being on mainland Australia. I looked out towards the ocean. To my left, the sea stretched for hundreds of kilometres, and I tried to digest the fact that I had traversed the entirety of it by paddle. Swivelling around to the right, I felt the breeze on my face, the southerly wind announcing its presence. Focusing my sights on the body of water that lay ahead, I felt a sense of trepidation. After the Bight, I'd had several weeks of calm conditions along the coast of Western Australia, which had allowed me to drop the intensity of the paddling. But I didn't have such a luxury here. I would need to back up the tough stint in the Gulf facing huge headwinds. No one in recorded history had paddled west to east across the Gulf until I did, nor had anyone I knew of ever paddled down the east coast in July when the southerly winds are at their peak. But I had no choice. Bulging disc or not, we hadn't come 10,000 kilometres to back down now.

By the time we returned to Seisia, the barge had come and gone, leaving an abundance of fresh food. The takeaway shop had a line out the door and we were able to top up our supply of fruit and vegetables. We planned to head off the next day. It was time to go home. With over 15,000 people following our journey across various social-media platforms, the hype around the paddle was building, and we needed to finalise a date for our arrival home to the Gold Coast. We eventually chose 28 August and we were informed that *Seven Sunrise* would be broadcasting the event live while media outlets from around the country would have the opportunity to interview me and the crew.

Locking in the date and alerting our contacts across various media platforms was both exciting and nerve-racking; it was a relief to know that in seven weeks it would be over, but it also gave us an intimidating deadline. With 2500 kilometres of paddling between Seisia and the Gold Coast, that would mean I had to paddle just under 400 kilometres a week on average. If Josh was correct, there would be times over the coming weeks where the wind would be too strong to paddle against, and we would be forced to anchor behind one of the hundreds of islands that were scattered along the east coast. The average total of paddling required on any given week realistically might be much higher than 400 kilometres. This was going to hurt.

On 5 July, it was time to make the last right-hand turn. Setting off from Seisia at lunch, it was not with my regular crew: Ben had taken the place of Blake. Mentally and physically spent after the Gulf, Blake had asked for a reprieve. For the second leg of the Gulf, I'd barely seen him; the attacks of nausea so bad he was forced to lie flat on the back deck to limit the vomiting. Now almost seven months into the trip, Blake hadn't backed down from a single challenge, but over the past few weeks I'd seen him start to falter and knew he needed the time off to reset and return for the final stint. Tina rejoined us because the open-water section was done for now and it was safe for her to board without the prospect of painful migraines.

Rounding the Cape, I looked up to the sign where I'd had my photo taken the previous day. The northernmost tip of the country; what an experience it was to paddle around it. Savouring the moment, I heard the wind whistling above the crashing of the ocean as rocky cliffs dropped into crystal-clear waters below. I was inspired to confirm the promise I had made in the Pilbara. When this was all over, I wanted to come back to places like this and appreciate them from the perspective of land, where I could look out to the ocean and feel grateful for what the experience taught me. But for now, it was time to put my head down and paddle harder than ever before. Though I'd been hustling since 2020 after first committing to the circumnavigation, I now had just six weeks remaining. *No matter how much it hurts*, I thought to myself as I angled south to begin my first kilometre down the east coast, *you are ready.*

Over the next week, my speed averaged seven kilometres an hour as I put my head down and took on the full force of the southerly winds. Though still in crocodile territory, I knew the risk of an attack was lower because we were 50 kilometres out to sea, where fewer crocodiles ventured. The prehistoric reptiles were not top of mind as I pushed hard to make whatever small forward progress I could manage. I had completed just 40 kilometres on the first day since setting out from Seisia, and the following days were equally unimpressive: 66 kilometres, 51 kilometres and 68 kilometres respectively. My speed had essentially dropped to half the pace I would hold during strong tailwinds. I decided that the task was largely a battle with my mind, and I turned the music up to block out the pain. I tried not to stress about making it home in time for the scheduled arrival date, but I knew it was going to be tight.

On 9 July, I paddled into the waters of Lockhart River, a tiny coastal Indigenous community 800 kilometres north of Cairns. The weather forecast predicted winds of 40 knots hitting the coast on 13 July and hanging around for a week. We would have to find an anchorage by the 13th to wait out the rough conditions. By this stage, my aching fingers presented the biggest threat to ending the trip. Once more swollen and an agony to touch, I begged Josh for a few days off to let the swelling settle down.

From Lockhart River, we had two options for our targeted destination. The first was Lizard Island, 250 kilometres further south, which was home to a luxury resort where we could spend the week sipping cocktails on the beach and enjoying massages at the spa. The second option was a little closer but far more remote: Flinders Island, 213 kilometres away, would provide protection but offered no civilisation. Lizard Island sounded far more appealing, but by the time we left on the 12th we only had 24 hours until we needed to be safely anchored in protected waters before the gale-force winds hit. If I was to successfully complete the paddle to Flinders, I would need to paddle further in one day than I ever had before, cracking the 200-kilometre barrier in 24 hours that I had previously thought unbreakable. The 250 kilometres to Lizard Island was nearly unthinkable. Following discussion with Josh and the crew, I decided to set out for Flinders, with Lizard Island as a blue-sky target.

But for now we needed food. Currently demolishing our fresh produce at a rate of knots, we were nearly out of staples such as milk and eggs. Following a treacherous ride to shore in the tinny in huge swells, Josh dropped Jaime and me onto the beach at Lockhart River, and from there we intended to hitch our way to town to look for a grocery shop. We waited 15 minutes before realising no cars were coming, so we decided to run the five kilometres into town. We had to be careful not to slip on the gravel as our legs were unaccustomed to running. Up the road, we spotted a white car whipping up dust as it sped towards us and we immediately stuck our thumbs out to signal for a lift. The car sped straight past, so we set off running once more but soon spotted a Toyota ute heading our way. Waving dramatically, I prayed the driver would have the heart to help us; much to our relief, the vehicle slowed to a stop beside us.

Winding down the window, a middle-aged man stuck his head out.

'Hey there, you want a lift?' he asked, flashing a toothy grin. Hardly believing our luck, we quickly accepted his offer and clambered into the back of the vehicle next to two other men. The driver's name was Coco, and he'd lived in the area his whole life, recently commencing work on the new Telstra tower that was being installed there. They'd been returning from their lunch break when they saw us madly running up the road. Coco and his colleagues not only did a U-turn and dropped us at the shops, but waited outside while we collected our groceries and then drove us back to the beach to be picked up by Josh.

After everything the previous weeks had dished up, this simple act of kindness filled our hearts with a warmth that can only be experienced through genuine, heartfelt connection with others. When I think of Lockhart River, I don't remember the stress of running low on food and the panic to restock the boat but the generosity of some of the locals.

CHAPTER 14

TRAPPED IN PARADISE

THE THOUGHT OF PADDLING THOSE KILOMETRES IN 24 HOURS was sending my nerves into a frenzy. To keep myself calm that afternoon, I continued bingeing the movies and television shows I'd missed while at sea for the better part of a year and found I had no clue what was topical in popular culture. As a person who had always made a habit of listening to podcasts and watching evening news bulletins, I now felt completely naive due to my lack of exposure.

When I was unable to focus on the screen of my phone any longer, I headed to the galley to bake. I'd picked up several packet mixes during our whirlwind trip to the supermarket in Lockhart River, and selected vanilla cupcakes as my recipe of choice and got to work. The process took longer than usual because my hands weren't working at full capacity, but one hour later I had 24 warm cupcakes sitting on the kitchen bench. Placing a piece of white chocolate in the icing of each cupcake, I offered them around to the crew who thoroughly enjoyed the hit of sugar. Then I retreated to my cabin to prepare my paddling gear for the following day.

As the sun began to set, the intensity of the challenge ahead hit me. Sitting on the back deck, looking out over the water, I rang Matt to inform him of the 200-kilometre target Josh and I had discussed, but the reception kept cutting out and our exchange was brief. This was the perfect analogy for our relationship since the trip had begun. Hanging up, I accepted that a fluent chat was not possible, and the reassurance I was seeking from Matt wouldn't be coming. Despite my positive mindset as we'd rounded the Cape, I was now filled with self-doubt. Frustration and anxiety were getting the better of me, and I began to sob, covering my face with my hands to prevent Ben and Jaime from seeing. But sailing boats are far from the most private of places, and it didn't take long for Jaime to notice I was upset.

Ambling over, he prepared to speak but I beat him to it.

'I'm not ready to put myself through the pain again, mentally and physically,' I mumbled through my tears. 'The 173 kilometres in the Gulf took everything I had. I'm not ready to go back to that place again.'

'I know what it took from you to get the 173 kilometres done,' he said. 'But you can do this. We get a whole week off afterwards, chilling out at a deserted island. That will be pretty cool, hey?'

I hoped he was right. Though the boys weren't aware of my issues with Matt, they were incredibly astute and I think they knew there were problems. So far, I'd managed to ignore the guilt that slowly crept up when I remembered the conversation I'd had with Matt in Weipa, but now that we were separated by hundreds of kilometres of ocean, it was eating away at me. We had said our goodbyes with so many issues unresolved, and the burden of a relationship hanging by a thread combined with chasing a world record had started to become too much.

There was also another issue that had been bothering me. After completing 173 kilometres in the Gulf, I'd posted the achievement to social media, recognising the distance as the furthest ever paddled by a woman on an ocean ski. The previous record of open-ocean paddling in one day for a woman had stood at 150 kilometres. But in the comments section on Facebook, Instagram and via direct message, one man was quick to point out that the furthest distance paddled by a woman in one day was in fact 201 kilometres, which had been achieved in flat water on a kayak. Comparing paddling a kayak in flat water and an ocean ski in open water was like comparing apples and oranges; they were two separate classes entirely, and therefore there was a separate world-record division for each. Though I had pointed this out, I continued to receive abusive messages from this particular person and was forced to delete the comments on my public pages after my followers jumped in to defend my efforts and the whole situation risked turning nasty.

But the fracas lit a fire within me. *201 kilometres is the record on a kayak?* I mused. *Well, why don't I just beat that and shut them up for good?*

Once my tears had dried, I began to visualise the task ahead. Even though my back was in constant pain, I felt a determination settle over me as 202 kilometres in 24 hours became the new goal. Studying my hands, blisters from the Gulf freshly healed, I prayed for the top layer of skin to hold. I knew the inconceivable pain I'd experience if the skin broke and I was forced to repeat thousands of strokes with raw wounds slamming against the carbon fibre of my paddle.

The next morning, as I changed into my swimwear and windbreaker jacket, a sense of calm descended over me. It was the type of assuredness felt by athletes on the morning of a big race, when everything aligns for the perfect performance. Somehow I had shed the doubts of the previous evening and now I had a sense that I was going to bank some big kilometres and paddle us to safety. I knew that we would outsprint the gale-force winds closing in on us, and that I would paddle further in 24 hours than any woman had ever done, period.

Ascending the stairs from below, I found Ben and Jaime already on deck laying out my gloves, booties, watch and the food I'd need for the ultra-marathon ahead. They were doing everything they could to help me through what was coming.

'Let's do this. Time to go and check out that deserted island,' I said.

Jaime nodded his approval at my change in attitude, and as I sat down on the bench to put my sunscreen on, we shared a look. I knew we were both thinking the same thing: *Today we are going to achieve something special.*

It was 4.30am when I lowered myself into my ski to begin the first kilometre of paddling. For the next 24 hours Jaime and Ben swapped shifts on Bonnie Watch, and I switched up between tracks by 50 Cent and Eminem as I worked my way through each kilometre. If the 172 kilometres in the Gulf had been hell, I was now in paddling heaven. Feeling strong and sitting tall in my ski, I lifted my hands higher than I'd been capable of doing in the past, rotating through my core to gain maximum efficiency with each stroke. Now into July, the temperature had dropped to a cool 18 degrees, but my windbreaker jacket kept me warm. In the Gulf, I'd made the mistake of wearing tight thermals and had paid the price with excessive chafing. Now wiser, I donned a light windbreaker, which was loose enough to give my skin a reprieve, and this time I smiled while answering the trivia questions Jaime had once again prepared.

During the first 50 kilometres, I had light headwinds to contend with, but this time I wasn't bothered. *Bring it on*, I silently challenged Mother Nature. Having faced so much adversity over the 11,000 kilometres of paddling since I'd left home, and with my new mindset, I was feeling battle-hardened.

Josh had been following the forecasts and had been anticipating a change in the wind. At the 50-kilometre mark, the breeze on my face lessened and the paddling became easier. 'Here we go, just as predicted,' the skipper called from the helm. 'It will only get flatter from here.'

It was as though someone had suddenly turned off the

enormous natural fan that had been blasting me in the face since Darwin, and I found myself paddling on a silky-smooth surface.

'How good!' I called out. I no longer had to contain my emotions and stifle frustration but instead felt a genuine sense of joy. It reminded me of when I'd caught my very first wave on a surf ski at the tender age of 17. How far I'd come since then. That same girl, who'd once had to drag a heavy second-hand surf ski down a sandy beach track to the water, was now mowing down kilometre after kilometre in the middle of nowhere, gaining speed as she went.

'Hey, Benny, can you grab me one of those cupcakes?' I called, the familiar signs of low blood sugar starting to hit. Carried away with paddling fast, I hadn't eaten enough throughout the morning, and suddenly needed some fast-release carbohydrates. Hurrying below deck, Ben returned with a sealed plastic bag containing one of the vanilla cupcakes. Grabbing the bag extended to me, I placed the cupcake into my mouth, savouring the sugary icing.

'Yum!' I squealed, mouth full of cupcake. 'They are even more delicious today!' Perhaps it was because I was in a mood to see the glass half full, or maybe because the sugar provided a welcome relief from the taste of salt water; whatever the cause, the cupcake was the most delicious thing I'd eaten in my life. Licking the bag clean, I silently thanked my past self for making the treats, which had given me an extra energy boost and resolved the issue of low blood sugars.

Jaime had come onto Bonnie Watch by the time I finished the cupcake, and as he adjusted the volume on the speaker that hung over the side of the boat, I informed him of my new plan.

'Every 50 kilometres, I'm going to ask for a cupcake,' I told him, creating my own reward system.

'No worries by me,' Jaime said. 'You just let us know when you hit 50 kilometres. Then it's cupcake time.'

Sure enough, 50 kilometres of paddling later I ate my next cake. Just as delicious as the first, it was a perfect reward for another block of five hours of effort, and as I devoured the vanilla icing of the baked treat, I already looked forward to the next one.

I ate the next cupcake around sunset, as the first dramatic streaks of orange made their way across the pale sky, the colours magnified by the absence of light pollution. Now 150 kilometres down, I knew if I could complete just 50 more kilometres, the 202-kilometre mark I was so desperate to reach would be within sight. The endorphins from the start of the paddle were beginning to fade, and I found I was now powered by the hate I'd received on social media. *Stuff you*, I thought, bringing to mind the profile picture from my critic's Facebook page. *I'll show you what a world record looks like.*

The skin on my blisters finally burst open and the open wounds stung in the salt water. I thanked my critics for the extra motivation. If there had been any prior doubt in me about reaching the double century, I now knew the only uncertainty lay in how far past 201 kilometres I would get.

As darkness fell, Ben affixed torches to the side of the boat to help guide me, and we recommenced a debate begun at the start of the trip. Both keen sports fans as well as athletes, Ben and I had argued over whether sprinter Usain Bolt or marathon runner Eliud Kipchoge, both the greatest of all time in their fields, was the better athlete.

'Kipchoge is the better athlete,' Ben insisted. 'He could cross into what Bolt does easier than the other way around and his margin of winning is greater.'

'No way,' I retorted. 'Bolt's margin of error is far less. One mistake and he loses. Kipchoge could muck his start up and still win.'

The argument continued for some time before we decided neither of us would change the other's point of view, so we switched topics to talk about nicknames.

'I still like LeBon James for you,' Ben said, reminding me of the moniker he'd developed early into the adventure. 'Or Bonald Trump.'

At 2.30am, with two hours to go until the 24-hour time limit was up, I hit 202 kilometres. Glancing down at my watch, with Jaime studying the spare watch hanging on the boat, we both let out a loud cheer. I'd done it. The furthest distance paddled on a ski or kayak by a woman in any conditions, ocean or flat water.

'How do you feel?' Jaime asked me on camera.

'Relieved,' I answered honestly. 'Mainly relief.' Though the reaction might be considered an anti-climax, I no longer had the energy to celebrate. As though a relentless desire to reach the set target had blocked feelings of fatigue, I was suddenly spent. Although I expected the heaviness in my arms, I realised my hands were bleeding, with blisters giving way to deep cuts. Deep chafing was stinging my underarms. I also became aware of windburn on my lips, and I wondered how long it had been there.

In surpassing the 202 kilometres I felt vindicated, but I now wanted to send a clear message to my doubters. In putting a buffer between my new mark and the old one, I would let the critics know to never give an athlete extra motivation.

At 3.30am, with one hour to go before the 24 hours was up, I decided to call it. The rap music blasting from the speakers had been downgraded to pop, and I sang loudly to James Blunt's 'Beautiful'. I forced my muscles to keep moving, but my pace had dropped to a snail-like three kilometres an hour. *Just get to the island*, I'd told myself at 205 kilometres when my lips cracked and I tasted blood. *Just get to the island.*

And now, for the first time in 23 hours, I stopped paddling. Hitting stop on my watch, I looked up to see Ben and Jaime, huge grins spread across their faces. Tina had again been forced to lie down for the day due to migraines, but Josh had manned the helm for the duration of the paddle, monitoring the chart plotter to check our line and providing me with regular updates. Looking down at my illuminated watch face, I saw a total of 213 kilometres.

I had needed my body and mind to step up, and they had more than delivered. Years as a professional athlete had paid off when needed. My emotional meltdown the day before had acted as a release, ridding me of all doubt when it counted.

Some critics had said I'd never make it past Sydney. Then, when I paddled past Sydney Harbour, I'd been told the remote waters of Victoria would be far too dangerous. In reaching Adelaide and preparing to cross the Bight, the doubters had said an east to west crossing couldn't be done, and in walking out of hospital after a successful Bight crossing, I'd read a message saying the crocodiles would get me before the Northern Territory. When I stood in front of a crowd after paddling to Darwin, I'd been told I'd never make it across the Gulf against the southerlies, and when I did, I'd been slammed on social media by a person who tried to question my credibility. Finally, as I gritted my teeth and forced my legs to carry me up the ladder to safety, my hamstrings locking up after 23 hours crammed into a seat measuring 45 centimetres wide, I knew that finally, no one could question what was fact. Against odds including headwinds, the most dangerous animals in the world and a global pandemic, I'd fought my way through and made it to Queensland. It had taken a mammoth effort to get to safety, but I'd done it. And now, as we motored towards the bay that would shelter us from winds that would threaten to de-mast the sturdiest of boats, I knew beyond doubt that in less than two months' time, I would be home.

'The winds are hitting in a few hours,' Josh informed me as he checked our position on the map. 'Let's make our way to our new home for the next week: Flinders Island.'

'Sounds good to me,' I replied from my position flat on the floor of the back deck, attempting to ease the muscles in my lower back that had begun to spasm. Wondering if the island had been named after the British explorer Matthew Flinders, who had sailed around Australia in 1802, I instead decided to use the last of my raspy voice to address a more pressing need. 'Can somebody please get me a cupcake?'

I was soon presented with a Tupperware box full of five cupcakes, which I proceeded to devour in world-record time.

As we motored into Flinders Island in the dark, I could barely make out the shape of the island. The curvature of the bay was evident in the glow of the half-moon that was now low in the sky and I was just able to make out the headlands.

When I emerged from below deck the following day, it was to a view of tropical rainforest meeting pure white sand running into crystal-clear water. This was paradise.

'Wowww.' Jaime's appreciation was audible from where he and Ben sat up the front of the boat, taking in the scenery. Tina's migraine had dissipated with our arrival in calm waters, and Josh appeared relaxed for the first time in weeks.

Wurriima (Flinders Island) has been home to the Yiithuwarra people for thousands of years. During World War II, the Australian Defence Force took over control of the seven islands within the Flinders Island Group, but the Yiithuwarra successfully claimed them back under the *Aboriginal Land Act (Qld)* in 1991. The islands are now jointly managed by the Cape Melville, Flinders and Howick Islands Aboriginal Corporation with the Queensland government. Evidence of the thriving community that once lived there can be seen in the dozens of painted images on the rock walls featuring native animals such as crocodiles, dugongs and turtles.

A popular anchorage for cruising yachts and fishing trawlers, Flinders Island offers protection from all directions except southwest storms in the wet season. When we arrived, there were two other private vessels anchored in the bay, seeking protection from the storms just like us. The larger catamaran belonged to a family with two young children, and the smaller yacht was owned by a Japanese woman in her fifties, who had sailed from her native country solo. Jaime and Ben introduced themselves to her when they took the tinny for a spin to check out the area, and they later shared her story with me, including about the running repairs she'd had to do while at sea on her own. I was amazed at the amount of resilience shown in such a situation. Clearly I wasn't the only woman in the area who was pushing the limits and defying the odds.

When Josh and Tina returned with the tinny after heading to land to stretch their legs, the rest of us hopped in to check out the beach for ourselves. Stepping off the boat onto the warm, soft sand, I giggled with joy as I twisted my feet from side to side and sank down further, luxuriating in the natural pedicure the beach provided. Taking a few tentative steps, it was as though I'd been hit by a train. I hadn't felt this sore since the Gulf or maybe even my first boxing session with Pat O'Keefe. I limped along the beach towards the mangroves, careful to keep a safe distance from the water, as per Josh's instructions.

'It may look beautiful,' the skipper had warned, 'but there's plenty of crocs in this place. Be careful. Don't even think of going for a swim.'

Heeding Josh's warning, I kept my head turned towards the shoreline, watching for any dark shapes. Crocodiles are fast across the land as well as in the water, and I wasn't keen on becoming one of the few tourists lost to a crocodile attack.

Returning to *Isabella* in the evening, we found Josh preparing a roast to celebrate our arrival in safe waters. For a man who had spent most of his life fixing equipment and maintaining a 60-tonne yacht, Josh was an excellent cook and took pride in what he was able to create in the kitchen. Each time he entered the galley, we knew in a few hours' time we'd be treated to a flavour bomb of herbs, spices and meat cooked to perfection. My hands were still only functioning at half of their usual capacity, so I was grateful to be relieved of the expectation to use a grater or whisk. Instead my focus was on conserving as much energy as possible so I'd be ready to take on the ocean again when the time came.

The following day, Josh dropped the boys and me to the beach at neighbouring Stanley Island to view carvings created thousands of years ago. Admiring the art and learning about the strong Indigenous history in the region, we took pride in writing our names in the guest book. That evening, under the light of the moon, we danced around the fire we made on the beach and toasted homemade damper in the ashes. Returning to the boat after the last embers had died, we were treated to a delicious pasta for dinner, made with the scallops and prawns Josh had bought from some trawlers that had anchored next to us in the bay.

On day three, the mood on the boat started to change as people grew restless. With no reception on the island, Ben, Jaime and I turned to watching movies from Josh's hard drive on the flat-screen television in the living room of the boat. Beginning with *The Hobbit*, we made our way through each of the sequels in the franchise. Josh and Tina, meanwhile, watched films on the television in their room, as everyone tried to pass the time until it was safe to head back out to sea. For now, the safest place for us physically was tucked in between the two islands as the 40-knot winds whipped through the area, but I could see the mental wellbeing of those around me starting to decline.

The only form of communication with anyone on the mainland was via the satellite phone and Garmin inReach, a satellite device that was designed for adventurers to take with them as a tracker but on which you can also send short messages. Shaped like a radio, the inReach was small but bulky, and anything beyond a simple message took a painfully long time to construct. I was initially hesitant to use the device as there was no urgent need after Josh had informed Matt of our safe arrival via satellite phone. But by day three, I picked up the inReach and asked Ben to teach me how to use it.

The first message took 20 minutes to type, but I soon figured out how to use the device more efficiently.

Hi. Safe here on the island. Have been checking out the carvings and watching movies. Hope you're all good. Bon x

Hitting send, I made the first contact with Matt in over a week. His reply was immediate.

So good to hear from you, it read. *All good here onshore. I'm in Townsville. What else have you been up to?*

The next message I typed took ten minutes but was worth the investment as Matt and I corresponded for the next few days. He filled me in on what was happening in the world and I tried to sound upbeat as I spoke of the beauty of the island, not dwelling on the reality of the situation.

The truth was that if on day three we were restless, by day four tempers had grown short, and people had begun isolating themselves from each other. Too much time spent with any one person isn't healthy, but spending all day every day with five people on a boat? It was a recipe for disaster. With Ben spending more and more time alone in his cabin, Jaime took to driving the tinny to the island for solo time. On some days, Josh and Tina spent most of the day in their cabin, and I found myself looking for tasks to keep me occupied.

On day five, I chose to handwash all my clothes and dry them on the line, as opposed to using the perfectly good washing machine Josh and Tina had invested in. Choosing a more labour-intensive method that took twice as long seemed to make sense at the time, but in looking back now, I realise that, like the others around me, I had also started to lose the plot. My fingers had regained much of their strength during the break, so I began baking in an attempt to stay sane, making carrot cake, scones and a bircher muesli for breakfast. With so much of my time and energy invested in paddling, I'd been unable to give back to my crew in the ways I would have liked, and the baked goods were a small token of my appreciation for them.

On day six, the flat screen in the living room broke amid our viewing of the third *Lord of The Rings* movie, and we knew our sanity was on the line. We sat dejectedly watching the thin grey line work its way across the screen, as our main form of entertainment was taken from us. Each of us was terrified to tell Josh that his beloved flat screen was broken, but he took the news surprisingly well.

'Ah well, it's been on the way out for a while,' he reassured us, after a few unsuccessful attempts to bring the television back to life. Relieved, we moved on to Uno, but no longer had the same enthusiasm as when we'd played the card game seven months earlier on the east coast.

Our island paradise was now feeling like a prison, and for every day we were stuck on the boat, our food supplies dwindled a little further. Already low on butter and cheese, Josh informed us that if we were stranded for three more days, we'd be forced to move on to rations of beans and rice.

'But we'll worry about that when we get there,' Josh muttered as he closed the hatch that led to the stores of rations. 'The wind looks to be dropping in a few days. Hope you're ready to paddle again.'

I was more than ready. In fact, I'd been ready after two days on the island. My body had repaired the muscle tissue I'd damaged through the recent 23-hour stint. Each day we spent at Flinders Island was eating into the buffer I'd worked so hard to build up by cutting across the Bight and Gulf, risking my life to save time and distance. The aching around my lumbar discs was also worsening, and I wanted to give myself every chance to recover before the next push towards home but I was limited in what I could do to help myself. A daily trip to the beach was proving helpful, but I wished I could dive into the water to loosen up my muscles with a swim.

Continuing to bake and wash clothing, I tried to stay patient. Though the wind had dropped to 35 knots out at sea, we needed a maximum reading of 25 knots before Josh would consider going back out there. Fortunately, the forecasts predicted our next window to be the following day, and as Josh ran me through the charts, I prayed the forecasts would be accurate.

And so, on day seven, after a week of waiting for the wind to drop, it was time. As we motored out to the mark where I'd finished one week before, spirits were high, and Josh was in a particularly good mood.

'Finally!' he exclaimed. 'It's time to head home.'

Pulling my gloves on, the task easy now thanks to the reduced swelling in my fingers, I smiled at his enthusiasm. We were back.

What's that saying about best-laid plans? As it turned out, I needn't have bothered putting on gloves or changing into my paddling gear. As soon as we motored beyond the protection of the island, the wind picked up well beyond the 20 knots predicted. *Isabella* quickly began rolling from side to side, and it became evident I'd be unable to make any forward progress in the angry conditions. Dejected, Josh turned the boat around and began sailing back the way we'd come. Flinders Island was not yet ready to release us from her clutches.

The mood on our return was low, and we each retreated to our separate quarters to wait out another day of minimal productivity. If we had one more week without paddling, I'd be disqualified from my world-record attempt. In a cruel twist of fate, I was physically able to continue, but Mother Nature wasn't giving an inch. Perched at the dining-room table, I turned to my journal to detail the events that had transpired over the past week and to release the immense frustration that had washed over me following the failed attempt to escape. I was ready to work harder than I ever had in my life, to not play board games and watch movies, and the unsuitable conditions had relegated me to a couch potato.

To everyone's great relief, the following day, 12 July, we were able to break the hold Flinders Island had over us. Feeling a sense of déjà vu, we motored out to the starting mark, but this time the wind had dropped significantly and instead of being forced to turn back, I climbed into my ski and powered forward. Pushing into the 20-knot winds, my body pulsing with energy after a week of lethargy, my muscles relished the opportunity to do what they'd become conditioned to.

The deserted island had been an excellent social experiment. The remote location had seemed like heaven for the first few days, but then as we began to crave all of the luxuries of life on land and the hustle and bustle of civilisation, the place had turned into a prison. Instead of the lethargy and intense boredom experienced on the island, I was grateful to be back bashing into the headwind, my fingers quickly increasing in size from the fluid that filled my joints. Ten kilometres in, the agony in my back returned, but I no longer resented it. I welcomed the pain now, as pain was associated with paddling, and every metre of paddling put more distance between us and the prison in paradise from which we'd escaped.

And with every metre of paddling, we edged closer to the Gold Coast.

Turning around to see that Flinders Island had faded to a speck in the distance, I now felt safe to focus my attention on the task at hand and let the reality sink in.

Finally, we were heading home.

CHAPTER 15

FULL CIRCLE

It took seven days to paddle the 377 kilometres from Flinders Island to Cairns, and by the time I reached the busy coastal city, the swelling and pain in my fingers made it impossible to pick up a pen, write in my journal or even open the fridge door. I now wore Josh's thick trawling gloves made of Kevlar, which gave me more grip on the paddle than the spearing gloves. I could relax my fingers and hands better in these gloves, but the headwinds averaged 15 knots most days, and I still found myself gripping the paddle tightly to prevent myself from tipping off my ski, as the ocean flung me around like a rag doll.

Reaching Cairns on 25 July left us with just over one month to get to the Gold Coast in time for the welcoming party on 28 August. It would have been a breeze to complete 1200 kilometres in 33 days with a tailwind, but the relentless headwinds were slowing the speed of my paddling significantly. A standard day saw me completing 50–60 kilometres, as opposed to the

120 kilometres I would have liked. I realised that rather than an easy homecoming, the final stretch would require me to push myself to the extreme once more.

We had initially planned to only have a short break in Cairns before beginning the push home, but Josh brought us some bad news after dropping anchor.

'The winds are picking up.' The skipper's tone was serious as he showed me the weather forecast on his iPad. 'It's too windy to paddle for the next few days at least. We may be here for a week.'

A sense of anxiety washed over me. I dropped back down on the back bench so Ben and Jaime could remove my gloves, sunglasses and back brace to wash them in fresh water.

What was a tough but achievable task in reaching the Gold Coast by the end of August had just become a whole lot harder. If we were holed up in Cairns for a week, it would be tight. Previously, our timeframe of 33 days required 37 kilometres of paddling a day on average. The forecasts predicted big winds over the next few weeks, so we would likely face further stints of being forced to seek shelter behind an island or headland until the ocean settled. Any days off would push the average daily kilometres required upwards, increasing our chances of missing the all-important 28 August deadline.

There was thankfully far more to distract us in the bustling tourist destination of Cairns than there had been on remote Flinders Island. What I didn't expect, however, was my difficulty in assimilating back into civilisation. Wandering slowly up the busy main street on the first day after so much time at sea, every shout and blast of a car horn seemed amplified. Crossing the road was a challenge; not only were my legs weak from lack of use, but my sudden exposure to this high amount of stimuli was overwhelming. A lack of stimulus on the island had made me lethargic, but the city was too much. As I wandered up the various aisles at the chemist to stock up on cream for my rashes and anti-inflammatories for my back, I knocked items off the shelves as I bumped into them. After nearly eight months on the ocean, it was difficult to walk in a straight line, and no matter how hard I tried, I couldn't seem to coordinate my arms with my lower body.

Later in the day, I sat in a cinema for the first time in nearly a year, as Blake, Jaime and I watched Australian director Baz Luhrmann's critically acclaimed biopic *Elvis*. As entertaining as the movie was, there was a special reason for the outing. Jaime had worked as a production assistant on the film. The three of us clapped and cheered when we spotted Jaime's name in the end credits and, for a few moments, I forgot the burden of the enormous load of kilometres left to paddle.

After five days in Cairns, the wind decreased to 15 knots, meaning it was time to pack the dresses away and put the paddling gear back on. It was 31 July by the time we left Cairns Marina. Every day on land had fuelled an increasing sense of desperation to get back in the water and I was relieved to get moving.

Throughout the last eight months, I had noticed an unfavourable pattern in my moods on days that I wasn't paddling, and the feeling of depression and anxiety that I again experienced in Cairns concerned me. I was reminded of several messages received on Instagram and Facebook over the past month. Sent from various adventurers and ultra-endurance athletes, they had warned of the anti-climax often experienced once a journey is over.

'Be careful of the low,' a successful ultra-marathon runner warned me. 'Keep yourself busy and make sure you don't come back to nothing.'

'Don't just spend the days lying on the beach,' a world-record-breaking ultra-endurance swimmer had advised. 'You need to keep yourself mentally and physically engaged.'

The advice alerted me to a harsh reality. So busy with the planning and execution of the expedition, I hadn't put any thought into the aftermath. How would I feel the day after arriving home, when there was no need to slide trawling gloves onto aching fingers or strap a back brace around my waist? How would I feel when I didn't constantly have a team around me to assist with whatever I required, my every wish their command? How would I manage when I didn't have a tangible goal each day? Would I hit a low? Would I know how to keep myself busy as a regular person, not the world-beating athlete I'd been for eight months? Though I didn't yet have the answers, I took the warnings seriously. I promised myself to take their advice and ensure I didn't come back to 'nothing'.

As a young ironwoman, much of my self-worth had been placed in my ability as an athlete. Even if I had a great result, I was incredibly hard on myself, picking my performance apart and often experiencing an extreme low the day after a race. Now aged 32, I was determined that whatever happened – if I got the world record or not, if the global pandemic shut the project down in the last few weeks, or if we were stuck behind an island for two months and I didn't meet the deadline – I would be okay. I knew I'd still have my friends, family and a lifetime of incredible memories made over the space of eight months. No matter what happened, I wouldn't come home to nothing.

*

Thinking I'd seen everything the Australian coastline had to offer, I didn't realise there were more surprises in store. Each year from June to August, Australia's east coast becomes a 'humpback highway' as around 40,000 humpback whales make their way north after a summer of feeding in Antarctic waters. Reaching a maximum of 16 metres, these majestic creatures can be seen travelling in groups led by young males, with pregnant females or females with their calf bringing up the rear. Humpbacks are known for putting on spectacular displays of acrobatics as they throw themselves out of the water, and we began looking out for the iconic species.

Five kilometres out from Townsville, we spotted a mother and calf splashing about, 500 metres directly in front of us. Without thinking twice, I paddled towards the pair to get a closer look.

'Be careful!' I could just make out Josh's words of caution as he manoeuvred *Isabella* further out to sea as per the maritime regulations that advise boats to stay 100 metres away from whales.

Before long, I was just 50 metres from the massive creatures and I slowed down until I was floating, careful not to startle them. A giant bubble appeared on the water's surface as both whales disappeared out of sight. They were likely getting a closer look at the foreign pink and white ski that had appeared next to them. Gently placing my paddle onto my knees, I didn't feel scared, because by now I had spent so much time on the ocean it felt comfortable and familiar.

Suddenly noticing how quiet it was without the continuous hum of *Isabella*'s engines or the crash of my paddle as I bashed into another incoming swell, I realised the wind had dropped and for the first time in months, the surface of the ocean was glassy. It was the perfect day for whale watching. *But where have they gone?* They'd been within touching distance just a minute prior, and I now couldn't see the whales anywhere.

Placing my legs into the water on either side of my ski to balance, I looked directly below and saw an enormous white belly. *Stay calm*, I told myself, desperately trying to remain steady on the ski. The mother was getting a better look at me, perhaps assessing whether I posed a threat to her baby. I was aware of stories of paddlers who'd been knocked from their ski or board by a whale, and I knew my fate was out of my hands; if the 500-kilogram creature chose this moment to surface, there was little I could do.

Obviously deciding I wasn't a threat, the enormous humpback soon retreated, angling down as a gentle swish of her tail propelled her towards the ocean floor. Surfacing 50 metres away with her calf safely beside her, she disappeared once more before performing a spectacular leap out of the water, crashing back down into the ocean with an almighty splash. I was very grateful she hadn't performed the manoeuvre one minute earlier, and I was able to enjoy the show, my respect and admiration for the beautiful creatures increasing even more. Coming face to face with a humpback whale remains one of the most special experiences of my life. Along with dolphins and seals, I see whales as the peacekeepers of the ocean and in the presence of these animals, I always feel safe.

Loud cheers erupted from *Isabella*, and I looked up to find the crew had witnessed the event, capturing it on film. Nearly eight months into the expedition, I was still enjoying first-time experiences. The leap of faith I'd taken in starting this expedition had led me to a private show featuring one of the most fascinating creatures on earth. More than ever, I appreciated my fateful discovery of Freya's book in the library that day. While paddling in the Bight, I had been treated to a sky full of stars so bright I felt I could touch them, and now here I was, within reach of one of the ocean's most elusive creatures. The paddle had brought me so many incredible experiences, and though I was excited to be almost home and soon be able to have my injuries tended to, part of me didn't want the adventure to end.

Word of my expedition had reached the community of Townsville, and as I made my way to the area, local paddlers joined me for the last few kilometres of the day. Turning to my right, I saw the Townsville women's outrigging team grinning as they kept pace with me, and to my left, several ocean paddlers urged me on as they stroked alongside. The support helped me finish off another huge day on the ocean. It had been months since I'd had extended interaction with anyone outside of my crew, and it was invigorating to hear new voices, see new faces and catch up on what had been going on in the world outside our bubble. Like a puppy taken to the park for the first time, I lapped up every conversation. I answered hundreds of questions about the paddle and also asked questions of my own, desperate for new stories and information. Without realising it, I was slowly beginning my assimilation back into civilisation.

Paddling into Seaforth off Mackay on 8 August, it was the first time I'd felt safe since we'd entered crocodile territory around Broome over three months before. Mackay marked the southernmost point on the east coast where crocodiles were considered a risk. A huge weight lifted from my shoulders. Somehow, through keeping my speed high and perhaps some sheer dumb luck, I'd paddled over 5000 kilometres in crocodile-inhabited waters without being attacked. Often asked post paddle whether I'd do the circumnavigation again, my answer is always no, not least because paddling an ocean ski in the Northern Territory and Far North Queensland is like tempting fate. I was running the gauntlet every time I climbed into my ski at night in regions known for the lethal predators, and I'm not naive to the fact that I got very, very lucky.

We were to spend three days in Mackay, where I met up with Matt. We headed to his parents' place while Blake and Jaime went to visit Blake's family. Meanwhile, Ben had taken a brief trip back to the Gold Coast and would rejoin us in a few days. The days off provided the perfect opportunity for Matt and me to address the conversation in Cairns, but even after all this time, neither of us knew what to say. The truth was that we had been apart for the majority of the previous eight months, and now we felt like married strangers. Rather than excitedly sharing stories of our experiences on land and on the ocean, we spent most of the break in silence, as though on an awkward first date.

It was impossible to do justice to everything that had happened at sea when I tried to explain it to Matt, and by the time I saw him, I'd already debriefed with my boat crew. The crew and I had shared celebratory dinners after treacherous open-water crossings, planned world-record-breaking feats together and witnessed fascinating creatures up close. We shared a bond forged by weeks without seeing land, debilitating seasickness and successfully achieving what had never been done before. All Matt wanted was a first-hand account of the journey he'd devoted two years of his life to, but I didn't know where to start. In the same room but feeling worlds apart, we were unsure what the future held. Both as individuals and together.

*

Josh had made a promise in Darwin to escort us back to the Sunshine Coast, and he made good on his word. Since my humpback whale encounter, the wind had swung to a northerly, which allowed us to make solid progress from Mackay past Rockhampton, Bundaberg and Hervey Bay. As we did so, local paddlers from the various locations joined in for short legs, and slowly but surely my social skills returned, as did my physical coordination thanks to spending more time on land. My ears were still sensitive to the sound of a speeding car, and I couldn't handle buttons or zips on my own because of the ongoing swelling in my fingertips, but I knocked over items far less frequently and no longer found everything a trip hazard.

At Inskip Point, south of K'gari (Fraser Island) and just 250 kilometres from the Gold Coast, it was time to say goodbye to Josh and Tina. Matt had contacted Darren Mercer of Noosa Heads Surf Life Saving Club and had organised a catamaran to accompany us back to the Gold Coast. The catamaran was owned by a Noosa family called the Thompsons, with dad Novak and mum Jo often spending time on the water with their teenage sons, Kai and Finn. The entire family were active members of the surf club. Kai showed promise across both beach and water events and stated his intention to join me for part of the final stint. It was fitting that I'd complete the last few hundred kilometres with a promising young athlete by my side. For the past eight months, I'd pushed my mental and physical boundaries well beyond what I'd thought possible, and I hoped that somewhere, someday, a kid of Kai's generation would read my book and be inspired to push their own limits.

As was in Josh's nature, his parting words were brief. After enjoying a reflective dinner on the boat the evening prior,

I'd presented him with one of my spare paddling t-shirts, emblazoned with my key sponsors. When he dropped our gear to Inskip Beach with the tinny, he proudly wore the shirt, and I felt grateful that he'd signed up as part of our team. A gruff goodbye from the tinny was all I received as he restarted the motor to tear off into the distance, back to Tina and *Isabella*. But words weren't needed, as Josh had validated me the night before as we enjoyed our last supper together.

'That was a bloody good effort,' he'd told me in between mouthfuls of roast lamb. 'You did good. You did real good.' Though he had a different way of showing it, I knew Josh was pleased to have met us too.

Paddling out from Inskip Point, it was strange not to have *Isabella* beside me, and for the first few kilometres I felt a little lost, searching for the vessel that had kept me company for several thousand kilometres. Fortunately, I was joined by Ben, Jaime and Blake on the jet ski, but with the roar of the engine, the ability to hold a conversation with the crew was very limited. Peering up ahead, I could just make out the silhouette of our final support vessel as she sliced through the water towards us. The Thompsons were the last of my guardian angels who would help guide me safely home.

Finishing the 59-kilometre paddling day at the stunning Double Island Point, I climbed aboard the Thompsons' boat for the first time, and into a family vibe comparable to the Kiwis'. The environment was exactly what I needed to settle my nerves as I prepared for my big arrival back on the Gold Coast.

The following day, skipper Novak set the autopilot on a direct line to Noosa Beach located 60 kilometres away. As I climbed into my ski and began the first kilometre of the day, a pod of dolphins popped up to join me. It was as though I was floating on water, and the paddling was easy in the slight cross wind. The knowledge that we were just a few days from home gave me a burst of energy and put a genuine smile on my face for the first time in months. With the worst of the headwinds behind us, the strength in my hands and forearms built up from previously bashing into southerlies made paddling in the favourable conditions a breeze.

Noosa is recognised as one of the most beautiful locations in Australia, attracting hundreds of thousands of tourists annually to its pristine beaches, and it didn't disappoint. Ironman legend Darren Mercer and his daughter Jordie, another icon of surf lifesaving and ocean ski paddling, know the Noosa coastline like no others. I soaked up their enthusiasm as I was escorted into the beach by them and other members from the Noosa squad, including Coolangatta gold champion Carla Papac.

Heavily pregnant at the time, Jordie was still paddling a ski better than most. She had been my original inspiration for taking up long-distance ocean ski paddling in addition to surf lifesaving, so paddling with her now made it feel like things had come full circle. Though only 30, Jordie possessed a certain wisdom, like she just *knows things*. Paddling alongside this champion athlete, I was struck by the fact that Jordie always looked blissfully happy in the ocean, taking time to surf, stand-up paddleboard and enjoy the ocean in a way that went far beyond how fast she could move through it.

Looking in to shore, the surface of the water glistening in the sun as though covered in crystals, I made a silent pledge to view the ocean as more than a training ground. Moving forward, I would value the ocean as providing a chance for cleansing, allowing me to wash away previous worries and connect with nature in its purest form. Each plunge into the sea would be a chance to start again.

'If you look further south, you'll start to make out the high rises of the Sunshine Coast,' Jordie briefed me, as we rounded the Noosa headland. And sure enough, as I peered into the distance, I could just make out the skyline of Mooloolaba and Maroochydore.

'It's time for me to go,' Jordie gently informed me, as she and the rest of the Noosa squad prepared to turn back towards the surf club. 'You've got this.'

Turning back to watch the paddlers fade into the distance, I knew Jordie was right.

It was 24 August and I had just 163 kilometres to paddle. I was going to make it home in time.

True to his word, Kai accompanied me over the following two days as I paddled past the Sunshine Coast and Brisbane. Occasionally he switched with Novak and Jaime to allow them a paddle, but for the most part, he ground out the final kilometres of the expedition alongside me, and I greatly welcomed his positive attitude.

On 26 August, I saw the Gold Coast skyline for the first time in eight months. Dave Gardner, one of the early backers of the project and the man who had provided us with the Ranger, joined Matt on the jet ski to witness the moment. Paddling inside North Stradbroke Island, I'd spent most of the morning choosing songs to blast on the boat speaker. The whole crew was singing and dancing to early 2000s hits, and the sounds of Beyoncé and Chris Brown were carrying across the ocean.

It was lunchtime when I rounded a corner to glimpse the iconic Q1 tower of Surfers Paradise, which stands well above neighbouring buildings. A few days before, we'd reacted with excitement prematurely as we mistook the Logan skyline for the Gold Coast. But this time there was no doubt about it. Dave and Matt cheered from the jet ski on my left and the boat crew whistled and hugged to my right. I knew we were home.

During my last few kilometres of paddling into the anchorage at South Stradbroke Island, just ten kilometres north of the finish line, I was surprised by some special guests. Mike Janes's giving nature was on full display once more as he motored towards me in his fishing boat, accompanied by two athletes from his squad at Mermaid Beach Surf Club. Mike had departed from the expedition following his stint on the Cruising Kiwis' boat in the Kimberley but had organised for his squad to join me for a day's paddling in Hervey Bay. Now he was joining me at K'gari. Luke and Christian, two of the squad's senior ski paddlers, accompanied me as I zig-zagged between the flurry of boats and speeding jet skis in the busy Gold Coast Seaway. Once the boys had departed, I spotted a jet ski heading directly towards me with two people sitting atop of it. Quickly recognising the driver as Matt, I strained to make out the additional figure on the back. I hadn't been told of anyone else who'd be joining me. Who could it possibly be?

It wasn't until Matt pulled the jet ski right up alongside me that I realised my sister Courtney was onboard. My training partner and role model as a young athlete, my big sister was here to help me once more. Climbing into the Thompsons' spare ski, Courtney paddled up next to me, making my last kilometre of paddling on the penultimate day of the expedition incredibly special. Seeing Courtney made me realise how much I'd missed my family. Blocking out my emotions for the best part of eight months to keep a cool head in the face of danger, I could finally let my guard down. Back in familiar waters, the burden I'd carried in knowing I had to perform at an elite level every day dropped away. Safe and happy, I was now home with the people I loved.

'I'll see you tomorrow,' Courtney promised as she left, leaving me to climb aboard the catamaran, which had anchored up in the seaway. With a clear view of the entire stretch of Gold Coast high rises, the end was literally in sight.

'I'll be there,' I said, smiling. I was looking forward to the hugs that would be waiting once I'd crossed the finish line.

After setting 28 August as the date I'd run up the beach to cross the finishing tape, I'd developed two objectives: the first, to make it back in time, and the second, to have a day off before the big event. I'd already booked rooms at the luxurious Sheraton Grand Mirage for myself and the crew in anticipation of our early arrival. I wanted to get ahead of the game and relax before the big grand finale.

The boys and I headed to shore, our rooms at the Sheraton awaiting. After living at sea for the better part of the year, Blake and Jaime didn't think to put shoes on to walk into the foyer of the five-star resort and I couldn't help but giggle as I realised I wasn't the only one having to adapt back to civilisation. In my room, I turned the air conditioning on for the first time in eight months and flicked through stations on the television, struggling to keep up with the fast pace of the words and images as they sped across the screen. In the shower I lathered my body in the expensive complimentary body wash, then wrapped myself in a fluffy towel and painted my toenails, slowly feeling human once more. Stepping back to assess my appearance in the mirror, I realised it was the first time I'd had access to a full-length mirror since beginning the expedition. I was 15 kilograms lighter than when I'd started and physical scars were etched into my skin from paddling thousands of kilometres with rashes and chafing. I was viewing the evidence of what I'd put my body through. But rather than looking at the imperfections with disgust as I might have done in the past, I wore my damaged skin with pride. *I earned these scars*, I thought, visions of the Bight and Gulf burnt into my memory.

At a shop across the road from the hotel, I bought a deep-green long-sleeved number to wear to dinner with the crew at the seafood restaurant I'd selected for the evening. Rather than a rambunctious affair, the dinner would be a low-key celebration of what we had achieved as a team, a quiet reflection before the day of festivities to come. Sliding my feet into high heels, I noticed how soft my soles were, a side effect of countless hours in salt water. After touching up my makeup, I met the boys in the lobby to call a taxi, pleased to see my crewmates had found footwear for the occasion.

Arriving at the restaurant, I sat down with Jaime, Blake and Ben to wait for Matt. After running around all day organising the finer details of the following day, Matt had informed us he had one last job to do but would meet us in time for dinner. Looking at the menu, I saw the list of cocktails and mulled over whether to indulge in one. It had been five years since I'd had a drink. Sobriety was not a decision I'd made abruptly but something that had happened naturally. I'd realised I didn't need alcohol to be social and so I'd begun to sip lime and sodas in between vodkas, soon removing alcoholic beverages from my repertoire altogether. But on the eve of the final day of the expedition, I decided to treat myself, choosing a fruity cocktail and sipping it slowly.

Twenty minutes passed at the restaurant and I wondered where on earth Matt was. Perhaps traffic was slow down the southern end of the coast, and he'd been held up? My stomach was growling, and I was keen to order from the divine-looking menu.

Sensing a figure at the restaurant entrance in my peripheral vision, I glanced over, and though I recognised the face instantly, it wasn't Matt's. The grey beard was unmistakable and the sight of Goatee's wide grin and flushed cheeks made me instantly emotional as I realised he'd travelled across the country to surprise me for the last stint. Behind him, Ryan looked equally delighted to be there and I ran across the room for a group hug. My guardian angels of the west were here, and I suddenly couldn't imagine finishing the journey without them. Looking around to find Matt so I could thank him, I realised he wasn't in the room. Strange. Hadn't he given the men a lift?

I didn't need to wait long to find an answer, as Rob and Rachel walked in two minutes later. The Cruising Kiwis, my protectors of the north, had come to join the party. Embracing Rachel and Rob, my excitement about the day ahead grew. It wouldn't be just about crossing the tape. It would be a celebration of everyone who had been part of the paddle, those who had watched over my shoulder as predators lurked, carrying me through each section of coastline physically and mentally. This was about all of us. The people who refused to believe in 'impossible'.

The final person through the door was Matt, appearing frazzled but pleased his grand plan had come to fruition. This had been his final job of the expedition: to deliver my guardian angels to me. Looking at Matt, I realised the extent of his selflessness, the work he'd put in to ensure I not only completed the expedition but finished it in a memorable way. When he married me, Matt hadn't known I'd pick up a particular book and head hundreds of kilometres out to sea on my ocean ski within a year of our vows. He hadn't signed up for eight months apart with minimal contact, nor had he factored in his wife shutting down emotionally during rare moments spent together in that time. But he'd done it. Putting his own needs aside, Matt had gone above and beyond to ensure I had every opportunity to succeed.

Crossing the room to thank him, not just for the evening but for everything, I hugged him. Properly. Not a light embrace to tick the box as I'd been guilty of in the past eight months but a different type of hug. The type of hug that said *Thank you.* The kind of hug that said *I love you.* As we pulled back from the embrace, a different emotion spread over his face, one that I hadn't seen since the start of the expedition. Relief. Though no words were spoken, he finally knew, as did I, that we were going to be okay.

*

The next day was picture perfect inside the seaway, and I posed for photos with the crew before the final leg of my big adventure. The welcome-home party was taking place at Northcliffe Surf Club because it was much larger than Mermaid Beach and the perfect place to host a large gathering of supporters. Then I was to enter the ocean one final time to complete the final few kilometres into Mermaid Beach, which was two kilometres further south and the official finish line of the expedition. It was quite fitting that I would first be coming into shore at Northcliffe, the place where I'd carved out a career as a professional ironwoman all those years ago. And finally, to bring the story full circle, I would complete the last stint of the paddle into Mermaid Beach, my new surf club, where I was known as a ski paddler.

With Mother Nature again ensuring nothing came easy, I felt the southerly breeze growing stronger as I headed out through the seaway towards deeper, unprotected waters. Glancing over at Ben, Blake and Jaime on the jet ski, I couldn't help but let out a belly laugh; of course I had a headwind to contend with. Except this time I knew it was my final challenge.

Leaving myself with 90 minutes to complete the short paddle, I casually chatted to the 15 paddlers alongside me, waving to the dozens of spectators who had lined the seaway. Enjoying myself a little too much, I eventually glanced down at my watch and was shocked to see how much time I had wasted. I was now under the pump. With the live television crossing beginning at 8.30am, I only had one hour to get to the finish line, and the wind was picking up with every stroke.

'What if I don't make it?' I called to Ben, who pulled the jet ski alongside me to check in.

'Don't think about that just yet,' he answered, slight concern in his voice. 'Just make sure you keep the pace up.'

Increasing the pressure on my paddle, I drove my ski forward, pulling away from the paddlers who'd given up their morning to support me. All but Mick remained, and as he sprinted to keep pace, I was pleased to have him beside me.

Squinting into the distance, I could see the outline of 15 paddlers making their way towards me and as they grew closer, I recognised the faces of Olympic kayaker Alyce Wood and ironwoman Lizzie Welborn. They informed me I was just three kilometres from the finish. Paddling up between the two, it was a thrill to be in the company of some of the best female athletes in the country, and a novelty to share the water with them outside of racing. Reaching Northcliffe, they headed to shore, leaving me on my own with the boys on the jet ski.

'This is it,' Ben said. Ten minutes remained until I was due in front of the cameras. 'We'll see you in there.' One pull up on the throttle and the boys were gone, speeding towards the beach to take up their positions.

Looking around, I found myself completely alone. Other than the sounds of commentary from the finish line floating towards me and the water gently lapping at my ski, it was almost eerily quiet.

Finally, I could accept what was now reality. I'd done it. I'd become the fastest and youngest person to paddle around Australia. After 32 years, I finally had my big win. Not in a single race but over 254 days of competing against the toughest opponent I'd ever met: the ocean. Though she'd tried everything to defeat me, refusing to relent even in the final round, all the losses I'd suffered prior had shaped me for the fight. Backed up against the ropes, I hadn't surrendered but instead I'd stepped forward into the full brunt of her punches, my refusal to throw in the towel an asset second only to the unwavering team in my corner.

Glancing down to see 8:29am on my watch, I began paddling towards shore. Pulling off a heavy wave that dumped hard on the bank, I stroked hard to catch the one behind it and was relieved to feel the white water crumble gently underneath me, providing the perfect ride to shore. Hitting the beach, adrenaline took over as I sprinted towards the finish line with the cheers from the crowd roaring in my ears. Lifting the finishing tape, I was met with an onslaught of hugs from Gus Worland, Earl Evans and my family.

'How does it feel?' the first reporter asked, her microphone held out for my answer.

'I can't believe I finally get to say this,' my words tumbled out quickly. 'But it feels great to be home.'

Two hours later, after a whirlwind morning of celebration and interviews, it was time to close the last chapter of my big adventure. Just two kilometres to Mermaid Beach, the wind had dropped, and I was excited to paddle home.

Climbing into my ski for the very last time, I stroked slowly out to the smooth water behind the breakers. Looking back at the newly built towers on the beach, I marvelled at how they glittered in the sun, their green-tinted windows reflecting the light and creating the illusion of a precious stone. Had the buildings always appeared so magnificent? Or was I viewing the world in a new way, everything more beautiful after what I'd been through?

'Slow down,' Rob had advised of the final paddle. 'Make sure to take it all in.'

Heeding his advice, I lowered my stroke rate, in no rush to reach my final destination. For the first time since I was a child, I slowed down and made friends with the ocean.

The sun was now high in the sky and its reflection caused a shimmer on the ocean, creating the illusion of hundreds of stars dazzling in the water. Having spent countless hours craning my neck to admire the stars glowing in the night sky, it was as though they were now lighting up the ocean, guiding me to my final destination. I ran my hand over the surface of the water and a child-like excitement took over as I envisioned myself collecting the ocean's stars, each one providing a light to combat the darkness I'd encountered in finding my way to the finish line.

Splashing my face with the cool water and letting the enormity of my achievement finally sink in, I had a sudden realisation. In finishing the expedition, I didn't feel any more fulfilled than the day before, or even eight months prior. Though I'd been searching for a big win my whole life, what I'd uncovered on the expedition turned out to be far more valuable.

It had been in clear view all along, but I'd previously been in too much of a rush to see it. But it was suddenly overwhelmingly apparent. Overcome with emotion, I found myself crying; my tears weren't shed through fear of failure but deep appreciation of what I'd found in the ocean when I slowed down long enough to appreciate its beauty.

My happy place.

EPILOGUE

'Okay, girls, let's get ready for a start.' The starter's voice rings out clear above the roaring ocean of Northcliffe Beach, directing me and the other 15 female ski paddlers on the line to move our skis into the water. We're getting ready for the start of the race, the red-hot field stacked with the best female ski paddlers in the country. I share a smile with the young competitor on my left, before looking over my shoulder to appreciate the huge crowd that lines the beach to watch us battle each other and the ocean.

We prop our skis up onto our hips, paddles in hand, and walk towards the water. At the starter's gun, we will leap up into our skis and begin to paddle out to sea. Then we'll round the turning markers located beyond the break and navigate back to shore as quickly as possible.

A week after finishing the expedition, I'd received a call from the club and was offered a job coaching the nippers at Mermaid. Initially hesitant to accept because I hadn't made any solid plans for my short-term future, I eventually agreed, remembering the advice I'd received from fellow elite athletes about ensuring I kept busy when I got home. Saying yes to the coaching gig turned out to be one of the best decisions I've made. The opportunity allowed me to tie in with a community of all ages upon returning, and the joy I receive from helping the next generation of surf lifesavers grow their confidence and achieve their goals is infinitely rewarding.

It's fitting that my first race back since returning from my circumnavigation is being held at Northcliffe. Now February, it's six months since I sprinted across this very sand to the cheers of the crowd as I reached the Gold Coast after eight months of paddling. Not having intended to return to racing, I was pleasantly surprised with my body's ability to recover relatively quickly from the paddle.

In fact, two weeks after returning to the Gold Coast, I'd managed to break another world record. Having completed 213 kilometres in 24 hours as we made our way back down the north Queensland coast towards the end of the expedition, I wondered if I could better that mark. I wanted to see what I could do in favourable conditions.

Getting the crew back together, we travelled to the tropical waters of Airlie Beach in north Queensland, known for high winds. After a few phone calls to contacts, we had located a catamaran and skipper to escort me for the new record attempt, and on 12 September at 2:28pm, I lowered myself into my ski to address my last bit of unfinished business.

By the same time the next day, I had paddled 235 kilometres and bettered my world record for the furthest distance paddled by a woman on a ski or kayak in 24 hours. Though I'd gotten the record, it hadn't been pretty. At 70 kilometres, I'd sustained a grade one tear to my left bicep, which gradually increased in pain. I'd spent the last hour of the paddle stroking primarily on my right side as it was agony to take a stroke using my left arm. When the tear happened, perhaps due to the fact that I was pushing my body so hard to break the record, I had a decision to make. Pull out or keep pushing through the pain? Choosing the latter, I'd spent the next 165 kilometres gritting my teeth in agony as my worried crew watched on, but I'm so glad I made the decision to keep going.

*

Though I felt incredibly at home on the ocean following the circumnavigation, it took several weeks to get used to the pace of life back on land. At first, I felt overwhelmed by the sound of traffic and large groups of people talking. Eventually, I reassimilated into everyday life on the Gold Coast, but it was several more weeks until I could confidently walk long distances, as my lower body had deconditioned significantly through lack of use. Thankfully, my fingers started to settle down as soon as they had a break, and I could slide my wedding ring over my knuckle once more.

It feels good to wear my wedding ring after eight months without it. After returning to Mermaid Beach, Matt and I spent the time getting to know each other once more. Finally letting him in, I recounted all the details of the paddle that he hadn't witnessed, sharing the wonderful parts, those that were more challenging, and finally, the ugliness of the Bight and the Gulf. I described what we faced and what the crew and I had to do to get through. And Matt shared stories from travelling around Australia by land: his favourite stretches to drive, the stress of organising extra financial support and the impact our separation had on him. We've got our marriage back, and he is on the beach for my return to racing, cheering from the crowd as I prepare to take on the ocean once more. He's also back at his beloved Southport Sharks, with a well-earned promotion.

As major sponsors of the surf-lifesaving carnival, Earl and Allan of Shaw and Partners Financial Services are also in the crowd, as well as Gus and Vicky Worland, the founders of Gotcha4Life. Following the expedition, I reached the $100,000 target for Gotcha4Life, which had been set before I left the Gold Coast. Furthermore, the charity has asked me to come onboard as an ambassador, a role that will enable me to assist in delivering mental-fitness workshops to Australians, an opportunity I couldn't be happier about.

Peering out to sea, I pray for Mother Nature to take care of me, to part the seas and give me a safe passage through the enormous walls of white water. With cyclone activity in north Queensland creating 6–8-foot swells on the Gold Coast, the organisers had considered moving the event to a sheltered bay 20 kilometres further south. Much to the delight of the competitors, however, we were eventually given the green light to stay at the open beach. The chance to race in huge seas is something surf lifesavers train for all their lives; the unpredictable nature of open water meaning anyone in the final has a chance to win.

After finishing first in my heat earlier in the day, I feel confident. Three months into training on my surf ski, I've recently had a breakthrough, my strength and speed returning to levels beyond what I'd anticipated.

Placing my paddle alongside my ski, I remember what my coach has told me: *Power off the start; be aggressive but smart.* The only way to take on seas this big is with an equal dose of patience and aggression, sitting and waiting for a gap, then turning on a burst of speed to manoeuvre over and through the waves, around the cans and back to shore.

This time last year, I was two days from finishing my crossing of the Great Australian Bight. No longer able to walk, I'd crawled from the boat to my ski, forcing myself through kilometre after aching kilometre with acid reflux burning in the back of my throat.

The crack of the starter's gun is a sound I've grown up with and I react quickly, my mind and body shifting into a predator-like mode, reflexes sharp and senses heightened. Jumping into my ski, I force the blade of my paddle into the water, focusing on getting the ski moving quickly through the water. The start is a good one, clean and drama-free, and I shift my gaze to the waves ahead, looking for a gap in the swells.

The wave in front is caught by the one behind and I have a split-second decision to make. Do I stay or do I go? Sit back and wait or charge towards the wave, looking for the sweet spot that will launch me up and over like a ramp? Backing myself, I pick up the pace and grit my teeth as I quickly slice my paddle through the water, reaching maximum speed to give myself every opportunity to go through cleanly. Reaching the base of the wave just in time, I hit the top of it and crash down on the other side, the nose of my ski plunging into the water with huge force.

Picking my way through and around the big waves, I get beyond the break into clean water. By the time I reach the can, I'm joined by just two other competitors, and it's a race of three. A fourth paddler is too far behind to win, so all I need to do now is outsmart the two near me.

I can see the finishing arch on the beach, and a ripple of excitement floods through my body at the sight. Wary not to count my chickens before they hatch, I shift my attention back to the present as the three of us paddle towards the beach, each taking our own line. Angling my ski further south towards the deeper water of a rip, I hope to get a smoother run into the beach.

There's a big set building out the back, so I put my head down and pick up my stroke rate, paddling hard to put maximum distance between myself and the waves. It's a near impossible task to hold an 18-foot ski straight on the enormous waves once they've broken, so the best chance of getting to shore safely is to outsprint the waves, choosing the right time and paddling in the gap between the sets.

Fifty metres from shore, a smaller swell picks up underneath us and we chase it, urging our skis to pull down the front, knowing that this is the winning wave; whoever holds it will cross the tape first. Gripping my paddle, I push hard, forearms burning. I can feel the nose of my ski start to bury, so I work hard to hold the ski stable. Thousands of litres of ocean are moving beneath me, the swirling sand colouring the sea brown.

Suddenly, I hit dead water. The ocean is no longer pushing me forward; instead it bubbles around me, holding me back from launching down the wave. Seeing my competitors surging ahead, I fight to stay with them, but I know it's too late. They disappear, carried to shore by the white water, the race to the tape now a battle of two.

Hitting the beach, I look up to see the two girls in front sprinting towards the finish arch, the huge crowd cheering them on. My position will be third.

As a young ironwoman, I'd put so much pressure on myself to win that when I didn't achieve the goal I had set, I'd been devastated. But now, as I round the turning marker and run towards the finish arch in third, it's with an immense sense of pride.

Turning to the left, I spot a group of Mermaid nippers waving at me from the sidelines. Running across to give them high-fives before crossing the line, I have a big grin on my face.

Standing on the podium afterwards, I scan my surroundings, taking in the moment. This wasn't just any third place. Months earlier, I'd crawled up the back stairs of a catamaran 500 kilometres out to sea, battled huge headwinds that led to a bulging disc and shared the ocean with sharks and crocodiles, and all the while there'd been a worldwide pandemic that threatened to end the expedition at any minute.

I feel grateful to be back racing, let alone able to compete with the best of the best once more.

And even though I can wash the salt from my hair and body, the memories of my paddle around Australia will remain with me forever.

ACKNOWLEDGEMENTS

Though it is my name on the certificate, I wish I could share the world record with the dozens of people who helped me to the finish line.

So now it is my opportunity to recognise the people who were instrumental in the journey, and the incredible humans who helped turn my vague idea to write a book – conceived while paddling 100 kilometres off the Western Australian coastline – into a final product I am immensely proud of. As we say at Gotcha4Life, this is my village.

To Mum and Dad. Thank you for being the first people in my life to empower me. For the sacrifices you made that allowed me to explore my passions.

To my sisters, Georgia, Courtney and India. Thank you for keeping my feet on the ground. For giving me something to aspire to. For being my first role models.

To Ben and Phillip, Cath and Dig, Kaylah and Jack. I am so lucky to call you family. Thank you for believing in me.

To Earl Evans and Allan Zion of Shaw and Partners Financial Services. Without you, I would never have got to the start line. Your willingness to take a chance on me has changed my life.

To Gus and Vicky Worland, and the rest of the Gotcha4Life

family. Thank you for inspiring me to do good in this world. I am so grateful my adventure led to us meeting each other.

Blake. You were there for me on some of the toughest days of the journey. Thank you for showing me silver linings in the middle of the ocean. Daw Island.

Jaime. Your courage provided a shining light. Thank you for your creative genius and adventurous spirit. Wedge Island.

Ben. Thank you for making me feel safe in the scariest of situations. Your humour and honesty were so important. King George River.

The Cruising Kiwis. In two weeks, you made me a better person. Thank you for guiding me through the most dangerous waters in the world.

Goatee and Ryan. Our paths crossed by fate, but by choice we became friends. Thank you for the good times.

Graham and Lovell. My crew and I didn't know how much we needed you until we met. Thank you for loving us like your own.

Josh and Tina. I'll never forget the lengths to which you went in getting me home. Thank you for taking on the headwinds with me.

Mike. I needed a coach and you didn't hesitate in answering the call. Thank you for lifting me to heights beyond what I could have imagined.

The Thompsons. I couldn't have planned a better final week than the one spent with you. Thank you for reminding me how much I love the ocean.

Thank you to all those who helped with safety, support and instilling self-belief within me, including Mick and Tina Herden, Frederick Lindstrom, Sir Roger Badham, Dean Gardiner, Greg and Sheree Young, Kate Cranage, Darian Quinlan, Brett and Kim Richardson, Dave Gardiner, Pat Langley and the Vaikobi team, Nick Marshall, Greg and Marie Bennett, Michael Weiner, Justin Ryan, Steve, Tracey and Liv at Queensland Car and Truck Rentals, Steve Major, Paul 'Gilly' Gill, Erin Wallace, Simone Haugh, Jordan Mercer, Darren Mercer, Carla Papac, Lizzie Welborn, Rebecca Marshallsay, Rachel Condos-Fields, Lisa Ketjen, Carol Fox, Beau Emerton, Tugun Family Medicine, Sophie Richardson and Sarah Kelly along with the Minerva Network, Surf Life Saving Queensland and Mermaid Beach Surf Life Saving Club.

To Jessica Watson, Sally Fitzgibbons, Leisel Jones and Libby Trickett. I have looked up to you all since I was a kid. Thank you for being among the first people to read this book.

To Selwa Anthony, literary agent extraordinaire. Thank you for taking a chance on me and allowing me to see what I am capable of away from the ski. Your belief has made all of this possible.

To Mary Rennie (non-fiction publisher), Madeleine James (editor), Stuart Henshall (publicity), Kimberley Allsopp (marketing), Karen-Maree Griffiths (sales) and the entire team at HarperCollins. Thank you for allowing me to share my story. Your guidance and encouragement for this athlete turned rookie author has been inspiring.

To Ingrid Roepers. Your passion and dedication are admirable. Thank you for directing those qualities into my projects.

Finally, to Matt. For eight months you put your own needs aside so I could achieve this record, but you've been empowering me for eight years. It took me 12,700 kilometres to realise that my favourite adventure is any one when I'm with you.

QUICK GLOSSARY OF OCEAN SKI AND BOATING TERMS

Spec/surf lifesaving ski: An 18-kilogram, 6-metre ski made of carbon fibre and fibre glass. Used in ironwoman and surf-ski races within surf lifesaving. Built for crashing through the surf and catching waves.

Ocean ski: A 9-kilogram, 6-metre ski made of carbon fibre. Used in professional ocean ski races. Designed for downwind surfing and longer distance races.

Paddle: Generally 500 grams in weight and made of carbon fibre, a double-bladed paddle is used by a paddler to stroke on both sides of the ski to propel the ski through the water.

Pedals: Made of carbon fibre, the two foot pedals in a ski are connected by a system of wires to the rudder. By pressing with the ball of the foot, the paddler can steer the ski left or right.

Footplate: The footplate, also made of carbon fibre, sits below the pedals and provides a structure for the paddler to place their heels against, allowing them to gain maximum power with stroke.

Ketch: A two-masted sailboat on which the larger mainmast is stepped forward of the smaller aft-mast.

Tender: A small inflatable boat that acts as a vessel to run to shore when the water depth is too shallow for the main boat.

Starboard: Right side of a boat when you face the bow (front).

Port: Left side of a boat when you face the bow (front).

Dry entry: Technique of getting into an ocean ski without getting wet. Involves one crew member holding the ski stable while the paddler steps in, with another crew member passing the paddle to the paddler. This entry can be performed in calm conditions or in small swells.

Wet entry: The technique of getting into ocean ski when conditions are too dangerous for a dry entry to be performed safely. It involves pushing the ocean ski away from the boat, requiring the paddler to leap into the water and pull themselves up into the ski using the remount technique (see below). A safety line between the paddler and the ski is recommended in case the ski is carried away from paddler by the wind.

Remount: This technique is used to get back into an ocean ski after falling out. With both arms over the seat of the ski, the paddler hauls themselves up and, twisting sideways, places their bottom into the seat of the ski and swings their legs and feet into the footwells. It is recommended paddlers practise the remount in calm waters before attempting in open ocean.

If you have been inspired by Bonnie's story, you might like to donate to Gotcha4Life, a not-for-profit foundation dedicated to building a mentally fit future. Gotcha4Life develops and delivers preventative mental fitness campaigns, workshops, programs and resources in schools, sports clubs, workplaces and communities Australia-wide.

www.gotcha4life.org